Between "Race" and Culture

1

Stanford Studies in Jewish History and Culture
Edited by Aron Rodrigue and Steven J. Zipperstein

Contributors

Murray Baumgarten

Bryan Cheyette

Maud Ellmann

Jonathan Freedman

William Galperin

Sander L. Gilman

Eric Homberger

Phyllis Lassner

Andrea Freud Loewenstein

Marilyn Reizbaum

Jacqueline Rose

Between "Race" and Culture

Representations of
"the Jew" in
English and
American Literature

Edited by
Bryan Cheyette

Stanford University Press
Stanford, California 1996

Stanford University Press
Stanford, California
© 1996 by the Board of Trustees of the
Leland Stanford Junior University
Printed in the United States of America

CIP data are at the end of the book

Stanford University Press publications are distributed exclusively by Stanford University Press within the United States,
Canada, Mexico, and Central America; they are distributed
exclusively by Cambridge University Press throughout the rest
of the world

In memory of Jack Cheyette
(1931–1994)

Preface

The idea for this volume was first conceived at a Modern Languages Association conference when I was struck by the many and varied approaches to the representation of "the Jew" in English and American literature. After a decade of working single-handedly in this area, my isolation had, at last, come to an end. Following the response to my *Constructions of "the Jew" in English Literature and Society*, I came to realize that there was, after all, a community of like-minded scholars treating this subject matter with the seriousness it deserves.

This sense of community, however, has been under attack in the 1990s as the study of literary racism and antisemitism has been mistakenly demarcated into broadly defined "politically correct" and "liberal humanist" positions. What is ironic about these supposedly antagonistic divisions is that they are, in fact, mirror images of each other. On the one hand, "liberal humanism" believes that the ameliorating western canon has, by definition, nothing to do with racism or antisemitism. On the other hand, "political correctness" wishes to exclude from the academy any literary text deemed to reinforce oppressive stereotypes. Both sides, in other words, moralize racism as a peculiar evil that is beyond rational discussion. In this way, they simply reproduce the complacent self-image of a civilizing Anglo-American liberal culture that considers racists or antisemites to be pathological fanatics banished to the margins of society.

The phony war between "liberal humanism" and "political correctness" has, inevitably, generated a good deal of heat and not much light. What is more, in practice, the polarization of this debate has stifled any genuinely open dialogue about the complex nature of racism and antisemitism within literary texts. For this reason, the diverse essays in this volume aim neither to excuse nor accuse the many writers that are examined. It seems hopelessly counterproductive to compose a latter-day "index of forbidden works" of authors who are peculiarly evil and who should, therefore, no longer be read. Such censoriousness simply continues the cycle of hatred that all thinking people, at least, should want to end. At the same time, the authors in this volume treat, with rigor, the many different forms that Anglo-American literary racism and antisemitism took in the nineteenth and twentieth centuries. In this way, it is hoped that valuable connections can be made within and between writers and other social and political contexts. The collection does not impose a schema or new orthodoxy, but instead encourages a plurality of approaches to a difficult and always contentious subject. Above all, it challenges the misguided notion that this area is really a matter of common sense and personal experience and does not need the discipline of hard thinking.

The initial interest of Steven Zipperstein in this project resulted in an early commitment from Stanford University Press that enabled me to approach the contributors to this volume with confidence. During his time at Oxford University in the early 1980s, Steven Zipperstein bolstered my research interests when others, in English literature departments, were dismissing them as overly "narrow." The anonymous readers of the typescript were equally encouraging and insightful. Norris Pope, Amy Klatzkin, and Ellen Stein, at Stanford University Press, have been exemplary editors who have made the publication of this book as smooth and as stress-free as possible. Although this enterprise spans the Atlantic Ocean, I have often felt that it has been handled with remarkable intimacy.

Since moving to Queen Mary and Westfield College in 1992, I have been fortunate enough to work closely with Jacqueline Rose, who has been a constant source of intellectual stimulation and who has, in particular, prevented me from many infelicities in this collection. Lisa Jardine and Jacqueline Rose, at QMW, both accepted me because of my research and not in spite of it. My thinking has therefore been invigorated by students and colleagues at QMW who have not been afraid to slaughter any number of sacred cows and who have stimulated me to rethink many of my most favored beliefs. Zygmunt Bauman, Janina Bauman, David Cesarani, Todd Endelman, David Feldman, Gabriel Josipovici, Tony Kushner, Laura Marcus, Benita Parry, Gillian Rose, and Nadia Valman have all made this book better than it might have been. I offer, in particular, my heartfelt thanks to the contributors to the volume, who have been a pleasure to work with. Now that there is no longer any need to chase deadlines, I will happily stay in friendly correspondence with all of them. My wife, Susan Cooklin, has once again created a loving and supportive atmosphere in which to write and, along with my mother and sister, has continued to keep my feet firmly on the ground.

This book is dedicated to my father, who, sadly, died during its production. His response to its publication would, as ever, have been honest and full of warmth. I will dearly miss our conversations about where we should go from here.

Contents

Contributors

Murray Baumgarten teaches English and comparative literature at the University of California, Santa Cruz, and is the founding director of the Dickens Project at Kresge College. His many publications include *City Scriptures: Modern Jewish Writing* and, as coauthor, *Understanding Philip Roth*. He recently coedited *Homes and Homelessness in Victorian Literature*, and he is the editor of *Judaism: A Quarterly Journal*.

Bryan Cheyette teaches English literature and Jewish cultural studies at Queen Mary and Westfield College, University of London. He is the author of *Constructions of "the Jew" in English Literature and Society: Racial Representations, 1875–1945*, and has completed a critical history of British Jewish literature in the twentieth century. He has also recently coedited *Modernity, Culture and "the Jew."*

Maud Ellmann teaches English and American literature at King's College, University of Cambridge. She is the author of *The Poetics of Impersonality: T. S. Eliot and Ezra Pound* and *The Hunger Artists: Starving, Writing and Imprisonment*. She has also recently edited *Psychoanalytic Literary Criticism*.

Jonathan Freedman teaches English and American literature at the University of Michigan, Ann Arbor. He is the author of *Professions of Taste:*

Henry James, Commodity Culture, and British Aestheticism and is currently working on literary antisemitism, and Jewish intellectuals' responses to it, at the turn of the century.

William Galperin teaches English literature at Rutgers University. He is the author of *Revision and Authority in Wordsworth* and *The Return of the Visible in British Romanticism* as well as numerous articles on romanticism and related topics.

Sander L. Gilman is Henry R. Luce Professor of the Liberal Arts in Human Biology at the University of Chicago. He is a cultural and literary historian and the author or editor of over forty volumes, the most recent in English including *Jews in Today's Germany* and *Kafka: The Jewish Patient*. He is also a past president of the Modern Languages Association.

Eric Homberger teaches American literature at the University of East Anglia and is the author of *American Writers and Radical Politics* and *John Reed and the Russian Revolution*. He has also recently published *Scenes from the Life of a City: Conscience and Corruption in Old New York* and *The Historical Atlas of New York City*.

Phyllis Lassner teachers women's studies and writing at Northwestern University. She is the author of two books on Elizabeth Bowen, a study of her novels and her short fiction, as well as articles on British women's writing of the 1930s and 1940s.

Andrea Freud Loewenstein teaches writing and literature at Medgar Evers College, New York. She is the author of two novels, *This Place* and *The Worry Girl*, and a critical study, *Loathsome Jews and Engulfing Women: Metaphors of Projection in the Works of Wyndham Lewis, Charles Williams, and Graham Greene*.

Marilyn Reizbaum teaches British and Irish literature at Bowdoin College. She has published widely on the work of Djuna Barnes and on Scottish writing and has completed a study entitled *Joyce's Judaic "Other": Texts and Contexts*. She has also recently coedited *Engendering "Ulysses."*

Jacqueline Rose teaches English literature at Queen Mary and Westfield College, University of London. She is the author of *Sexuality in the Field of Vision, The Haunting of Sylvia Plath*, and *Why War? Psychoanalysis, Politics and the Return to Melanie Klein. States of Fantasy*, the 1994 Clarenden Lectures, has recently been published.

Between "Race" and Culture

CHAPTER ONE

Introduction: Unanswered Questions

BRYAN CHEYETTE

> They do not grudge us, we are musing, our prosperity;
> when suddenly, turning the corner, we come upon a
> bearded Jew, wild, hunger-bitten, glaring out of his mis-
> ery; or pass the humped body of an old woman flung
> abandoned on the step of a public building with a cloak
> over her like the hasty covering thrown over a dead horse
> or donkey. At such sights the nerves of the spine seem to
> stand erect; a sudden flare is brandished in our eyes; a
> question is asked which is never answered.
> —Virginia Woolf,
> "Street Haunting: A London Adventure" (1927)

Midway through her aimless "ramble" across London in search of a "lead pencil," Virginia Woolf is shocked into a recognition of the poverty and misery that separate her irrevocably from the "hunger-bitten" "bearded Jew" and the homeless "old woman" whom she accidentally stumbles across. Up until that point, "Street Haunting" had been a quintessentially modern "adventure" of Woolf as *flâneuse*. In this Baudelairian guise, Woolf was able to glimpse fleetingly the cityscape as both an anonymous partici-pant and a privileged voyeur. No longer performing the role of a re-spectable member of the bourgeoisie, Woolf, in her essay, is able to irre-sponsibly identify with whomsoever she happens to encounter. Out of the ugliness and grotesqueness of the city the *flâneuse*, supposedly indistin-guishable from her male counterpart, attempts to crystallize those transi-tory moments of aesthetic transformation: "For the eye has this strange property: it rests only on beauty; like a butterfly it seeks colour and basks in warmth."[1]

Just before she turns the corner and confronts these dispossessed "dere-licts" — the "bearded Jew" and the "old woman" — Woolf seems to have an unequivocal affinity with those captured by her aestheticizing eye. The search for fragmentary beauty both determines and structures her seem-ingly arbitrary ramblings. After seeing an abnormally small woman in a shoe shop, she asks, "What, then, is it like to be a dwarf?" (p. 157). Woolf answers by focusing on the "dwarf's" feet as she imagines that "perhaps . . . the rest of the body was of a piece with those beautiful feet" (p. 158). As women were often "loved for their feet alone," Woolf thinks of this par-ticular woman as being in a state of "ecstacy" due to the "beauty" of her "perfectly proportioned foot" (p. 158). Later on, she speculates, "in what crevices and crannies . . . did they lodge, this maimed company of the halt and the blind?" (p. 159). This benevolent sense of empathy is extended to the "maimed company" who haunt the streets as "the dwarf" leaves the shoe shop: "all joined in the hobble and tap of the dwarf's dance"; all be-come "humped," "twisted," and "deformed" in her presence (p. 158). But the grotesquely beautiful transformation of both the "dwarf" and those nearby, including Woolf herself, is quickly shattered by the sight of the "misery" and "poverty" just around the corner. As a "prosperous" con-sumer, a "dwarf" can be utterly transfigured into a thing of beauty. Yet the irredeemable abjection of those lying in the street, unable to undergo even this momentary transformation, freezes Woolf, who is no longer the voy-euristic *flâneuse*: "At such sights the nerves of the spine seem to stand erect; a sudden flare is brandished in our eyes; a question is asked which is never answered" (p. 159).

If Woolf, as modern *flâneuse*, is able to briefly assume any guise and identify with even the most grotesque of consumers, then her sense of blindness, immobility, and inarticulacy — when encountering the "dere-licts" of London — shows starkly the limitations of this too easy and playful vision of modernity. Immediately after her sense of visceral powerlessness, in relation to those that the city has disgorged, Woolf notes that "these derelicts [often] choose to lie not a stone's throw from theatres" and the "shop windows" of Oxford Street (pp. 159–60). In this locale, at the heart of metropolitan role-playing, "commerce" offers a false "sprinkling" of beauty as if this "night cast up nothing but treasure" (p. 160).

*

Woolf's extraordinary essay serves as a prelude to this volume, as it pro-vides a powerful and redolent sense of the range of possibilities open to the writer when attempting to contain the Other within the imagination. The shift from the facile aestheticizing and easy identification with "the dwarf" to the shocked inarticulacy at the unexpected sight of the "bearded Jew" and the "old woman" indicates something of the flavor of the varied encounters with the Jewish Other that make up the collection. There are many occasions, in the essays that follow, when the writers who are considered are similarly paralyzed by their inability to transform "the Jew," especially when, as many contributors argue, this figure is deeply embedded in the unconscious.

Not that "the Jew" should ever be separated from the larger social, political, and cultural contexts through which he or she is viewed. As "Street Haunting" makes clear, it would be invidious to distinguish the "bearded Jew" from the "humped body" of the abandoned "old woman," whose poverty and gender shatter the dream of a transforming modernity no less than "the Jew." Such connections between supposedly distinct realms help define the various essays in the collection. Mark Twain's stunned observation of the "dwarfs" and "cripples" in Constantinople is, as Sander Gilman illustrates, intimately related to Twain's later understanding of the "diseased" Jews in Palestine. Marilyn Reizbaum also makes clear that exotic otherness, in James Joyce's "An Encounter," is associated as much with the "two labourers" as with the "little Jew with a bag" whom the two boys stumble upon when they attempt to escape on a ferry boat from the safe provinciality of Dublin. The conflation of Jews, art, and degeneracy was at the heart of Henry James's queasy fictional representations of "the Jews," as Jonathan Freedman demonstrates. While the fear of "degeneration" might well be a general concern of modernity, it does not, as Freedman shows, preclude a specific consideration of the role of "the Jew" within these more widespread preoccupations.

The multitude of arbitrary guises that "the Jew" assumes in the volume means that he or she is not conceived of as a static "myth" but is, instead, irrevocably shaped by the gender, aesthetics, and politics of a given writer. Whether it be the radical aesthetics of romanticism or modernism; or nineteenth-century constructions of "diseased" bodies; or theories of degeneration; or Irish nationalism; or the emancipatory politics of twentieth-century feminism or communism or liberal individualism; each essay situates "the Jew" in a specifically determining intellectual and historical framework.

Woolf, in particular, helps us to understand the associations and dissociations between different forms of oppression that lie at the heart of our argument. After all, it was Woolf who famously formed a "Society of Outsiders" in her well-known essay "Three Guineas" (1938), which specifically brought together women and Jews as victims of patriarchy and fascism. Woolf's diasporic feminism — "as a woman my country is the whole world" — is the starting point for Jacqueline Rose's reassessment of Dorothy Richardson's fictional construction of "the Jew" in terms of the language of assimilation and nationhood. Nation-building and feminist emancipation, more usually thought of as radically opposed histories, are interweaved in Rose's essay, although these histories are also shown to be, at key points in Richardson's *Pilgrimage*, irredeemably antagonistic to one another.

Both Rose and Phyllis Lassner affirm that feminist writing, no less than male socialist writing, has itself unwittingly reinforced the exclusivist race-thinking that has accompanied the rise of the modern nation-state. In addition to Richardson and Woolf, brief references to a significant part of the corpus of Margery Allingham, Djuna Barnes, Olive Schreiner, and May Sinclair in the twentieth century, and Maria Edgeworth in the nineteenth century, indicate in general that women writers have, not unlike the male canon, commonly utilized racial constructions of "the Jew." With this largely unacknowledged complicity in mind, Lassner shows the extent to which Woolf's ideals in "Three Guineas" remain unrealized in many of her fictional Jewish representations. Woolf's "Three Guineas" is also an important source for Rose's skepticism toward what she calls a "too easy metaphoric or troped identification between forms of outsideness, between—in this case—women and Jews." For both Woolf and Richardson, like their male counterparts, the characteristic tone is one of relentless uncertainty, as they both strongly identify with and absolutely distinguish the Jewish Other.

Although this ambivalence, rather than naked hostility or unqualified affinity, sets the tone for most of the essays in the volume, it is not as complete a predilection as it might at first appear. William Galperin, with reference to European romantic writing, has noted that ambivalence, by itself, does not fully explain a writer's inability to contain "the Jew." One might want to go further and insist on the need to fully particularize a writer in relation to the Jewish Other. In this way, one is able to avoid a bland universalization of a writer's unresolved identification or differentiation with the Jewish Other, which, as this collection demonstrates, takes radically differing cultural and political forms. Simply to point to ambivalence as an all-explaining predisposition is, in this regard, not nearly enough. That "the Jew" is, above all, a sign of confusion or indeterminacy should be clear from the essays that follow and from recent writings on racial discourse in general. But this is very different from saying that confusion or indeterminacy always assumes the same forms throughout time, irrespective of a specific historical or social context.[2]

*

If we return to the question of gender, we can begin to characterize ambivalence in more detail rather than merely deploying it as an all-embracing category. As Elleke Boehmer has recently reminded us, women are historically positioned in a mode radically different from that of men with regard to the dominant ideologies of the nation-state.[3] That supposedly "feminine" Jewish men were, however, also differentiated from patriarchal conceptions of nationhood relates them, interestingly, to the excluded position of women.

There are many examples of this commonplace feminization in the collection. Murray Baumgarten especially shows how the "sympathetic" Riah, in Charles Dickens's *Our Mutual Friend* (1864), is feminized to the extent that, like his mirror-image Fagin, he wears a skirt. Whereas what Baumgarten calls "Judaism as feminization" results in Riah directly helping women in their quest for emancipation, in *Oliver Twist* (1837) Fagin's not dissimilar lack of "masculinity" is represented in an unremittingly homophobic manner. The extent to which the supposed "femininity" of the male Jew can be read in either emancipatory or repressive terms may also be dependent on the gender of a given author. Riah and Fagin are two sides of the same coin precisely because they are both differentiated from the assumed authorial standard of a healthy Christian masculinity. That male romantic poets could dissociate themselves from the masculine norms of the nation, however, meant that they could appropriate Jewish women as figures of universal redemption, as Galperin shows with reference to William Wordsworth's "A Jewish Family."[4]

Only as objects of undiluted misogynistic and Judeophobic scorn in the pernicious fiction of William Gerhardi, which is examined by Andrea Freud Loewenstein, are women and Jews unequivocally interchangeable as categories of absolute alterity. As Loewenstein rightly observes, it would be a mistake to separate textual representations of women and Jews insofar as both are perceived as a threat to the supposed potency of the male author. That hatred can be self-consciously transferred from women to Jews in George Orwell's *Nineteen Eighty-Four* (1949) demonstrates, as Loewenstein notes, the extent to which Jewish racial representations are deeply implicated in dominant and dominating constructions of masculinity. With reference to Henry James, T. S. Eliot, and Ezra Pound, both Freedman and Maud Ellmann understand "the Jew" to be the "feminine principle" or, alternatively, the "negative principle" repressed in the unconscious of their respective authors. According to Freedman, "the Jew" is a "figure onto which can be loaded all the sources of [James's] inchoate anxieties and unacknowledged terrors," and, for Ellmann, both Eliot and Pound construct "the Jew" as a means of exorcising or displacing an "unknown self." Given that the fear of "feminization" was at the heart of these unknown "terrors" for many of the male authors under consideration, it is clear that male and female writers may differ radically in terms of their relationship to Judaism as a form of "feminization."[5]

As Lassner notes, Virginia Woolf eventually came to regard herself as a "Jew" after her marriage to Leonard Woolf and, at the same time, could comment on Leonard's "long and hooked" nose on a trip through Nazi Germany. By the time of her 1935 tour of Nazi Germany, Woolf was to write to Ethel Smyth and Margaret Llewellyn Davies that "we have got a letter from Prince Bismarck in our pockets, as people say we might be unpopular as we are Jews," and also, "our Jewishness is said to be a danger."[6] This form of uneasy acculturated Jewishness, based on custom and attitude, or experience and exposure, is precisely what many of the male authors who are discussed in this volume dread being "corrupted" by.

That this fear of Semitic degeneration was perceived to be an ever-present threat can be seen, for example, in James's *The Tragic Muse* (1890). In a key passage from this novel, explored in depth by Freedman, the artist Nick Dormer inadvertently finds himself speculating that Miriam Rooth's non-Jewish mother might well contain the "immemorial Jewess" within her. He goes on: "The late Rudolf Roth had been . . . so that . . . good Semitic reasons were surely not wanting to the mother" (pp. 25–26). The same Semitic reasoning meant that Virginia Woolf could openly contemplate her own "Jewishness" and, before her, Robert Browning, Matthew Arnold, George Eliot, and Olive Schreiner were all haphazardly "Judaized" according to a not-dissimilar logic.[7] Ellmann is surely right to argue, especially with regard to Pound and Eliot, that the "imaginary Jew" became the "mirror image of the poet himself." This reasoning goes some way to explain why Joyce in *Ulysses* (1922), as Reizbaum contends, could embrace "the Jew" as the "other" self of his artistic persona, Stephen Dedalus. While Joyce welcomed the subversive inexactitude of Leopold Bloom, Eliot and Pound were to try to impose a harsh clarity on precisely the same "Jewish" confusion. Galperin reminds us that this "mirror image" prevailed not only in the work of modern poets striving for a classical aesthetic order, at the expense of what Ellmann calls their repressed Semitic "diabolic *semblance*," but also in the writings a century earlier of romantic poets who had an equally fraught relationship with the Wandering Jew as their displaced and shadowy double.

This form of arbitrary Judaization, as Freedman maintains, both reinforces and undermines more biologically reductive race-thinking. The fear that Jews can supposedly "infect" absolutely everyone, not least the writers who struggle to understand them, is the pronounced focus of many of the essays in the volume and is especially at the heart of Ellmann's account of Eliot and Pound. Rather like "the dwarf" — whose presence makes those around her "humped," "twisted," and "deformed" — "the Jew" threatens to deform writers so that they can no longer see either themselves or their world with clarity. What unites the feminist modernism of Woolf and

Richardson with their male counterparts, such as Pound, Eliot, and James is, precisely, the implication in their texts that "the Jew" is bound up with an unfathomable confusion that haunts the aesthetic of all of these writers.

Such hideous inarticulacy, already endured in "Street Haunting," perhaps accounts for the extraordinary last section of Virginia Woolf's *The Years* (1936), considered in full by Lassner, when North's reading of Marvell's poetry to the hunchback Sara is interrupted by "the Jew," Abrahamson, taking a bath. As in "Street Haunting," Sara's physical deformity relates her to Abrahamson, a factory worker in the tallow trade, but this identification is immediately undermined by his all-too-apparent poverty. Woolf does not pull any punches when characterizing Sara's dread of being "polluted" by the "grease" left by Abrahamson in the communal bath that she is also expected to use. Sara's refrain, "all because of a Jew in my bath," which was even more obsessively repeated in early draft versions of *The Years*, interrupts her storytelling and is self-consciously associated with the "polluted city, unbelieving city, city of dead fish and worn-out frying pans" that she has been compelled to enter. The lines from Marvell—"Society is all but rude— / To this delicious solitude"—are in turn related to the boundary-crossing or "slimy" Jew who, above all, signifies Sara's social descent.[8]

The transformation of Sara's "delicious solitude" into the rudely polluting "Jew" connects *The Years* to the male canon of Jewish racial representations, but it should also be distinguished from this canon in important ways. In this regard, it is not a coincidence that "the Jew" in *The Years* is named Abrahamson, embodying a biblical patriarchy devoid of women. Just as Miriam Henderson in Richardson's *Deadlock* (1921) thought of Judaism in terms of the "social oblivion of women" (p. 224)—her reason for not marrying Michael Shatov—Sara similarly constructs "the Jew" as the gendered opposite of her sense of freedom. On the other hand, the recognition of "the Jew" as a kindred spirit, not unlike diasporic women who do not fully belong anywhere, can release a liberating set of oppositional values in the writings of George Eliot and Stevie Smith, discussed by Baumgarten and Lassner respectively, as well as those of Woolf and Richardson. The sense of mutual powerlessness at the exclusion of both Jews and women from the public sphere of the nation is, in the end, necessarily contrasted with the anxieties of male writers who tend to concentrate narcissistically on the corruption of a supposedly homogeneous masculinized body politic. After all, as Loewenstein makes clear, there is an enormous difference between the spurious victimhood of those with power and the actual victimization of those who are institutionalized as Other in relation to dominant national narratives.

*

By placing the racially and sexually marginalized at its center, "Street Haunting" shows, above all, the limitations of a too playful and transforming modernity. This sense of haunting restraint can be extended into an understanding of much contemporary Anglo-French theoretical criticism, especially as it impinges on the representation of "race," which is referred to throughout the collection. In, for example, her well-known account of George Eliot's *Daniel Deronda* (1876) Cynthia Chase, noted by Baumgarten, made out an influential case for reading this novel in deconstructive terms. Hans Meyrick's retrospective letter to the novel's eponymous hero, which establishes Deronda's Jewishness, confirms for Chase the novel's subversive logic. Meyrick tells Deronda that "whatever is best is for that reason Jewish," which, for Chase, has the following implication: "In renaming the novel's central issue as a matter of a substitution of terms, Meyrick's deconstructive gesture reconceives the significant action of human subjects as the purposeless play of signifiers."[9]

What prevents Deronda's Jewishness from being merely substituted for moral excellence is, in this reading, the "scandal" of his circumcised penis: "The plot can function only if . . . Deronda's circumcised penis is disregarded." Chase's argument is that the purposeless play of signifiers — which results in the erratic interchangeability of ostensibly different categories — is brought to a stark halt by the permanency of Deronda's "genetic" origins, which are metonymically signified by his circumcised penis. For all her deconstructive pretensions, Chase is in fact simply reinforcing the opposing narratives of "race" and "culture" in the novel, privileging a self-contradictory Jewishness as both a fluid, all-inclusive aesthetic realm and a racially reductive "nationalism."[10]

The racial fixity that Chase associates with circumcision is not, however, as self-evident as this reading assumes. As Gilman observes in his essay, with reference to Mark Twain, circumcision was itself allied to a wide variety of contradictory discourses and was not as stable and unchanging a racial signifier as is often supposed. In the case of Twain, turn-of-the-century American society was to associate being "uncircumcised" with being "uncivilized," whereas in Germany during the same period, as Gilman maintains elsewhere, male circumcision might well signify a deformed "feminization" in opposition to dominant notions of civilization or national superiority.[11]

Following on from Chase, other cultural critics have shown how circumcision in Victorian England was an "ambiguous sign" that could be accepted, historically, as a hygienic practice. It was not nearly as straightforwardly analogous with Jewish ritual as one might, at first, presume. The range of signifiers associated with circumcision in *Daniel Deronda* has been further elaborated in a recent reading of Gwendolen in terms of what has been called the "language of circumcision," which is gendered female. Gwendolen's first appearance on stage, it is said by the authorial voice, produces an "effect" rather like "a bit of her flesh — it was not to be peeled off readily but must come with blood and pain." Circumcision here, rather than being racially specific and gendered male, is, potentially, more inclusive and is a symbolic "effect" that, far from separating Daniel and Gwendolen, might bring them together.[12] As with the novel as a whole, circumcision can be understood simultaneously in both inclusive and exclusive terms. To reduce *Daniel Deronda* to the unbridgeable gulf between racial fixity and "purposeless play" is, therefore, to unquestioningly reproduce the novel's own unresolved oppositions.

Just as the categories of "woman" and "Jew" should not be simply collapsed into each other according to some supposedly deconstructive "play of signifiers," the figure of "the Jew" is always contested and equivocal: neither pure "play" nor pure "fixity." For this reason, racial immutability, in relation to Jewishness, is often projected onto a supposedly unambiguous "blackness." There are a number of key instances of this displacement in the literature under consideration. *Daniel Deronda* is once more instructive in this regard especially when the strangely incongruous but revealing authorial aside about the "Bosjesman" (or bushman) of South Africa is noted: "And one man differs from another, as we all differ from the Bosjesman" (p. 370).

In contrast to this imperious statement of an absolute "black" alterity, Deronda is affirmed immediately to have "something of the knight-errant in his disposition" as he ponders on the relative merits of Mirah and Gwendolen with respect to his "utopian" ideals (p. 370). At the same time as embodying an idealized European history, Deronda explicitly identifies in the following chapter with what Grandcourt calls the "beastly sort of baptist Caliban" (p. 376), who is said to have caused the anti-colonial uprising in Jamaica that was so viciously repressed by Governor Richard Eyre. Deronda, we are told, had "always felt a little with Caliban," and it is worth remembering, in this context, the extent to which Harriet Beecher Stowe's remarkably popular *Uncle Tom's Cabin* (1852) was a major influence on George Eliot's novel.[13] Palestine and Liberia, in these works, respectively enact the simultaneous assimilation and expulsion of the Jewish and black Other with regard to the dominant liberal values of the West. This narrative similarity might well explain why southern Africa, in Eliot's aside, is crudely denoted as a realm that "we all" differ from. To resolve Daniel's ambivalent positioning between a "barbarian" East and "civilised" West — the indeterminate location of a future Jewish nation-state — blackness becomes a structuring absence, an ultimate Other, onto which is displaced the potentially uncontainable otherness of Deronda's Jewishness.

Toward the end of Dorothy Richardson's *Deadlock*, published nearly half a century after *Daniel Deronda*, a stark example of this kind of displacement is made particularly explicit. In an extraordinary encounter in a small London teashop, Miriam Henderson and Michael Shatov postpone their mutual recriminations about the possibility of women's freedom in relation to what Miriam had earlier called the "mysterious fact of Jewishness" (p. 193). One "deadlock" is replaced by another, as Miriam finds herself "frozen . . . by the presence of a negro":

Miriam sat frozen, appalled by the presence of a negro. He sat near by, huge, bent, snorting and devouring, with a huge black bottle at his side. Mr Shatov's presence was shorn of its alien quality. He was an Englishman in the fact that he and she could *not* sit eating in the neighbourhood of this marshy jungle. . . . Yet the man had hands and needs and feelings. Perhaps he could sing. He was at a disadvantage an outcast. There was something that ought to be said to him. She could not think what it was. In his oppressive presence it was impossible to think at all. Every time she sipped her bitter tea, it seemed that before she should have replaced her cup, vengence would have sprung from the dark corner. Everything hurried so. There was no *time* to shake off the sense of contamination. It *was* contamination. The man's presence was an outrage on something of which he was not aware. (p. 217)

Miriam's paranoid sense of being "contaminated" and of being frozen into silence by an unexplainable but vengeful animal-like presence is precisely related to the Jewish racial representations of her day, many of which are examined in this volume. By displacing these representations onto a rampantly potent "negro" — "with a huge black bottle at his side" — Miriam is able, as she says, to no longer think of Shatov as a racial Other or even a threatening male: "Mr Shatov's presence was shorn of its alien quality." Shatov in his whiteness and assumed Eurocentricity is finally identical to Miriam in her Englishness, but only after his "alien" qualities have been so nakedly displaced onto the "marshy jungle" of Africa. It is the "black form in the corner" — no longer with "hands and needs and feelings" — who is said to "crush" Miriam's "thread of thought" (p. 217). This moment of overwhelming paralysis obviously prefigures Woolf's comparable passivity in "Street Haunting" when she comes across the "bearded Jew" and the "old woman." Not unlike "the dwarf" in Woolf's essay, Shatov's shifting status is such that it is now "the negro" who is the potentially "liberating" Other who must be faced before Miriam can speak:

In the awful presence she had spoken herself out, found and recited her best, most liberating words. . . . Light, pouring from her speech, sent a radiance about the thick black head and its monstrous bronze face. He might have his thoughts, might even look them, from the utmost abyss of crude male life, but he had helped her, and his blind unconscious outlines shared the unknown glory. (p. 219)

The interdependence between the "liberation" of the bourgeois woman and, in this case, the racial exclusion of the black Other connects in part, as Rose asserts in relation to Shatov, *Deadlock* and *Jane Eyre*. The self-immolation of the Creole woman, in Charlotte Brontë's novel, is the familiar prelude to Jane Eyre's own "independence," in the same way that the "unconscious outline" of "the negro" shares in the "glory" of Miriam's growing sense of separation from Shatov.[14] What is interesting, with regard to this volume, is the blatant arbitrariness of this form of othering, which positions "the negro" in exactly the same role that "the Jew" had occupied only a few pages before. When placed next to "the negro," Shatov is no longer an un-English "alien." He has moved from being "black" to being "white" and, by extension, from being "male" to being "female." By temporarily resolving her uncertain identification/differentiation with Shatov, "the negro" makes it possible for Miriam to see the "light" and realize, finally, why she should "liberate" herself from her Jewish admirer.

There are further notable instances of the ambivalent positioning of "the Jew" in terms of a racialized "blackness." That Jews were commonly conceived of as being both "black" and "white" can be seen from Baumgarten's reading of Trollope's anonymous *Nina Balatka* (1867). Trollope's description of his hero, Anton Trendellsohn, is significant in this regard: "Very dark — dark as a man can be and yet show no sign of colour in his blood. No white man could be more dark and swarthy than Anton Trendellsohn" (p. 11). Trendellsohn is, equivocally, as "dark" as a man can be who happens also to be "white." Where precisely the borders lie between "black" and "white" is also central to Gilman's understanding of Mark Twain's representations of "the Jew." Jews, for Twain, are neither "white" nor "negro," which is precisely why they are such a disturbing presence for him. Henry James, on the other hand, as Freedman shows, is untroubled by the fixity of "the negro" or the "Chinaman" when compared, as he saw it, to "the Jew" who spoke in the less predictable, more fluid "Accent of the Future."[15]

What is clear from these examples is that the racial identity of "the Jew" was not simply determined biologically but varied radically both between and within the literature under discussion. Even within the same "character," the otherness of "the Jew" was such that s/he could be simultaneously "male" and "female" and "black" and "white" and ultimately, as many essays illustrate, both "philosemitic" and "antisemitic." The protean instability of "the Jew" as a sign is, therefore, continually refigured by a wide range of differentiating discourses that complement the intertwining trinity of "race," class, and gender.

But one should not underestimate the extent to which "the Jew" could also be the ultimate and unchanging Other, threatening above all the coherence of any given narrative. Near the end of E. M. Forster's *Passage to India* (1924), for instance, Aziz reads an unopened latter from Heaslop to Fielding: "You are lucky to be out of British India at the moment. Incident after incident, all due to propaganda, but we can't lay our hands on the connecting thread. The longer one lives here, the more certain one gets that everything hangs together. My personal opinion is, it's the Jews" (p. 303).[16] Here "the Jews"—no less than "the Bosjesman" in *Daniel Deronda* or "the negro" in *Deadlock*—act as an all-explaining absence or "connecting thread" which somehow accounts for the increasingly uncertain future of "British India." Neither absolute alterity nor absolute mutability, "the Jew" might well explain everything or, as Forster intends, nothing. But despite his best "philosemitic" intentions Forster's authorial voice immediately adds: "thus far the red-nosed boy" (p. 303), which ironically turns Heaslop into a "red-nosed" Jewish stereotype. However hard he tries to expose the unacceptability of Heaslop's "antisemitism," Forster cannot escape from that which he would wish to expunge. Such is the anxiety generated by "the Jew" as the most tenacious of signifiers.

*

While the essays in this collection all attempt to historicize "the Jew" as an ambivalent sign, many also make an equally strong case for the liberating potential within this ambivalence. Eric Homberger's essay on some of the "uses for Jewish ambivalence," which concludes the volume, provides an important perspective on this subversive possibility with specific reference to the fiction of Abraham Cahan and Michael Gold. Homberger argues that "ambivalence has played a significant role in the emergence of Jewish writers in the United States" and he goes on to contrast this doubleness with what he calls the reification of "the Jew" or "the Other" in much contemporary cultural theory.[17] His essay is at pains to show that the early American Jewish novel attempted to work through the bittersweet emotions that many radical Jewish writers felt about the established values of the Jewish immigrant community in America. According to Homberger, Cahan and Gold both self-consciously colluded with and distanced themselves from the received and internalized stereotypes of the day. His essay illustrates the extent to which the "politics of ambivalence"—rather than "self-hatred" or "antisemitism"—provided a fertile means of undermining undifferentiated notions of "the Jew" or "the Other." Ironically, the productive irresolution of the American Jewish novelists in the interwar period also applies to Heinrich Heine's own "useful" Jewish ambivalence, which Galperin highlights in his opening essay.

What Galperin and Homberger expressly throw into relief, and it is implicit in all of the essays in the volume, is the limitations inherent in the entrenched historiography, which distinguishes absolutely between antisemitism and philosemitism. Galperin especially notes in his essay those points when antisemitism and philosemitism become indistinguishable in the poetry of Heine and Wordsworth. Freedman, similarly, discusses the "interplay" of these supposed irreconcilable states in the fiction of Henry James. If "antisemitism" is essentialized hostility that exists only on the margins of liberal society, then it is by definition a pathological form of expression that has little or no impact on a supposedly humanizing culture. In contrast to this approach, the representation of "Jewish" or Semitic difference within an apparently benevolent liberalism principally brings together the American and British literature in this collection. Enlightenment expectations, stemming from traditional Christianity, that Jews need to "convert" or assimilate into a superior culture are, as Galperin shows, as much a part of the history of western "antisemitism" as racial genocide in Nazi Germany or the medieval figure of the "Jew-Devil." Instead of a discrete and fixed series of "anti-Jewish images," the racial representations of "the Jew" under consideration assume a myriad of contradictory forms.

The overdetermination of "the Jew" within liberalism can be seen, above all, to have both an oppressive as well as an emancipatory aspect. What understandably tends to get emphasized is the violent resolution of "the Jew" as a perversely imprecise sign. Both Lassner and Ellmann, for example, in their essays stress the various ways in which the incommensurable "Jew" is bounded and fixed by an authoritarian political aesthetic, in the case of Pound and Eliot, or, in Woolf's case, by lavishly racialized characteristics. But other essays contend that literary texts are able to defuse this violent potentiality by directly exposing the insoluble "certainties" that make up "the Jew." Reizbaum illustrates how Joyce, by the time he came to write *Ulysses*, was to counter much of his earlier exoticized and eroticized demarcation of "the Jew" in *Dubliners*. That the colonized Irish could particularly identify with and differentiate themselves from the national liberation of diasporic Jewry is not insignificant in terms of the special place that "the Jew" had within Irish national consciousness. Joyce's refusal to elide the obvious differences of Jews and Irishmen as persecuted peoples — as well as his recognition of their similarities — was used to undermine nationalist mythologizing on all sides. The colonialization of Ireland and the hypocrisy of Empire, as well as Leopold Bloom's unrealizable Jewish assimilation, were all a part of the same historical "nightmare" of English liberalism. But if you place Jews and Irishmen in another historical context, such as New York in the 1920s and 1930s, as Homberger notes, then the supposed affinities between these two competing ethnicities become less and less apparent.

Many of the essays in the volume do, above all, attest rigourously to the possibility of overcoming dominant ways of constructing "the Jew." Orwell, in Loewenstein's account, begins to re-examine and question his own antisemitism after the Second World War, which in turn became a tangible aspect of his *Nineteen Eighty-Four*. One should not, in this regard, underestimate those authors such as Dickens, Virginia Woolf, and Graham Greene who rewrote a number of their key literary texts after recognizing their deleterious use of Jewish stereotypes in earlier editions or drafts.[18] Other novelists, such as Stevie Smith, deliberately set out to reverse the pernicious impact of "the Jew" on national consciousness, as Lassner makes clear. Smith's fiction deliberately interrogates the myths of Anglo-Saxon superiority and, in particular, Kiplingesque constructions of "the Jew." Whereas Kipling could write of the chosen Imperial relationship of "dark Israel" to the "Secret River of Gold," in *Puck of Pook's Hill* (1906), Smith, in *Over the Frontier* (1938), was to take exactly this mythologized language of Empire and expose its fascistic potential.

While literary texts might well help to change perceptions over a long period of time, they rarely have a transformative impact that is not in itself intimately related to wider social issues. The challenge of the literature under consideration, as many of the essays in the volume are at pains to emphasize, is to find a critical language that neither reinforces nor reproduces the racialized exclusions of the past. Most contributors to this collection, therefore, expressly refuse either to use the language of accusation or to validate a spuriously universalizing academic discourse that fails to recognize the specificities of, in our case, Jewish racial representations.

Finding a vocabulary that does not replicate the same processes of othering that one would wish to explore results, as we have seen, in an overriding need to radically rethink the dominant and received historiography of antisemitism (or, for that matter, philosemitism). The danger is that this historiography continues to essentialize Jews as uniquely timeless, unchanging victims and therefore positions the history of antisemitism outside of the social, political, and historical processes that gave rise to this history in the first place. All Jewish racial representations can, of course, be said to be ultimately "antisemitic." But instead of an aberrant hatred or affinity for "the Jews" by a particular author, this volume highlights more prevalent constructions of Semitic "difference" which, above all else, dispute the humanizing pretensions of the Anglo-American literary canon and liberal culture in general. In this, I follow Zygmunt Bauman, who has recently called for the term *allo-semitism* to be used to conceptualize anti-semitism and philosemitism as two relatively distinct aspects of a much broader process of differentiating Jews from other human beings.[19] The urgent task of finding a language and a way of thinking about the world that genuinely transcends past injustices is not, of course, the work merely of the academy but of everyone. Literary texts might, at best, provide the reader with a vision of the common identity of the oppressed and of how others have come to terms, either consciously or unconsciously, with the dehumanizing language of "race." But only when it is understood that no one is immune from the many and varied processes of othering will it be possible for the particular history of *allo-semitism* to be unlearned as a routine matter by teachers and students alike.

CHAPTER TWO

Romanticism and/or Antisemitism

WILLIAM GALPERIN

The conjunction of almost anything and the term *antisemitism* generally yields predictable results, and romanticism is seemingly no exception. From the generally benign neglect of Wordsworth and Coleridge (one recalls, for example, Coleridge's consignment of the Jew to the ship's "hold" in the account of his passage to Germany in the *Biographia Literaria*), to the offhand complaints of Keats and Byron, to the romantically inflected utopianism of Fichte, Marx, Hegel, and Fourier, romanticism apparently has had little trouble assimilating a conventional and sometimes virulent denomination of the Jew as Other (or as "jew," to use Lyotard's discrimination of the reviled Other and the actual people who are in this case made to represent it), to frequently revolutionary, even millenarian ends. Indeed, as Bernard Lewis observes, "the myth of a Jewish conspiracy to dominate the world, directed by a secret Jewish government of which all Jews are agents," is a late-eighteenth-century invention.[1]

There is, however, another account of romanticism and antisemitism in which the two are seemingly at cross-purposes. This narrative, which begins with Lessing and Schiller and the ideal of a universal humanity (in Lessing's exculpatory play *The Jews*, for example, the Jew is portrayed as no different from any other cultivated German), reaches a crescendo perhaps in the Berlin salons of Jews such as Rahel Varnhagen, who in the last years of the eighteenth century provided a "socially neutral" zone where, as Hannah Arendt notes, "all classes" could meet and "where it was taken for granted that each person would be an individual."[2] In more recent times this narrative has reappeared in the sympathetic reevaluation of romantic writing, chiefly British romantic writing, under the auspices of American critics—among them Harold Bloom, M. H. Abrams, Geoffrey Hartman, and even Lionel Trilling—many of whom are Jews.[3]

What this twentieth-century critical movement—the so-called romantic reassessment—has arguably reversed, then, what it has defended romantic writing *against*, is more than simply a poetics that may have found fault with romantic writing and its democratized aesthetics. Rather, what romanticism resists in this critical dispensation, particularly in conjunction with the strictures against Jews, both in the profession of letters at the time the reassessors were beginning their careers as well as in the very works (i.e., those of Pound and Eliot) by which English professors were at that time most influenced, is antisemitism itself.

According to Harold Bloom, for example,

the entire continuity of English poetry that T. S. Eliot and his followers attacked is a radical Protestant or displaced Protestant tradition. It is no accident that the poets deprecated by the New Criticism were Puritans, or Protestant individualists, or men of that sort breaking away from Christianity and attempting to formulate personal religions in their poetry. . . . It is also no accident that the poets brought into favor by the New Criticism were Catholics or High Church Anglicans Donne, Herbert, Dryden, Pope, Dr. Johnson, Hopkins in the Victorian period, Eliot and Auden in our time.[4]

Bloom may well be simplifying things in crediting Protestantism with greater tolerance (and, by implication, a greater tolerance toward Jews) than other sensibilities. If anything, it is Catholicism or a Catholic country—specifically France—that historically, and during the revolutionary period especially, was at the forefront of the Jewish emancipation in Europe. (It is sometimes difficult, on this score, to reconcile the image of Robespierre as defender of the Jews with the Robespierre of the Terror, or to recall that Napoleon did more for Jewish emancipation in Germany than did the Germans.)[5]

But regardless of its ahistorical bent, Bloom's reading of literary history suggests at the very least, in conjunction with other readings and *other readers* of romanticism, that romantic writing, or the displaced Protestantism that is romanticism (according to Bloom), is in the end less wedded to antisemitism than are other artistic movements. This does not mean, again, that romanticism is not ultimately ambivalent in its particular stance toward Jews and toward antisemitism. If anything, the romantic reassessment remains—in perhaps its most provocative formation—a call simply to suspend efforts in resolving this ambivalence. It is, at last, no longer necessary for criticism to reinvent romanticism according to Martin Buber (as Bloom does rather defensively in his study of Shelley), any more than it is necessary for criticism to imagine romanticism according to Martin Boorman (as Peter Viereck effectively manages in his classic analysis of the roots of the Nazi mind or as Philipe Lacoue-Labarthe has done more recently in stressing the romantic "schema of historiality" in Heidegger).[6] Indeed, it is the business of criticism *now* to come to terms with this ambivalence.

And here we are confronted with two alternatives, with two very different implications for our understanding and evaluation of the romantic achievement. Our first option, which has become increasingly available over the last fifteen years, would undoubtedly employ this ambivalence to demystify romanticism by underscoring the contradictions and defaults endemic to a putatively humanistic and revolutionary movement. The second, and for my part, more interesting option, regards this ambivalence as a consequence, not merely as a feature, of romanticism: as a moment of consciousness, if you will, where the confluence of romanticism and antisemitism is such that ambivalence is barely containable as ambivalence. This latter option, then, registers romanticism's own uneasiness regarding the ambivalence signaled in, among other forms, philosemitism or progressive humanism and constitutes, by turns, an ambivalence *toward ambivalence* — toward the very contradictions that many recent versions of criticism find so disturbing in romanticism. And as such, it generally takes the form of something remarkably uncontradictory and univocal: an antisemitism, sometimes, that is necessarily and unequivocally anti-romantic.

Antisemitism is scarcely the only time when romanticism turns on itself, or turns itself in, in this curious way. The conception of romantic irony, for example, encodes a rhythm of apostasy into romanticism as a way of confessing and thereby disabusing romanticism of its essentializing and contradictory tendencies.[7] But antisemitism is a useful moment to examine precisely because its instances are on balance so relatively scarce, because the relative absence of antisemitism in romantic writing would seem to distinguish romanticism on the very grounds it would claim distinction and apparently deserves recognition, according to Bloom and others: namely, as a revolutionary and humane movement with a special commitment to the significance and autonomy of individual human beings. There are precious few Bleisteins with their cigars in romantic writing, or Rachel Rabinoviches with their murderous paws, or "perfect Schnorrers" (in Pound's putatively knowing description). Instead, what we are apt to encounter in romantic writing whenever Jews appear, for example in Byron's *Hebrew Melodies* — or, more important, when they *don't* appear in, say, almost all of

Wordsworth's poetry—is something inimical to romanticism (and to its "revolutionary" program) *only* under pressure of interpretation.

In a virtually forgotten poem composed in the latter part of his career Wordsworth describes a Jewish family that he had occasion to observe while on tour in Germany. Initially invoking the painter Raphael, whose various renderings of Madonna and Child could easily be modeled on "this poor family," the poem lingers over the dyad of mother and boy before turning its attention—indeed its speaker's gaze—to the boy's sisters:

> Two lovely Sisters, still and sweet
>   As flowers, stand side by side;
> Their soul-subduing looks might cheat
>   The Christian of his pride:
> Such beauty hath the Eternal poured
>   Upon them not forlorn,
> Though of a lineage once abhorred,
>   Nor yet redeemed from scorn.
>
> Mysterious safeguard, that, in spite
>   Of poverty and wrong,
> Doth here preserve a living light,
>   From Hebrew fountains sprung;
> That gives this ragged group to cast
>   Around the dell a gleam
> Of Palestine, of glory past,
>   And proud Jerusalem![8]

The recourse to "Jerusalem" at the poem's close scarcely beclouds the fact that, like everything else here, Hebrew eschatology is merely, and not coincidentally, the *last* thing that has been appropriated by the poet or put to some other use.

The preliminary allusion to Raphael, though an acknowledgment surely of the family's extraordinary beauty, literally represents a conversion of the Jews; it is a surmise (to borrow Hartman's figure) in which the Jews are alternately recuperated as Christians and displaced as Others. It represents a conversion, that is, in which Jews are converted to Christianity because *as narrative figures* they are in need of conversion—for their sake as well as ours. No matter how much the speaker is disposed to credit the Jews, whether as types of the Holy family or as the fountains of hope for a better, more equitable world, he does so according to a logic that ultimately conflates Jews and "jews." He does so according to a Christian eschatology, or to a Manichean narrative, as Heine would later identify it, for which "Jerusalem"—no less than a Holy family comprising Jewish bodies—is a figure for something *other* than Jerusalem: for a Jerusalem, that is, *displaced* from "Palestine." As the poem's last word (literally and figuratively), "Jerusalem" marks a turning from, rather than a gesture toward, the actual place of origin.

This counterturn similarly informs the poem's philosemitism, which, as the passage shows, is indistinguishable finally from antisemitism. In the very way that the speaker can acknowledge the Jews only by recoiling from them, by decapitalizing the *J* in *jew*, so to speak, so his liberal acknowledgment of the general abhorrence of the Jews, of the very scorn that as the poem notes persists to the present day, is offered in virtual ignorance of the scorn of this moment itself. It is offered, then, on the very heels of the eroticism of the "two lovely sisters" (Nazi propaganda would later deem this subjection of the soul "sly Jewish eroticism") which, no less than the relocation of Jerusalem as a final plenitude, as a town *without* Jews, and no less than the recuperation of the family as the work of Raphael, echoes the logic — the logic of what is at once antisemitism and millenarianism — where praise and blame are necessarily indistinguishable.

It is not my purpose, of course, to excoriate Wordsworth for having written this poem, which is well-meaning, I think, despite its narrative structure. I bring it up simply to illustrate the kind of contradictory writing — a writing alternately anti- and philosemitic, alternately antinomian and orthodox — which it is easy, I suppose, to deem typical of romanticism in general. But there is another aspect to romanticism (and to Wordsworth, as I've argued elsewhere) that is perhaps not so typical, or is atypical only according to the fashions of literary history that are forever bent on containing romanticism in one way or another. And it is an aspect of romanticism one site of which is antisemitism.

Romanticism, in this aspect, is characterized less by contradiction, by the kind of philosemitism of Wordsworth's "Jewish Family," which disintegrates under pressure of reading. Instead, it is characterized by a remarkably unidirectional "excess," which in some sense blocks interpretation and ultimately proves a dead end. Romanticism in this manifestation "overflows" with antisemitism, the peculiar excess of which, to follow Lyotard's description of this phenomenon, "takes possession" of representation — of romantic narrative, to be precise — before narrative can ever take possession of it (Lyotard, *Heidegger,* p. 20). Thus, it is a romanticism alternately ironic and incomprehensible and also antisemitic, a romanticism no longer pitched toward a totalizing synthesis and meaning — toward "Jerusalem," as it were — and a romanticism no longer confused with philosemitism or progress. The coincidence of romanticism and antisemitism is in this sense part of a *negative* dialectic, whose ultimate function, I would argue, is the protection of all bodies from narrative. Akin now to what Jeffrey Sammons, in reference to Heine, has termed a "blind alley," the discourse of romanticism remains a discourse in which there is only interference and consequently no final solution, no new or second Jerusalem for which the conversion or extirpation of the Jews is otherwise a precondition.

The following example from Heine's famous essay, *Concerning the History of Religion and Philosophy in Germany* (1832),[9] will serve to illustrate this excessive, disruptive tendency. Remarking on the reversal by which Christ, disparaged by the Romans as "King of the Jews," finally became "God of the Romans" to whom both "heathen" and Christian Rome "had to pay tribute," Heine is inspired by the cunning of history into antisemitic fantasy:

If you, dear reader, during the first days of the trimester, will betake yourself to Lafitte Street, to the hotel at no. 15, you will see there in front of a tall gate a lumbering carriage from which a stout man will descend. He will go upstairs to a small room where a young blond man is sitting, actually older than he probably looks, in whose elegant, grand seignorial nonchalance there is yet something as solid, something as positive, something as absolute as if he had all the money in the world in his pocket. And indeed he *has* all the money in this world in his pocket, and his name is Mr. James Rothschild, and the stout man is Monsigneur Grimbaldi, a legate of His Holiness the Pope, and he is bringing in the latter's name the interest on the Roman loan, the tribute from Rome. (p. 194)

In the event that one was not aware either that Heine was a Jew or that he was a writer whose particular romanticism was predicated on an uneasiness with what he termed the "Romantic School," much of this — indeed, the curious amalgam that was Heinrich Heine — could be inferred from the way romantic narrative and antisemitic narrative are made synonymous here.

For the most remarkable thing about this passage is not that it could have turned up just as easily in the writings of Pound or Céline (both of whom share the same fantasy of Jewish dominance); most remarkable about this representation is a peculiar autonomy or overdetermination that appears to disarm even Heine himself. Here, in short, a narrative of triumph — specifically of the Jews by agency of their "king" over Rome — a rather stable narrative over which the speaker exerts fairly rigid control, modulates to a completely unstable (and, on the evidence of the tone here, completely incomprehensible) discourse in which the present-day version of the Jews' triumph is coextensive with a fantasy that demands, as the only possible closure, the annihilation of the Jews. In meaning to say one thing Heine ends up signifying something else that is no different, at the same time, from what he means. One triumph, that is, simply begets another.

The name for this discursive turn is, of course, irony. But it is an irony that must be distinguished from the stable irony in which Heine begins this passage—and not, I would urge, from the unstable or romantic irony to which the passage leads. In his famous essay on the romantic school Heine speaks of a "humorous irony," the apparent rage for which he correctly deems a "sign of our lack of political freedom." A humorous ironist is someone like Prince Hamlet who dissembles constantly but who is, according to Heine, "the most honest soul in the world":

> His dissimulation only serves as a substitute for external appearances. . . . In all his humorously ironic jests he intentionally lets one see through his dissimulation; in everything that he does and says his real opinion is quite visible for anyone who knows how to see. . . . And by feigning insanity he likewise does not want to deceive us; he is deeply aware that he actually is insane. (pp. 66–67)

If Hamlet, the prototypical ironist, is utterly transparent, then Heine, the Jewish antisemite, is utterly opaque. While Hamlet feigns insanity in the awareness that he is actually insane, so Heine—the progressive Jew—is actually an antisemite, someone who literally declaims against the Jewish ownership of the world, even as he is plainly feigning it or, more accurately, as he is narrating.

Nor should it surprise us, then, that Heine was Freud's characteristic jokester.[10] For in the very way that jokes (notably Heine's) are, as Freud conceives them, "uncompromising" (p. 172) irruptions, which, unlike dreams, reestablish "old liberties by getting rid of intellectual upbringing" (p. 126), so the irruption of antisemitism in Heine—the Jewish joke carried to a sublime or vertiginously ironic pitch—has a similar effect of exposing the latent or repressed content of representation so-called. Where dreams and narratives entail compromise in Freud's view, where Heidegger, as Lacoue-Labarthe recently insists, "compromised with a movement for which antisemitism was a fundamental principle" (p. 33), Heine's uncompromising Jewish joke renders audible what—either in the notorious example of Heidegger or in the barely noticeable example of teleological narrative—is otherwise silent or repressed.[11]

Thus, in "The Rabbi of Bacherach," an otherwise affectionate vignette of medieval Jewry, Heine is not only disposed to quicken the story's action by exposing his fictional rabbi to the threat of pogrom and annihilation; he is careful to link the narrative of Jewish culpability to the Jews' own narrative "of their deliverance from captivity in Egypt" as it is commemorated every year at Passover.[12] The ruthlessness of this particular effort to incriminate the Jew, on which the story ostensibly centers, involves the exploitation of the hospitality customarily extended to strangers who wish to join in the Passover festivities but who in this instance gain entry to the rabbi's home simply to deposit a child's corpse under the Seder table in order to incriminate him. Still, not even this hideous betrayal is sufficient to becloud the narrative logic, indeed the peculiar symmetry, that links one narrative of opposition and deliverance, specifically of the Jews from Egypt, to another narrative of opposition and deliverance in which the Jews are to be overcome.

Rather than compromising itself by adherence to a given narrative (however virtuous or judgmental), "The Rabbi of Bacherach" approximates Schlegelian irony in asserting both the impossibility and necessity of complete communication. For what is truly "uncompromising" in this story, and in Heine generally, is no more possible to see through, to comprehend as something merely intended, than to avoid. It is something altogether excessive and incomprehensible (to use another Schlegelian trope), something following which narrative, like the philosemitic narrative of the Jews' triumph over Rome or Egypt, is both madness and civilization. Thus, Heine's narrative must also be distinguished from the "Jewish self-hatred" that, according to Sander Gilman, simply reifies and preserves civilization's conception of the Jew.[13] Rather, antisemitism is a text that, according to Heine, must now cease, and which his unstable irony effectively brings to a halt (or sequesters in a blind alley) because *as a narrative* it is virtually consumed by a sense of an ending.

With this in mind, we can better understand Heine's oft-cited critique of romanticism, particularly his charge that romanticism is nothing more than a version of Catholicism. What Heine seems to be getting at by this capricious identification is not simply that romanticism can be read retrospectively in light of Schlegel's recent conversion, or that romanticism is overly spiritual and, as such, overly escapist (as Jerome McGann has recently construed Heine's complaint).[14] Heine is doing something far more basic, I think; he is trying, in the most obvious way possible, to save Jewish bodies (among others) *from* romanticism, which involves saving romanticism from a tradition (or "schema of historiality") in which Jews, no less than the Catholics who followed them, are equally implicated.

Heine, to be sure, had little quarrel with the liberationist agenda of romanticism and, despite his position regarding humorous irony, a far larger indebtedness to romantic irony than he would ever let on. The problem for him was in the Manichean narrative, with its opposing principles of good and evil. It was in the "cosmogony, the real idea of Christianity," that, as he remarks in his contemporaneous essay on the history of religion and philosophy in Germany, "spread over the entire Roman empire with incredible rapidity, like a contagious disease, at times a raging fever, at times exhaustion, lasted all through the Middle Ages, and we moderns still feel spasms and lassitude in all our limbs" (p. 133).

Romanticism, then, is the most recent name for this disease and the most modern by far of the Manichean narratives. All the same, to regard romanticism as the culprit in all of this is as pointless ultimately as tarring romanticism with the brush of Catholicism. The problem, once again, is with narrative itself — with a narrative of which Heine's own history of Germany is an example. That this is so, I think, is clear in the famous ending of Heine's *History*, which is often regarded (and usually praised) as a prophecy of the cataclysmic events involving Germany in our century: in short, as a prophecy of the Holocaust. According to Heine, the Germans, motivated by the "demonic forces" of "ancient . . . pantheism," "[will] with their old stone gods . . . arise from the forgotten ruins . . . and Thor will at last leap up with his giant hammers and smash the Gothic cathedrals" — "a crash such as has never been heard before in world history" (p. 243).

It is almost impossible, upon reading this (and there is, needless to say, much more in this vein than I have cited), not to credit Heine as the most perspicacious, perhaps, of all nineteenth-century German writers. Yet it is just this impossibility that I am asking us — that this passage is asking us — to consider. To regard these statements as truly prophetic merely grants stability and meaning by means of hindsight. It imbues what is monstrously unstable and excessive with a truth-value or transparency simply because something like what Heine hysterically puts forth here eventually took place. Such a reading, or retrospective ironization, overlooks the fact that, like Heine's own antisemitism, the irony here is immediately unstable, that this ending is no more than what narrative requires and what writing here both serves and resists. It overlooks the fact that cataclysm and conversion and "Jerusalem" — or the killing of the "jews," to be precise — is the only meaning that can be attached to this or any narrative, the only closure, in effect, that "history" can have. Heine, for his part, may have intended this prophecy in a more rational form. But like his antisemitism, these intentions are still a consequence of narrative and — despite exposing the consequences *of* narrative — of a "history" into which the historian is absorbed even as the reader is invited to resist it.

A similar ambivalence toward narrative is evident in a quite different, if still relevant, text of Heine's: his famous "Hebrew Melody" on the medieval poet and philosopher "Jehuda ben Halevy."[15] Here in the seemingly hagiographic account of this Jewish spiritualist, Heine accomplishes what Wordsworth could not accomplish in his poem on the Jewish family. He exposes and, ultimately, ironizes the narrative partnership of philo- and antisemitism, of the Jerusalem toward which Jehuda hearkens and the "Jerusalem" — the romantic plenitude — that costs Jehuda his life. Virtually all commentators on the poem agree that Halevy is more than a historical figure, that he is indeed a prototype of a romantic poet — indeed of the very speaker "in whose imagination he lives."[16] Where there is a problem is simply in the point of this connection: Is Heine vowing in some way to imitate Jehuda? Does he similarly hearken toward Jerusalem? Or is it more that Heine invests Jehuda with this nostalgia of a lost homeland, with both narrative *and* its consequences, in order to distinguish and thereby to save himself?

The poem, I think, is characteristically divided. On the one hand, it never ceases to be a hagiography. On the other hand, it never ceases to be ironic, or to require that we infer more, or less, from the paean than it yields. And this is due, I think, to the poem's excess, to the blind alleys (Sammons, p. 392) that sustain this division and — paradoxical as it may sound — allow Heine to move beyond it. The poem is divided, then, according to an excessiveness that ultimately brings the narrative — and the poem's ambivalence — to a crashing halt. Typical of this interruption would be the story of the pearls that were contained, according to the poem, in a casket of jewels initially won from Darius by Alexander the Great and subsequently passed from the dancer Thais, to Cleopatra, to Spanish queens — who wore them "at the bullfights and processions" and at "the autos-da-fe / where they sat on balconies / and drank in the refreshing smell / of old Jews being fried" — before finally passing into the hands of the Baroness Rothschild herself.

The gathering of owners here, all of whom are potentially victims and victimizers, is ironic enough, but the full import — and the full irony — of Heine's story is dependent still on what follows. For no sooner is this story told than it becomes an allegory or figure for Halevy's own poems: for the very works that, as the narrator tells us again and again, continually anticipate the consummation of the rabbi and his beloved Jerusalem. "I thought," he writes, "if I should ever / Gain possession of [Darius'] casket, / And was not compelled directly / By financial straits to sell it, / I should like to lock within it / All the poems of our Rabbi, / Of Jehuda ben Halevy."

Clearly, the material image of Halevy's poems as pearls before genocide, as ornaments to the actual destruction of Jews, is something of a shock, all the more in that they now bedeck — both literally and as a cultural legacy — the Baroness Rothschild. But what is even more remarkable about this passage — as it was earlier in Heine's antisemitic fantasy — is that this connection is barely made, that we are invited by the metaphor to *value* what the allegory discredits: namely, the transhistorical, transcultural disposition of Jehuda's millenarian narrative.

Jehuda's narrative becomes, then, in this radical instability, a song that, however beautiful, is death-dealing: a narrative that kills Jews, and that literally kills Jehuda, who, as we learn shortly, was fatally wounded by a Saracen, but not before "he calmly finished singing, / Sang his song out, and his death-sigh / Was the name Jerusalem!" Legend has it, of course, that this

Saracen was not evil, "but an angel in disguise," who slew Jehuda "to speed him painless / To the kingdom of the blessed." But this speculation — in the poem's curiously exteriorized stance to its own ambivalence — is simply another song. It is another Manichean jewel, which casts a blind eye — in a way that an excessive romanticism no longer permits — to the Saracen's own song, to the "Jerusalem" to which *the Saracen* was speeded, having killed Jehuda, the romantic singer of Jerusalem.

CHAPTER THREE

Mark Twain and the Diseases of the Jews

SANDER L. GILMAN

> In estimating the position of Israel in the human values
> we must remember that the quest for righteousness is
> oriental, the quest for knowledge occidental. With the
> great prophets of the East—Moses, Isaiah, Mahomet—
> the word was "Thus saith the Lord"; with the great seers
> of the West, from Thales and Aristotle to Archimedes and
> Lucretius, it was "What says Nature?" They illustrate two
> opposite views of man and his destiny—in the one he
> is an "angelus sepultus" in a muddy vesture of decay; in
> the other, he is the "young light-hearted master" of the
> world, in it to know it, and by knowing to conquer.
> —William Osler,
> "Israel and Medicine" (1914)

There has been increased interest recently in Mark Twain's essay "Concern-ing the Jews," which appeared in the September 1898 issue of *Harper's Magazine*.[1] Indeed, there has even been speculation that Sigmund Freud's last public statement on the nature of antisemitism was a paraphrase of Twain's work.[2] Twain's essay responded to a reader's inquiry following his ironic account in the August issue of the antisemitic rhetoric of the "de-bate" in the Austrian parliament concerning the bill mandating Czech as the official language of Bohemia. Twain's reasoned answer, along with the addendum concerning the role of the Jew as soldier, make up one of the most complex documents written against antisemitism in late nineteenth-century America. Yet it bears the hallmark of presuppositions concerning the special nature of the Jew that were noted even by Twain's contempo-raries, such as M. S. Levy, who wrote in 1899 that "from the many statements Mark Twain makes regarding the various traits of the Jews, it is plain that they are not only tinged with malice and prejudice, but are incorrect and false."[3] It is clear that Twain's intent in writing his essay "concerning the Jews" was to counter the growing antisemitism following the increase of Eastern European Jewish immigration to the United States. The shifting, sometimes contradictory positions that Twain occupied concerning the Jews were acknowledged by his contemporaries. What is important, and has not been noted by the critics, both contemporary and contemporaneous, is that Twain shifts the underlying rhetoric of his argument about the Jews from one that sees the nature of the Jews as immutable to one that understands it as socially constructed. This essay will examine three interrelated questions: (1) Twain's image of the Jew in his earliest writing and its affinity to the model of the "diseased Jew," (2) the various racial models of the diseased Jew that existed in European and American thought through the nineteenth century, and (3) the parallel and/or difference of Twain's later views to his earlier ones. To understand the differences and continuities in Twain's image of the Jew, the reader must be able to comprehend that there was an earlier, as yet unread image of the Jew in Twain's work, which was published decades before the more widely cited essay "Concerning the Jews."

My focus will thus not begin with this late "liberal" essay (though I shall refer to it later in this analysis) but with Twain's first extended representation of the Jews in his most popular book, *The Innocents Abroad; or, The New Pilgrims' Progress*.[4] What I shall be examining is Twain's pattern of representing illness in this work and the relationship of this model to contemporary discussions of the illnesses of the Jews. This travel account, published in 1869, represents a specific Reconstruction debate concerning the Jew's body. It reveals a set of presuppositions about the meaning of racial identity and the inheritability of such an identity that were widely debated at the time. *The Innocents Abroad; or, The New Pilgrim's Progress* recounts Twain's journey to Europe and the Holy Land during 1867. One of its central themes is the meaning of disease in the traveler's life and experience. Disease is a concept closely linked to religion and the exotic. This theme quickly becomes one of the structuring principles furnishing a philosophy of history that underlies Twain's account of his journey as moving backward in time as he and his friends travel ever eastward in space. And, as we shall see, no people is more ancient or more remote or more diseased than the Jews. For Twain, the tracing of disease becomes a commentary on the role of the Jews in western civilization. Such underlying views would seem to run counter to the stated intentions of Twain's essay of 1898.

Twain's Travels

The Innocents Abroad; or, The New Pilgrims' Progress begins with the reprinting of the announcement for the tour. This list of particulars included, as the fourth item following the description of the steamer, the *Quaker City*, the fact that "an experienced physician will be on board" (p. 18). It is, of course, not unusual that such provisions for medical care were attractive for extended cruises. But the theme of ubiquitous illness and disease is made an intrinsic part of the fabric of the trip. The relationship of the American visitors to the disease and death they experience as inherent in the exotic locales that they visit in Europe and the Middle East defines the Americans as the curable, if not the healthy, and a "white" United States as that place where, though there may be illness, there is also modern "scientific" medicine and the potential for remedy. (Twain, as we shall see, assumes that the Native American is predisposed to illness.) For, even with all of the minor illness experienced by the American travelers, there is no parallel in their experiences (at least on this trip) with the ever mounting roll call of horrors seen on their trip. Medicine is on their side, as is an unencumbered belief in that science. It is the reality of disease and death that haunts Twain's representation of his travels eastward.

Earlier American travelers on the Grand Tour had recounted their own fascination with the specter of disease, but always within the frame of the aesthetic. Among the standard stops on the Grand Tour were exhibitions of anatomical figures in the museums of Bologna, Florence, Rome, and Vienna.[5] Florence especially, and specifically the Royal and Imperial Museum of Physics and Natural History (called La Specola, because of its observatory), founded in 1775, became the mecca for travelers fascinated by the world of decay. Represented in the collection of the Florentine school were a number of the great masters of wax casting, especially the famed Sicilian wax modeler Gaetano Giulo Zummo. He, like many of the sculptors, was responsible for many of the anatomical exhibitions as well as religious artwork in this medium found throughout Italy and France. The traveler experienced these traditions as one, linking the anatomized body and that of the martyred saint, which the traveler saw through the use of the same aesthetic devices cast in wax.

These collections of anatomical art became a focus for the visits of Americans on the Grand Tour. Americans were offered a sense of the "sublime," the emotion of overwhelming sensation to be had within nature. This was nature frozen in the aesthetic form of the wax cast rather than in the stinking cadavers of the anatomical theater. Henry Wadsworth Longfellow, in the 1830s, saw these figures on his Grand Tour of the continent and sensed both their reality and the unreality that one must ascribe to the medium of the wax sculpture:

Zumbo [*sic*] . . . must have been a man of the most gloomy and saturnine imagination, and more akin to the worm than most of us, thus to have reveled night and day in the hideous mysteries of death, corruption, and the charnel house. It is strange how this representation haunts one. It is like a dream of the sepulcher, with its loathsome corpses, with "the blackening, the swelling, the bursting of the trunk, — the worm, the rat, and the tarantula at work." You breathe more freely as you step out into the bright sunshine and the crowded, busy streets next meet your eye, you are ready to ask, Is this indeed a representation of reality?[6]

The dream of the real, or perhaps the nightmare of death, of the body corrupt, of the body putrefied, is "real" only because it tricks the highest sense, sight; it is "unreal," a false representation, because it lacks the other senses. Longfellow's vision was of the permanence of corruption, of the immutability of mutability, all images so contradictory that they lead to a questioning of the very body itself. But Longfellow saw all of this in the work of art representing death and decay.

The world of exotic religion as experienced by these American travelers was also closely associated, through the wax cast, with the erotic and death. As late as 1858, Nathaniel Hawthorne (on his Grand Tour) sensed the close relationship between the religious use of such wax sculptures and erotic imagery: "And here, within a glass case, there is the representation of an undraped little boy in wax, very prettily modelled, and holding up a heart that looks like a bit of red sealing-wax. If I had found him anywhere else, I should have taken him for Cupid; but being in an oratory, I presume him to have some religious signification."[7] Twain's fascination, perhaps because of his western exposure to public images of disease and physical corruption, was not with this type of aestheticized corpse but with the dreary realities to be found in European daily life. For Twain, it is not the image of decay and the body that fascinates, but the dead and decaying body itself.

In Paris, one of their first stops in Europe, Twain's travelers in *The Innocents Abroad* first visit Notre Dame, where they are shown church relics similar to Hawthorne's little wax figure. But here they include the "bloody robe" of the Archbishop of Paris assassinated on the Parisian barricades in 1848 as well as "the bullet that killed him, and the two vertebrae in which it was lodged" (p. 105). Twain's comment that "these people have a somewhat singular taste in the matter of relics" links (as do the comments of Longfellow and Hawthorne) the representation of the body within the rituals of Christianity (here, especially Catholicism) and the barbarous dismemberment and display of the body. Little surprise that from the Cathedral the travelers' next stop is "the Morgue, that horrible receptacle for the dead who die mysteriously and leave the manner of their taking off a dismal secret" (p. 105). There they see the body of a drowned man, "naked, swollen, purple," which is gawked at by the passersby, "people, I thought, who live upon strong excitements, and who attend the exhibitions of the Morgue regularly, just as other people go to see theatrical spectacles every night. When one of these looked in and passed on, I could not help thinking: 'Now this don't afford you any satisfaction — a party with his head shot *off* is what you need' " (p. 106). Such a body would have been the body of the Archbishop of Paris as exposed in the Cathedral of Notre Dame. Twain has established the relationship between religion, especially exotic religions such as Catholicism, and the dead or dying body.[8]

Twain's sense of the horrors associated with the representation of disease and its relationship to the exotic is heightened the further east he travels. Thus, in entering Constantinople he is reminded about the "dwarfs" and "cripples" he had seen on the streets of Genoa, Milan, and Naples. His Italian experience was nothing compared to the "very heart and home of cripples and human monsters" that is Constantinople. There Twain sees in the very flesh the deformed and mutilated — a woman with three legs, two of them withered; a man with an eye in his cheek. The normally mutilated, "a mere damaged soldier on crutches would never make a cent. It would pay him to get a piece of his head taken off, and cultivate a wen like a carpet sack" (p. 285). All of these horrors of the flesh are seen by the travelers on their way to the Mosque of Saint Sophia. Again, the association between the diseased and the religious is made, but here exponentially. For in Paris the association was made between two isolated places in the city, which Twain linked to provide his readers with an association between religion and disease; in Constantinople disease, deformity, and dirt are everywhere, invading, indeed defining the very presence of the Mosque itself (p. 286).

The closer Twain and his party get to the Holy Land, the more the metaphors of disease and religion are linked. It is in Damascus — on the way to the Holy Land — that the very sight of the city first causes Twain to begin to quote from what is his (and his companions') true guidebook on this journey, the Bible. For the travels of the innocents in Twain's account are a disguised account of a pilgrim's progress, but the progress of a pilgrim already doubting the veracity of his own faith. The sight of Damascus evokes Paul's sojourn there and the origins of Pauline Christianity, "that bold missionary career which he prosecuted til his death" (p. 365). Twain's own ambivalence toward the meaning of religion in general takes on the coloration of his anxiety about the link between disease, death, and belief. Twain no longer sees this linkage as taking place in isolation or at a distance from himself. Rather, he slowly comes to understand that his own Christian belief system, the cultural perspective that forms his vision, is itself a

product of a religious worldview, the worldview of the Jews. It is, therefore, not in the New Testament that Twain finds the appropriate vision by
which he can comprehend the Holy Land.

The image that Twain uses to close this chapter and to introduce us to
the Holy Land is taken from the Old Testament; he quotes the words of
Naaman from 2 Kings 5, who praised the waters of Damascus as "better
than all the waters of Israel. May I not wash in them and be clean?" For
Naaman, "the favorite of the king," was a leper, and his house in Damascus
had been turned into a leper hospital where inmates "expose their horrid
deformities and hold up their hands and beg for buckseesh when a stranger
enters" (p. 367). Twain's response is one of horror: "One can not appreciate the horror of this disease until he looks upon it in all its ghastliness,
in Naaman's ancient dwelling in Damascus. Bones all twisted out of shape,
great knots protruding from face and body, joints decaying and dropping
away—horrible!" (p. 367). To this point Twain had distanced the horrors
of death. They were the fascination of others—of the visitors to Notre
Dame or the Rue Morgue, of those unfortunates who exposed their muti-
lations in Catholic Italy or Muslim Turkey. Here the horrors seen are immediately internalized. It is in Damascus, in the city of Naaman the Leper,
that Twain is struck ill.

Twain spent his final day in Damascus, after visiting the lepers' hospital,
suffering from "cholera, or cholera morbus" (p. 368). Given his symptoms,
it is clear that his intestinal complaint is what we today would call "turista"
or, perhaps, Naaman's Revenge. It was hardly cholera as understood in the
late nineteenth century.[9] His response to his symptoms was hysterically to
apostrophize his healthy, American audience—as if his stomach cramps
were the sign of his own corrupt nature. His association of the world he
has entered with disease has now infiltrated into his very being, into his in-
nermost sense of self. Twain comes to realize that his association of death,
illness, and religion is not merely the fancy of exotic practices (Catholicism) or religions (Islam) or of spaces that are unrelated to his sense of self
(Paris, Naples, Constantinople). Rather, he now has to struggle with the
image that his association belongs to his world, the world of backwoods
Christianity as represented by The Book that formed his sense of self, the
Bible. But Damascus, the gateway to the world of the Bible, becomes retrospectively, in contrast to the diseased nature of the Holy Land, his "one
pleasant reminiscence of this Palestine excursion."[10] The loathing Twain
comes to feel for the diseased world of the Bible confuses his text. The
hysterical discovery that the disease attributed to others was part of his
own sense of self creates physical symptoms, revulsion, and nausea, which
moves the text widely between the ancient past (which is part of Twain's
present world) and the present (which reveals itself to be a continuation of

the past). What was external and seen in Constantinople has now become internalized as a symbolic representation of the means by which Twain belongs to this world. Illness is real, and it exists in the very fabric of the world around him; it infiltrates into the very essence of his being. But illness is tied closely to religious belief, to "superstition," which the ironic Twain and his appreciative reader must see as remote from themselves. In this frame of mind, Twain sets off for the Holy Land. The very first experience he has "just stepping over the border and entering into the long-sought Holy Land" (p. 372) is that of disease.

On September 17, 1867, Twain entered the Holy Land with seven companions. There he finds that the very ground on which the Savior walked, "that Jesus looked on in the flesh" (p. 373), is the land of disease.[11] "Standing on ground that was once actually pressed by the feet of the Savior," Twain sees himself surrounded by "the usual assemblage of squalid humanity" which, in its passive suffering, evoked in him the image of the native Americans: "They remind me much of Indians, did these people. . . . They sat in silence, and with tireless patience watched our every motion with that vile, uncomplaining impoliteness which is so truly Indian, and which makes a white man so nervous and uncomfortable and savage that he wants to exterminate the whole tribe. These people about us had other peculiarities, which I have noticed in the noble red man, too: they were infested with vermin, and the dirt caked on them till it amounted to bark" (pp. 374–75). The children are covered with flies, and they suffer from sore eyes, which eventually leads to blindness in many of them. And in their passivity and acceptance of illness they are the very antithesis of the white American: "And, would you suppose that an American mother could sit for an hour, with her child in her arms, and let a hundred flies roost upon its eyes all that time undisturbed? I see that every day" (p. 375). Twain's "sight" is a mark of his American health, as opposed to the blindness of the inhabitants of the Holy Land.

Once the waiting multitudes learn that among the travelers is a physician, Dr. J. B. Birch of Hannibal, Missouri, they come in droves. (Are they not attracted by exactly that same faith that moved the steamship line back in the United States to so prominently advertise the presence of a physician on board the *Quaker City*?) "The lame, the halt, the blind, the leprous—all the distempers that are bred of indolence, dirt, and iniquity—were represented" (p. 375). And the doctor ministered to them with his "dread, mysterious power" and "phials . . . of white powder." For these diseased individuals, "he was gifted like a god" (p. 376). The physician as "god" is a mirror of one of the central metaphors of Christianity, that of Christ as physician: "And great multitudes came together to hear, and to be healed by him of their infirmities" (Luke 4:15).

And here Twain pulls out the card he had been waiting to play from the moment he and his companions had left the United States. For it is the very despair of these individuals that makes the very wonders of the historical Christ comprehensible, a factor understood in the abstract in western religion but written on the very skin of the inhabitants of the Holy Land:

Christ knew how to preach to these simple, superstitious, disease-tortured creatures: He healed the sick. They flock to our poor human doctor this morning when the fame of what he had done to the sick child went abroad through the land. . . . The ancestors of these—people precisely like them in color, dress, manners, customs, simplicity—flocked in vast multitudes after Christ, and when they saw him make the afflicted whole with a word, it was no wonder that they worshipped Him. No wonder his deeds were the talk of the nation. No wonder the multitude that followed Him was so great that at one time—thirty miles from here—they had to let a sick man down through the roof because no approach could be made to the door; no wonder His audiences were so great at Galilee that he had to preach from a ship removed a little distance from the shore; no wonder that even in the desert places about Bethsaida, five thousand invaded His solitude, and He had to feed them by a miracle or else see them suffer for their confiding faith and devotion; no wonder when there was a great commotion in a city in those days, one neighbor explained it to another in words to this effect; "They say that Jesus of Nazareth is come!" (p. 376)

Here is the secret of Christ's historical mission—he cured the diseased in a world tormented by infirmity. His miracles mirrored the needs of the world in which he found himself. But his audience was persuaded only by the reality of their experience of their own disease. They were materialists who could only understand the transcendental (if transcendental he was) if it were literally internalized and then written on their skins.

But Twain's mid-nineteenth-century Palestinian Arabs (whether Muslim or Christian is unstated) were not biblical Jews. He stresses the fact that he is speaking in the present about the Arabs of the Holy Land, for one of the children treated by his traveling companion, the physician, is the daughter of the local Sheikh. Nevertheless, Twain sees "this poor, ragged handful of sores and sin" now inhabiting the Holy Land as identical in all respects with the Jews who dwelt there at the time of Jesus (p. 377). Their physiognomy is unchanged, and this is also reflected in the unchanged nature of their diseased bodies. Christ preached to the biblical Jews, whose sorry state made them believe in him. In seeking the most efficacious way of persuading them of his mission, he cured them of their afflictions. But the Jews remain essentially uncured, as they remain unconverted to Christianity. The "blindness" that marks the inhabitants of the Holy Land is both an explanation of a perceived reality (the relationship between flies and blindness) as well as the reification of a health that emanates from the

American and is represented by Twain's Christian insight. This is the central Christian trope about the nature of the Jew, for he who "lacketh . . . [knowledge of our Lord Jesus Christ is] blind, and cannot see afar off, and hath forgotten that he was purged from his old sins" (2 Peter 1:8–9). For it is "that blindness in part is happened to Israel, until the fulness of the Gentiles be come in" (Romans 11:25). Jews are blind; Christians see.

For Twain, the image of Jesus is linked to his ability to heal. He ironically imagines the young Jesus in these terms: "Recall infant Christ's pranks on his schoolmates — striking boys dead — withering their hands."[12] Jesus as a child does precisely what the adult Jesus undoes — he strikes his playmates with illness and death. One can think of the account of the first Jews Twain ever saw in Hannibal, the Levin boys, and the "shudder" that went through all of the other boys in town as they discussed whether they should crucify the Levin boys.[13] Jews were automatically associated with the act of crucifixion and were literally seen as defiling the Christian world by their presence. But for Twain these Jews "were clothed in the damp and cobwebby mold of antiquity. They carried me back to Egypt and in imagination I moved among the Pharoahs."[14] The present evoked the past. In 1853 Twain could still speak of Jews "desecrating" two historical houses in Philadelphia.[15] This image of pollution is closely linked to the world of the Jews. Twain can and does draw a clear distinction between the Jews and himself — they are corrupt, and he (and all other Protestant Christians) are the antithesis. And yet in entering into the Holy Land, the inescapable fact, understood in abstract but here suddenly writ large for even Twain to see: all of those believed figures of the Old and the New Testament were Jews — Jesus as well as Naaman. But they were Jews like the present-day inhabitants of the Holy Land. They were diseased, just as was Twain himself in Damascus. Twain needs to separate his Christian-American identity from the image of the Jew that was part of his cultural inheritance. Everyone (including Mark Twain) has the potential to become ill, but the Jews are illness incarnate.

Thus the central question Twain presents in his image of the Jews, reaching from the biblical leper Naaman to their contemporary surrogates, is their diseased nature and its relationship to their essence. It mirrors Twain's own questioning of his internalization of the Judeo-Christian presuppositions of the Bible. Disease and religion are indeed linked, but they are linked in the very essence of the Jew. The racial identity of the Jew is unchanged across centuries, even though the religious identity of the people inhabiting the Holy Land may have shifted. Twain reads this not merely as a reflex of the space in which the Jews are located. There is a fin-de-siècle school of thought, best represented by the German anthropologist Friedrich Ratzel, which argued that the nature of a race is a reflex of the geographical space in which it is to be found.[16] The nature of the Jews is tied to the space they "naturally" inhabit. For Twain the movement into the Holy Land is also a movement back in time; the world he finds does not shape the peoples found in it but rather reflects their inherent nature. The nature of the Jews is tied not only to their space but also to their historical times. The Arabs of the Holy Land are merely unchanged biblical Jews in disguise. This view of Jewish immutability is a commonplace of late-nineteenth-century anthropological and medical science. In Richard Andree's 1881 study of Jewish folklore the central question is the relationship between ideas of who the Jews are and what their bodies mean. Andree's discussion centers on the permanence of the Jewish racial type, but more importantly, on its implications. He observed concerning the conservative nature of the Jewish body and soul:

No other race but the Jews can be traced with such certainty backward for thousands of years, and no other race displays such a constancy of form, none resisted to such an extent the effects of time, as the Jews. Even when he adopts the language, dress, habits, and customs of the people among whom he lives, he still remains everywhere the same. All he adopts is but a cloak, under which the eternal Hebrew survives; he is the same in his facial features, in the structure of his body, his temperament, his character.[17]

And it is the body of the Jew that is the sign of this immutability. This thesis of the immutability of the Jew is linked in the discourse of the late nineteenth century to the unchanging relationship of the Jew to the world of disease, pathology, and death. Twain is responding to a debate about the diseased nature of the Jews that was part of western culture and that took a striking turn in the latter half of the nineteenth century.

Jews Are Diseased

The signs of disease had long marked the Jew as different. The earliest modern images evoked their decrepitude as an essential aspect of their nature. It was seen as the physical sign of their guilt for the Crucifixion. Johannes Buxtorf, writing for a fearful Christian audience about the inner nature of the Jews in an account of their nature and practices, catalogued their diseases (such as epilepsy, the plague, leprosy) in 1643.[18] Johann Jakob Schudt, the late-seventeenth-century orientalist who was *the* authority on the nature of the difference of the Jews for his time, cited their physical form as diseased and repellent:

Among several hundred of their kind he had not encountered a single person without a blemish or other repulsive feature: for they are either pale and yellow or swarthy; they have in general big heads, big mouths, everted lips, protruding eyes and bristle-like eyelashes, large ears, crooked feet, hands that hang below their knees, and big shapeless warts, or are otherwise asymmetrical and malproportioned in their limbs.[19]

Schudt's view saw the diseases of the Jews as a reflex of their "Jewishness," of their stubborn refusal to acknowledge the truth of Christianity. What is striking about Schudt's early comment is the tradition of seeing the diseased Jew as "swarthy." The Jews are black in their illness.

How intensively this image of the black Jew haunts the imagination of European society can be seen in a description by the "liberal" Bavarian writer Johann Pezzl, who traveled to Vienna in the 1780s and described the typical Viennese Jew of his time:

There are about five hundred Jews in Vienna. Their sole and eternal occupation is to counterfeit (*Mauscheln*), salvage, trade in coins, and cheat Christians, Turks, heathens, indeed themselves. . . . This is only the beggarly filth from Canaan which can only be exceeded in filth, uncleanliness, stench, disgust, poverty, dishonesty, pushiness and other things by the trash of the twelve tribes from Galicia. Excluding the Indian fakirs, there is no category of supposed human beings which comes closer to the Orang-Utan than does a Polish Jew. . . . Covered from foot to head in filth, dirt and rags, covered in a type of black sack . . . their necks exposed, the color of a Black, their faces covered up to the eyes with a beard, which would have given the High Priest in the Temple chills, the hair turned and knotted as if they all suffered from the *plica polonica*.[20]

The image of the Viennese Jew is of the Eastern Jew, suffering from the diseases of the East, such as the *Judenkratze*, the fabled skin and hair disease also attributed to the Poles under the designation of the *plica polonica*.[21] The Jews' disease is written on the skin. It is the appearance, the skin color, the external manifestations of the Jew, which marks the Jew as different. Here Pezzl argues by analogy—the Jews are like the Blacks. When this tradition is transferred into American culture during Reconstruction, the question of the analogy between the Jew and the Black has an even greater salience. For if the Jews are to be understood to be black, how does the Christian white reader, especially the Christian white physician, relate to the idea of the marked nature of the Jew's body? This complex American reading of the Jew's body is the tradition in which the image of the Jews in *The Innocents Abroad* can be best placed.

The very charge of the diseased nature of the Jews—whether diseased because of their essence or because of their experience—was highly debated in the United States following Reconstruction, when the racial question was differently constructed. If the Jews were equated with Blacks within the European tradition, in the United States they clearly were not Blacks, even though they were understood as different. Twain's early image of the diseased Jew, and its relationship to models of Jewish "infiltration" into other arenas of modern life, such as the economy, is reversed for his contemporary American readers. In an exchange of letters in 1874, in the prestigious Philadelphia *Medical and Surgical Reporter*, Madison Marsh, a physician from Port Hudson, Louisiana, put forth the argument that Jews had a much greater toleration for disease than the general population. He based his view on the supposed Jewish immunity from tuberculosis. Marsh argued that the Jews "enjoy a wonderful national immunity from, not only phthisis [tuberculosis] but all disease of the thoracic viscera."[22] The Jew does not suffer from tuberculosis because "his constitution has become so hardened and fortified against disease by centuries of national calamities, by the dietetics, regimen and sanitas of his religion, continuing for consecutive years of so many ages."[23] This view was generally held during the latter half of the nineteenth century. Lucian Wolf, in a debate before the Anthropological Society of Great Britain and Ireland in 1885, stated categorically that "figures could also be given to prove the immunity of Jews from phthisis," and Dr. Asher, in that same debate, observed that "Jews had an extraordinary power of resistance to phthisis."[24] Jews (at least Jews in the Diaspora) live longer, have a lower child mortality, and are generally healthier than Christians. The Jew's "high average physique . . . is not less remarkable than the high average of his intelligence."[25] Jews are the "purest, finest, and most perfect type of the Caucasian race."[26]

This view was one widely espoused by American Jews in the late nineteenth century. Rabbi Joseph Krauskopf informed his Reformed congregation in Philadelphia that

eminent physicians and statisticians have amply confirmed the truth: that the marvelous preservation of Israel, despite all the efforts to blot them out from the face of the earth, their comparative freedom from a number of diseases, which cause frightful ravages among the Non-Jewish people, was largely due to their close adherence to their excellent Sanitary Laws. Health was their coat of mail, it was their magic shield that caught, and warded off, every thrust aimed at their heart. Vitality was their birthright. . . . Their immunity, which the enemy charged to magic-Arts, to alliances with the spirits of evil, was traceable solely to their faithful compliance with the sanitary requirements of their religion.[27]

Marsh added one new twist to this equation. Jews are healthier, live longer, are more immune to disease, and are more intelligent because of their healthful practices, such as diet, and the fact that they belong to the "white" race. Or at least so the Jew was seen from the standpoint of a rural Louisiana physician during Reconstruction.

A month after this report was published, it was answered in detail by Ephraim M. Epstein, a Jewish physician practicing in Cincinnati, Ohio, who had earlier practiced medicine in Vienna and in Russia. He rebutted Marsh's argument point by point: Jews have no immunity from tuberculosis, or any other disease, including those long associated with Jewish religious practices: "I am sure I have observed no Jewish immunity from any diseases, venereal disease not excepted."[28] Jews do not have "superior longevity"; they have no advantage either because of their diet or because of their practice of circumcision. But Jews do possess a quality lacking in their Christian neighbors. What makes Jews less at risk is the network of support, the "close fraternity, one Jew never forsaking the material welfare of his brother Jew, and he knows it instinctively."[29] It is indeed the "common mental construction" of the Jew that preserves his health. And, in addition, "the constitutional stamina which that nation inherited from its progenitor, Abraham of old, and because it kept that inheritance undeteriorated by not intermarrying with other races."[30] Group dynamics and racial purity are the source of Jewish health, such as it is.

Here the battle was joined: The southern, Christian physician saw in the Jews' social practices and their race a key to universal health. He, of course, defines race in terms of his own ideological understanding of the primary difference between the "Negro" and the "Caucasian" races. The Jews, according to the standard textbooks of the period, such as that of the Viennese biologist Carl Claus, are indeed "Caucasians."[31] But in American terms, following the close of the Civil War, this concept was given a special, intensely political association. Whites have the potential, with good diet and the fortitude to bear oppression (such as Reconstruction), to be healthier, more intelligent, more immune from disease than. . . . And here Marsh's readers would understand—than . . . Blacks. The Eastern European Jewish physician saw any limited advantage accruing to the Jews lying in their inherited nature and sexual practices to which the non-Jews could have absolutely no access, indeed which by definition exclude them.

Marsh's intense, vituperative response came in August of 1874.[32] Initially, he called upon the statistical evidence from Prussian, French, and British sources to buttress his argument about Jewish longevity. He then dismissed Epstein's argument about Jewish risk of disease completely and turned to the question of "the moral cause that had prevented intermarriage of the Jews with other nations, and thus preserved intact their health and tenacity of life" (p. 133). It was circumcision as a sign of the separateness and selectivity of the Jews that Epstein evoked as the proof for his case about Jewish difference. Circumcision for Marsh is a "sanitary measure and religious rite . . . in practice by the ancient Egyptians. . . . It never became a Hebrew institution until friendly relations had been established between Abraham and the Egyptians. Then it was initiated by the circumcision of Abraham and Isaac by the express command of God" (p. 133). Circumcision was an Egyptian ritual, and "Moses, the great champion, leader and lawgiver of the Hebrew race, was himself an Egyptian priest, educated in

all the deep research and arts of the Chaldean Mage and mystic philo-
sophic development of Egyptian and Oriental science, and all that was then
known of the science of medicine, in its general principles and in its application of details for the preservation of health and prevention of disease"
(p. 133). It is through the impact of this philosophy with "a slight tinge of
Egyptian and Indian, or Asiatic philosophy, and shadow of its teachings
[which] pervade all the books of Moses" (p. 133). The ritual practices of the
Jews are but an amalgam of the combined knowledge of the West. They are
in no way the special product of this inbred and haughty people. And indeed, Marsh, like Mark Twain, is immediately brought back to Egypt, to
the "damp and cobwebby mold of antiquity" in which the Jews continue to
be understood.

What could Epstein know about real medicine? Marsh simply dismissed
Epstein as merely a Jew, whose authority is solely drawn from this very
fact: "What evidence or authority does he bring to support his pretensions
to superior knowledge? His being himself a Jew, per se" (p. 134). And he
affirmed his view that the Jews possessed the secret to greater health, which
they were unwilling to share with the rest of the world. The subtext to
Marsh's argument is that the Jew has a special immunity, which is the result
of accident and which gives them immunity to disease. But the true secret
is that this gift is not theirs at all; it was taken from the peoples among
whom they lived. Jews, like Epstein, are charlatans who try to disguise
their true nature. It is the Jewish body that lies at the heart of antisemitism.
In the late nineteenth century it was the claim of the special nature of the
Jewish body that evoked the anger of the non-Jew toward the Jew's sexual
selectivity or *amixia*.[33] Marsh reversed this, as he, too, wished to share in
the special status of the "healthy" Jewish body.

Circumcision had become a major issue within the medical practice of
the United States. Indeed, in the 1870s the American physician Peter
Charles Remondino noted that "circumcision is like a substantial and well-
secured life annuity; . . . it ensures them better health, greater capacity for
labour, longer life, less nervousness, sickness, loss of time. . . ."[34] And indeed, by the 1890s, an American association had begun to be made between "uncircumcised" and "uncivilized."[35] In this context it is of little
surprise that circumcision, an intervention that could be made by the
physician, came to have a function in the definition of "hygiene." But it is
in no way to be understood as a Jewish practice, in the terms that Epstein
had outlined. The debates about the "health" or "illness" of the Jews centered on the inherent nature or social practices of the Jews. The image of
the Jew as different was always juxtaposed with the unstated understanding
of the diseased and inferior nature of the African American. Twain's views
about the diseased nature of the Jews in biblical times can be placed within

this long-standing and complex debate about where the true boundary of inferiority is to be placed. Twain's focus on the religious aspects of disease and the corrupt body reflects the perimeters of this debate. Like Marsh, Twain sees the world through the model of a Christian understanding of the nature of the Jew. That the Jew is different from the Christian in terms of his understanding of the world is exemplified by the very nature of his body.

Twain Sees the Diseased Jew

Twain's contrast between the Jews he represents in his essay of 1896 and those he saw in 1867 is striking. He had, in *The Adventures of Huckleberry Finn,* parodied the assumptions of the relationship between African Americans and mental illness that dominated the medical discourse about African Americans from the 1840s on through Reconstruction.[36] The late 1890s marks the high point of both antisemitic and anti–African American hysteria.[37] In his 1898 essay on the Jews, written in the heat of antisemitic outbreaks in the United States and in the light of the debates he had experienced in Vienna, there seems to be a more liberal, more benign view of the Jews. Certainly they, like Nigger Jim, are in no way to be associated with images of disease. Or at least not overtly. For Twain's concern in the 1890s is to present a positive image of the Jew in terms of the Jew's awareness of the Jew's civil responsibility. For Twain, the Jews may still be diseased, like other peoples, but they at least take care of their own. The Jews are never beggars; indeed, they create "charitable institutions" like hospitals (p. 14) to take care of their afflicted. They are quite unlike the diseased multitudes that flocked to the tent of the western doctor in Palestine some three decades earlier.

For these Jews are the victims of society. As Susy Clemens recorded in her notebook, Twain "decided that the Jews had always seemed to him a race much to be respected; also they had suffered much, and had been greatly persecuted, so to ridicule or make fun of them seemed to be like attacking a man who was already down."[38] The debate between those who believed that Jews' illness was an essential aspect of the Jewish race and those who saw it as a reflection of the social status of the Jews is worked out in Twain's own texts. Twain saw, at the fin de siècle, the nature of the Jew as a reflection of neither space nor race but of the oppression inflicted upon the Jews by western culture. The rationale for writing his essay on the Jews in 1898 was a letter from a Jewish American lawyer who asked Twain about the cause of antisemitism. The Jews are seen as the victim, especially in the context of his experience in Vienna. Twain sees contemporary Jews as little different from all of the other inhabitants of Europe and the United States, except that they are self-consciously aware of their status as victims. Once Twain moved from the past to the present some thirty years later, the focus of the argument shifted from the origins of Christianity to the nature of late-nineteenth-century capitalism and the role of the Jews. But these two aspects of the Jew are linked, as we have seen in the arguments about the Jew's nature in the eighteenth and nineteenth centuries. Initially the Jews were, for Twain, the afflicted and superstitious Jews of the past, Naaman the Leper, incarnate in Twain's experience entering into the Holy Land. These Jews are thus the originators of Christianity. But the miracles of Christ, recounted in detail in Twain's commentary, seem not to have helped the Jews very much over time, for they seem to still be in the same diseased state as they were two thousand years before Twain arrived in the Holy Land. It seems to be American science, rather than the mysteries of the past, that the sufferers in the Holy Land need today.

Twain differentiated between the corrupt Jews of the Bible and contemporary Jewry. But he also unconsciously linked them. Twain found it impossible to hold these two categories apart. In his essay of 1898, Twain evoked his own southern image of the Jew and noted that "religion [i.e., Christianity] had nothing to do with" the hatred of the Jew. During Reconstruction, the Jew had opened "shop on the plantation, supplied all the Negro's wants on credit, and at the end of the season was proprietor of the Negro's share of the present crop and of part of the share of the next one. Before long, the whites detested the Jew, and it is doubtful if the Negro loved him" (p. 18). The category "Jew" has nothing to do with religion, as Marsh noted, but is a racial designation. In his system, Twain, like Marsh, can differentiate between "whites," "Negroes," and "Jews." Jews are designated as different from "whites" and "Negroes" on the basis of their racially marked character and practices. Here the question is whether the Jew was white or not, a question that reappeared in the debate about the social position of the Jew in the South during the Leo Frank case.[39] This distinction is important. For just as Twain needed to separate his identity from that of the diseased Jews and their progeny, so too does he need to see himself as different from the Jews. For as Clara Clemens commented, Twain's "eloquent . . . defense of Christ's race" was turned by his enemies so that "it was rumored at one time Father himself was a Jew."[40] Indeed in Vienna, while he was observing the debates that triggered the essay on the Jews, he was labeled by the antisemitic press as the "Jew Mark Twain."[41] Just as Twain needed to create a diseased inheritance for the Jews in the 1860s so too does he need to distinguish himself from the corrupt Jews of the 1890s.

The Jews are diseased, but their infection is the desire for capital. Twain's answer to antisemitism returns to the central theme of his earlier writing, to the image of the Jews in the context of the Holy Land. Twain supports the political aims of Theodor Herzl. But he ironically fears the in-gathering "in Palestine, with a government of their own — under the suzerainty of the Sultan, I suppose." For "if that concentration of the cunningest brains in the world was going to be made in a free country (bar Scotland), I think it would be politic to stop it. It will not be well to let that race find out its strength. If the horses knew theirs, we should not ride any more" (p. 27). It is this cunning that marked the Jews in the South and it is this cunning that Twain sensed in the origins of Christianity. And this cunning is a sign of the inherent difference of the Jews as a race, a mark of their corruption and disease. For in the science of the late nineteenth century, this corrupt genius was as certain a sign of pathology as the physical symptoms of the leper.[42] Twain's rhetoric about physical disease has been transformed into rhetoric about psychological predisposition, which is as far as he was able to go in rethinking the meaning of the diseases of the Jews. Twain sees the diseases of the Jews as markers for the Jews' difference but also for the difference which they (as individuals who have experienced death and disease in their own world) see in themselves. And yet, in his own estimation, he is not as "ill" as the Jews, and that redeems him.

CHAPTER FOUR

Seeing Double: Jews in the Fiction of F. Scott Fitzgerald, Charles Dickens, Anthony Trollope, and George Eliot

MURRAY BAUMGARTEN

In F. Scott Fitzgerald's classic novel, *The Great Gatsby* (1925), the Jew is a criminal. In the course of this fiction many things are imputed to Meyer Wolfsheim, including that most heinous and un-American of crimes, the fixing of the 1919 World Series. It is thus not surprising to learn that this fictional character has been linked to Arnold Rothstein, the founder of Murder, Incorporated. Nevertheless, even in a novel set in post–World War I America that maps the jazz age and uses the landmarks of highways, bridges, billboards, and most notably, the Plaza Hotel to define its psychic geography, there is never any doubt that this Jewish gangster is Jay Gatsby's double.

Both are elusive characters. Gatsby is said to have killed a man, something that is not foreign to Wolfsheim's character and is part of the reason both men are perceived by the choral voice of the narrator to share shady pasts from which they cannot quite emerge into the brighter light of WASP America. More damning than murder, in the eyes of the gatekeepers of society seeking to maintain at least the semblance of social order after the upheavals of the war to end all wars, is their social aggressiveness.

Wolfsheim and Gatsby are the arrivistes demanding entrance. What they have done is take advantage of their meager opportunities. The resources they have carved out of their marginal worlds by the bluff and bravado of their self-transformation have been made into the forceful levers of wealth that will, they believe, propel them into society. Hegemony will give way to heteroglossia; the Yale of Tom and the southern debutante society of Daisy will make room for the school of hard knocks of the daring desperado of the Midwest. By the end of the novel, the failures of Jay Gatsby that prove to society his vulgarity boomerang, in the eyes of Nick, the novel's narrator, and the reader, into an indictment of the postwar hypocrisy of the American East Coast Establishment.

The price paid by Gatsby for the moral devaluation of society and his moral regeneration is death. In Nick's telling, however, Gatsby's becomes the ultimate sacrifice, martyrdom rescuing him from the meaninglessness Tom expected his death would produce. This concluding religious imagery echoes patterns central to the novel's subtext though little remarked critically — consider, for example, the moment when the kiss of Daisy and Gatsby becomes the incarnation of the American dream of success — locating Fitzgerald's novel in the mainstream of the American romance tradition. Doubled, Wolfsheim and Gatsby reinforce each other's situation. The novel's structure thereby locates Jew and criminal as central to its strategy of moral reevaluation, as it articulates an ideology of self-sacrifice and Christian love. He who was marginal has decentered the culture that sought to return the parvenu to his pariah status.[1]

By contrast, almost a century earlier, the Jew, Fagin, in Charles Dickens's *Oliver Twist* (1838), stands alone; he has no double. (A fellow Jew, though mentioned, plays no role in the dramatic action of the novel.) Although an argument might be made to link Fagin with Oliver, the narrative logic of the novel works to deny the connection. Instead of seeing Fagin, like Oliver, as the outsider, his Jewishness placing him at even more of a disadvantage than Oliver's orphaned status, and suggesting that both characters echo each other in asking for more, they are placed in opposition, so that for Oliver to claim his rightful place in society Fagin must die.

Dickens's text and Cruikshank's illustrations reinforce each other. As J. Hillis Miller notes, "The relationship between text and illustration is clearly reciprocal. Each refers to the other. Each illustrates the other, in a continual back and forth movement which is incarnated in the experience of the reader as his eyes move from words to picture and back again, juxtaposing the two in a mutual establishment of meaning."[2] Consider, then, the iconic illustration, generally acknowledged as one of Cruikshank's greatest pictures, inserted in apposition to Oliver's visit to the condemned Fagin in his cell (Fig. 1). At this point in the fiction, the Jew-Devil is crazed, muttering and incoherent, and caught in the same circle of insanity that beset Sikes before he slipped and hanged himself in an apparent suicide-death. Yet unlike Bill Sikes running from the hue and cry, Fagin in his prison cell is alert enough to bargain with Brownlow and Oliver for his life.

Revealing to Oliver where the papers attesting to the birthright are, he thinks to get him to help in an escape attempt.

Oliver offers to say a prayer for Fagin, and urges him to join in. "Say only one, upon your knees, with me, and we will talk till morning." But Fagin the Jew is impervious to these Christian entreaties, just as he has earlier rejected the appeal of his compatriot: "If I hoped we could recall him to a sense of his position," Mr. Brownlow notes. "Nothing will do that sir," replies the turnkey. "You had better leave him." Christian love has no taker here. Instead, as "the door of the cell opened, and the attendants returned," Fagin clutches Oliver, certain he can help him to negotiate even this gauntlet. "Press on, press on," cries Fagin. "Softly, but not so slow. Faster, faster!" Only main force holds Fagin back.

By contrast with Fagin's inability—or is it the willful Jew's refusal?—to understand what is about to happen, the chapter ends with Oliver's participation in the narrator's meditation on death.

It was some time before they left the prison. Oliver nearly swooned after this frightful scene, and was so weak that for an hour or more, he had not the strength to walk.

Day was dawning when they again emerged. A great multitude had already assembled; the windows were filled with people, smoking and playing cards to beguile the time; the crowd were pushing, quarreling, joking. Everything told of life and animation, but one dark cluster of objects in the centre of all—the black stage, the cross-beam, the rope, and all the hideous apparatus of death.

"No Escape," the running head of this page proclaims. Not only life but even the incipient gesture of remorse that seemed to have animated Sikes at the last moment is absent. This character is unredeemable. Where others have a soul, he has an absence.

The Cruikshank figure is again instructive. In its isolation in the cell, in its presentation of Fagin as Jew-Devil stuck without maneuvering room in the condemned prisoner's cell, the stylized caricature proclaims one signal: evil will now be banished from this realm. In contrast to Cruikshank's illustrations of Oliver's progress, which, as Anthony Burton notes, recount the narrative "by composing the figures in his designs so that certain patterns of grouping and gesture recur," Fagin in his cell "ironically" sits "beneath a barred window" which "admits only the peaceful light of day and no danger from outside, for Fagin, heedless of the light, has evil deep within him."[3] In terms of the novel's plot, Fagin now bears the burden of not only his own criminal behavior but the villainy of Monks, Oliver's half-brother. He has become the Jew as scapegoat.

Ironically, Dickens's effort to locate Fagin as scapegoat has an implicit boomerang effect. When Christian tradition makes Jesus the ultimate

Fig. 1. "Fagin in the Condemned Cell," by George Cruikshank. Reprinted from Charles Dickens, *Oliver Twist*, ed. Andrew Lang (New York: Scribner & Son, 1907), opposite p. 502; originally published as "Oliver Twist; or, the Parish Boy's Progress. By Boz," *Bentley's Miscellany*, Feb. 1837–March 1839.

scapegoat for humanity, dying for the sins of the human race, it brings him forward from the subtext to the center of the action. The only way to avoid this boomerang effect is to cordon Fagin off and separate him in all possible ways from Oliver, who has played the Christian scapegoat's role prior to this moment. This also accounts for the uneasiness that many readers have felt at Fagin's sentence and the sentimentality of the concluding passages of this chapter's meditations on death.

Even more surprising is the impact of isolating Fagin, the Jew. When, as Jonathan Grossman notes, Oliver calls Fagin "The Jew! The Jew!" at the beginning of chapter 35, he not only "naturalizes his position in the middle class, with Mr. Brownlow, who also later privileges the term 'the Jew' over Fagin's name,"[4] he is also severing any link that might have existed between them. In a novel of doublings and splittings so full as to be representative of Dickens's fictional world-making, this epithet ensures that Fagin is alone.

Thus unlike the other characters in the novel, his is a life that is unsayable and unnarratable. His existence is ontologically different in kind from that of the other characters, despite the ongoing process of secularization of Christian myth that helps to articulate Oliver as the child-innocent speaking the Queen's English. The heteroglossic world of the Artful Dodger or Nancy does not extend to Fagin. His language of ingratiation, including the "My dear" and "deary," is not theirs, just as the thieves' argot linked to Ikey Solomons and the marginal world of fences and old-clothes-dealers does not mark him, for example, as part of Mayhew's sociological explorations. When he includes Jews as members of the criminal underworld Mayhew the journalist does not use a stereotyped caricature of a Jew to illustrate and clinch his point.[5] Mayhew's description of Jewish life in the London streets is an ethnographic account. The racial epithets in his account are not his but the reported conversation of observers and apparently biased individuals. Furthermore, he notes that the supposed criminality of the Jews is untrue. The picture of the Jew as Old-Clothes Man is not a devilish, isolated figure but that of one of the London street-people going about his daily business (Fig. 2). By contrast, in Dickens's world and Cruikshank's vision, Fagin is not one of a group or class, not martyr or victim, but Mephistophelean tempter of Christians.

Existing outside the Dickensian world of doubling and splitting, Fagin is an anomaly. The impact of his isolation depends on the ways in which every other character in the novel is part of a group. Current discussions of typologies offer a clue to the central meanings of this isolation. Much in evidence among contemporary visual artists, typologies are ways of grouping situations through repetition and variation. The detail of an individual image is framed as part of an implicit discourse, thereby making single moments part of a syntax of many. "A typology is a collection of members of a common class or type. Like natural scientists, who assemble taxonomies of living things based on genus and species, the photographers in this exhibition seek to document, in a consistent manner, examples of a specific type of subject matter for the purpose of comparison. The work is fully effective only when viewed as a suite of images, allowing the dialectic between the class and the specific member of the class to become apparent." We see "differently when [the] affinities" of one photograph "are explored in a group" linking it "to urban spaces worldwide."[6] As part of a suite, each member in the typology can now be narratable; each is part of a discourse. It is worth noting that this contemporary artistic habit echoes strategies at work in Dickens's era, deployed by scientists like Lyell, Babbage, and Faraday, and

Fig. 2. Illustration by Archibald S. Henning, modeled on a daguerreotype by Richard Beard. Reprinted from Henry Mayhew, *London Labour and the London Poor*, 4 vols. (London, 1861; reprint, New York: Dover, 1968), 2: opposite p. 73.

that led, in Darwin's hands, to revolutionary transformations of worldview and social understanding.

Note also how the impact of these city scenes in the typological structure makes them akin to streets whose functions are inextricable from the urban whole. The analogy to Dickens's urban art is apt: in typologies, single figures make visible the mechanical reproduction of repetition in fiction and in city-building. We have entered the world articulated by Walter Benjamin's analysis. The structures of repetition elaborate the movement of narration and demystify uniqueness, be it of single image or romantic godlike art-creator. In this city-as-totality, urban repetitions of character, scene, and situation orient the one as part of the discourse of the many; the fiction of juxtaposition of opposites defines the assemblage of possible meanings.

In this changing, shifting world, to leave one figure dangling without doubling is to stereotype him and make him available as the screen for the Rorschach projection of all that is to be excluded. Like Malvolio, he is the enemy of the revels and must be imprisoned, and even banished, for the feasting and festivities to come into their own. To place the Jew outside this city discourse, as Dickens does, is to stereotype him as the incarnation of evil, and articulate a literary economy of antisemitism, thus preparing the way for the racialist representations that defined general cultural images of the Jews for better than a hundred years of English and European culture since the publication of *Oliver Twist* in 1838. It is also to understand the continuities of that image of the Jew with the more religiously rooted anti-semitic tradition of medieval, Crusader, and Renaissance productions, including Barabbas and Shylock.

It is no surprise then to read contemporary Jewish responses in which praise of the generosity of Dickens's fictional sympathies leads to a complaint that is registered as a request: Is it possible for the Jew now formally emancipated to find a different cultural representation? Can someone in the century and cultural tradition that prided itself on the ability to give the unspoken masses voice and tell the stories of those so long deemed unworthy of having them — think only of Carlyle and the Chartists, Dickens and the homeless, Arnold and Wragg, the abandoned widow — also strike off a fictional world that will tell the story of the Jews as something other than victims or demons? This is the burden of the query of the *Jewish Chronicle* in 1854, asking "why Jews alone should be excluded from 'the sympathizing heart' of this great author and powerful friend of the oppressed." In his reply to an invitation to attend the anniversary dinner of the Westminster Jewish Free School, Dickens pleaded innocence: "I know of no reason the Jews can have for regarding me as 'inimical' to them," citing the "sympathetic way in which he had treated the persecution of the Jews in his *Child's History of England*" in 1851. Choosing to ignore the evidence of Fagin, he noted that "on the contrary . . . I believe I do my part toward the assertion of their civil and religious liberty, and in my Child's History of England I have expressed a strong abhorrence of their persecution in old time." Arguing against religiously based antisemitism, Dickens emphasizes his championing of the rights of English subjects whatever their religious beliefs. The terms in which he phrases his stalwart repudiation of religiously based antisemitism locate him in his historical moment. Clear and forthright, Dickens's phrasing nevertheless indicates his lack of awareness of the growing impact phrenology was to have on the formation of a racialist rhetoric. We cannot fault him for being only a writer, not a prophet; rather, we need to recover the moment of his understanding of the situation of the

Jews — at the moment when it is about to become that Jewish problem, so poisonously defined by the racialist rhetoric of the later nineteenth- and twentieth-century ideologues.

A more personal appeal led to a different and fuller response. When Eliza Davis, "who, with her husband James, a banker, had bought Dickens's London home, Tavistock House, three years earlier," wrote him about Fagin, her questions and urgings are credited with his invention of the Jewish character, Riah, in the last novel he lived to complete, *Our Mutual Friend* (1864). As Deborah Heller notes, "the Davises were Jewish, and . . . Mrs. Davis gave voice to the distress of Dickens's Jewish readership: 'It has been said that Charles Dickens, the large-hearted, whose works plead so eloquently and so nobly for the oppressed of this country . . . has encouraged a vile prejudice against the despised Hebrew. . . . Fagin I fear admits only of one interpretation: but (while) Charles Dickens lives the author can justify himself or atone for a great wrong.'" The evasions of Dickens's response are aptly underlined by Heller's analysis.[7] For my purposes what is appropriate is to rephrase the queries of the *Jewish Chronicle* and Mrs. Eliza Davis: Can the remarkable heteroglossia of the Victorian and nineteenth-century novel extend its linguistic and generic resources to those not only excluded but defined by previous religiously based habits as the to-be-banished? Or are the Jews to be inscribed and ever re-inscribed into the role of scapegoat of this imperial racialist thrust of western culture? the first and continuing victims of its orientalism?

What is at stake here is whether the story of the Jews is possible within this secular discourse of the novel. The question leads us perforce to a discussion of Riah and the role he plays in *Our Mutual Friend*, and then to other Victorian novels and novelists. It is revealed in the phrasing Dickens used in his defense. The referential argument that Jews were criminals in the nineteenth century has been demolished in its own historical terms by many critics, Harry Stone and Edgar Rosenberg among them, while the issue of novelistic rights — "the assertion of their civil and religious liberty" by the Jews — though touched on by Heller deserves further elaboration. To put it another way, is the story of Riah, whose name means friend in Hebrew, narratable in the same discourse as the one that recounts the adventures of Lizzie and Charlie, Eugene and Mortimer, Bradley Headstone and Rogue Riderhood, Wegg and Venus and Sloppy?

The argument made by both the *Jewish Chronicle* and Mrs. Davis centers on how Fagin is not just a representation of one Jew but bears the weight of all. In his letter responding to Mrs. Davis, Dickens claims that Fagin, like the Christian characters, is but one of many, an assertion belied by the absence of any other Jews in the novel. Furthermore, Dickens does not engage the ways in which Mrs. Davis and the *Jewish Chronicle* speak out of the concerns not only of any immigrant group seeking entry into a caste society rethinking itself as a class society—with some few hedged-in, limited, and conditioned, yet actual, points of entry for newcomers—but as representatives of a people for whom individual achievement, given the conditions of their political and social subjection in diaspora/exile, meant inevitable abandonment of a people's heritage. In other words, can Riah play a role in a world that damns him for being one of the Jews and that might at best sneer at him with faint praise for any single acts of individual merit? The inquiry reveals its own result: in this world of doublings and splittings, to keep Riah separate, to make him the *only* Jew, is to scapegoat him *as* a Jew, whatever benefit results from particular actions he takes. In other words, it is not just exclusion and absence that are ideologically motivated but also singularity and non-comparability. It is a version of that French motto coined at emancipation: "To the Jews as a nation we must grant nothing; to the Jew as an individual we must give everything," which Stanislaus de Clermont Tonnerre, a delegate from Paris to the French National Assembly, responded to on December 23, 1789, by arguing that what the Jews wanted was "to be considered citizens."[8]

It is thus no surprise that, for most of the novel, Riah takes the role of usurer because he is the Jew, even though by the end he is revealed as the unwilling front man for Fledgby of Pubsey & Co. In effect, Riah acts the part of miser that Boffin only plays at being, in order to teach Bella a lesson in a version of the pious fraud deriving from the theatrical traditions of the commedia dell'arte.[9] Furthermore, the individual actions he takes, which include the central ones of sheltering Lizzie not only from the pursuit of the murderous Bradley Headstone but also from the libertinism of Eugene Wrayburn, are situated—like the traditional Jewish garb he wears—in the gender-marked axis of the novel as feminine.

Like Jenny Wren, who also seeks to shelter a potential victim, in this case her father, as well as Lizzie, Riah wears skirts, a detail emphasized in text and illustration throughout the novel. And even so, he is, like Fagin, the only Jew in the novel, a condition that makes him the talisman of the fictive discourse, the screen on which the absence of Christian love is projected. And in his isolation, the impossibility of any kind of Jewish story being told about him becomes manifest, for the Jew is defined via his or her Jewish reference group, with its customs, festivals, traditions, and cultural values. Alone, Riah too is non-narratable. Even in *Our Mutual Friend*, the Jew is outside discourse and thus in his or her isolation vulnerable to caricature.

In his skirts, Riah bears the mark of his Judaism as feminization. Fagin too wears them, and there is some gender ambiguity in his first appearance, when he provides food, education, and fun for Oliver. One could then argue that the power women exercise in *Our Mutual Friend*, from Betty Higden to Jenny Wren and Lizzie, extends to him. Perhaps this is the force of that episode when Jenny and Lizzie discover that Riah is not the usurer he seems to be. Fledgby has forced him into the role (though we never discover the full particulars of the case). Once this is grasped, Jenny and Lizzie find in Riah an ally. Welcomed to their roof garden, he too can join them in "playing dead" — the only world in which they too have rights and freedoms. Thus, it is appropriate that Lizzie and Jenny learn to read and write with the help of a tutor he provides, thereby gaining potential access to the rights of citizenship which they have the possible chance to exercise in the larger world of the living. What Riah learns, however, is that their hope is not his. In having agreed to serve as Fledgby's front man, as he tells Jenny Wren,

in bending my neck to the yoke I was willing to wear, I bent the unwilling necks of the whole Jewish people. For it is not, in Christian countries with the Jews as with other peoples. Men say, "This is a bad Greek, but there are good Greeks. This is a bad Turk, but there are good Turks." Not so with the Jews. Men find the bad among us easily enough — among what people are the bad not easily found? — but they take the worst of us as samples of the best; they take the lowest of us as presentations of the highest; and they say "All Jews are alike." If, doing what I was content to do here, because I was grateful for the past and have small need of money now, I had been a Christian, I could have done it, compromising no one but my individual self. But doing it as a Jew, I could not choose but compromise the Jews of all conditions and all countries. It is a little hard upon us, but it is the truth. I would that all our people remembered it! Though I have little right to say so, seeing that it came home so late to me. (pp. 795–96)

Perhaps this is Dickens's reprise of Shylock's famous speech, though here it is not the rhetorical question of "Hath not a Jew eyes?" but the self-evident answer that there is no such thing as an individual Jew in Christian countries. Given that condition, the best Riah can do is accept Jenny's invitation and enter their utopia in the world of "Come up and be dead."

Riah's Jewishness, like Fagin's, is evident in and through his body. In this world, character, as John Jordan notes of *Oliver Twist*, "is something written or printed on the body, a textual effect like the designs and patterns printed upon nineteenth-century handkerchiefs."[10] The reading of their bodies to which we are thus invited has no internal textual context, since both are outside the fictional discourse. Both are extraordinary. Where Fagin is the manifest racialist caricature, Riah is its latent obverse, the unmanned Jew. Sander Gilman has taught us to read the way in which foreground and background are reflections of the larger context, so clearly evident here: the psychic geography of Dickens's fictional world excludes the

Jew and thus casts him out as available prey. His is the world of what Wolfgang Iser has called "the unsayable" and what D. A. Miller has characterized as "the unnarratable." What is abundantly clear is that in this city, the Jew has no address.

The contrast to the fictional worlds created by George Eliot in *Daniel Deronda* (1876) and Anthony Trollope in *Nina Balatka* (1867) is evident along all the axes of comparison. To begin with, Eliot and Trollope devise worlds inhabited by many Jews. Their characterization also describes the Jewish characters in the same terminology as the non-Jews. Even the use of physiognomic and phrenological references are general and applicable to all. Furthermore, whatever the involvement of Jewish characters in the non-Jewish world, they are also interwoven into the fabric of their Jewish communities, be it through Daniel Deronda's discovery of vocation and mission at the end of the novel or through the power of communal celebration in articulating heterosexual love even across boundaries as elaborated by Anton and Nina from the beginning of Trollope's tale. This multiplicity of images engages their discourse in typological terms: in these novels the Jews are part of sets that have more than one member and thus engage categories of narration and patterns of social meaning.

Edward Alexander's brilliant analysis of George Eliot's practice elaborates the issue in terms parallel to those I develop here, though with a different central focus. Of particular interest in this connection is the impact Jewish Prague made on George Eliot and her beloved G. H. Lewes.[11] Furthermore, Eliot's understanding of Jews and Jewish culture as different from a "race fellowship" and more akin to her own ideal of a community was brought about in large measure by her friendship with Emanuel Deutsch. Their friendship led not only to the writing of *Daniel Deronda* but as well to her important essay, "The Modern Hep! Hep! Hep!" which argued for "a renovated national dignity" to be accorded the Jews as a right as it is to every other nationalism embraced by English liberals. The impact of Eliot's work is not to be gainsaid. It includes, as Alexander notes, the inspiration for Eliezer Ben-Yehuda's decision to leave the academy and proceed to Paris and then Eretz Yisrael where he was to take up his "'mad' dream of Jewish national revival" and claim his place as the "father of modern colloquial Hebrew" (Alexander, p. 31). We might even regard George Eliot's fiction as an answer to the queries put to Dickens by the *Jewish Chronicle* and Mrs. Eliza Davis. And despite the stereotyping of the Jew that Trollope extends from the single Jew to the community as a whole we can in part see Trollope's *Nina Balatka* in a similar light.[12]

Though the male protagonist in this love story is linked to Shylock at the beginning as a defining feature of his "race," there is at the same time another model at work, the one of antisemitism as a social construct. Bryan Cheyette notes that Trollope's fiction "includes the racialized 'other' only to exclude or contain it within his construction of 'the real.'" Furthermore, his "all-inclusive 'realism'—showing the world as it 'really' is—is an attempt to contain those forces that are 'other' to an authentic Englishness rooted in the past." Of particular importance here is the "commercialism" that in Trollope's fiction threatens the "English nation." His "Jewish representations are, in this way, 'balanced' precariously between inclusion in the world of 'realism' and exclusion from the authentic world of a racially fixed 'feudal' England."[13] By contrast with the efforts of Dickens in *Oliver Twist* to isolate Fagin and thus proclaim his identity as Jew-Devil, Trollope's doubling calls to mind, though in a simpler mode, the method of Philip Roth's *Operation Shylock* (1992), in which mirroring effects serve to decenter all certainties of identity and antisemitic definitions.

At the novel's opening, Nina, despite her father's prohibition, finds a way to visit her Jewish lover in Prague's old city. To get there she must pass from Cathedral to Synagogue, and thereby chart the physical space of the psychic geography of this tale. Musing upon his father's house, "as she sat there waiting for her lover, she wished that it had been her lot to have been born a Jewess. Only, had that been so, her hair might perhaps have been black, and her eyes dark, and Anton would not have liked her. She put her hand up for a moment to her rich brown tresses, and felt them as she took joy in thinking that Anton Trendellsohn loved to look upon fair beauty." Trollope's handling of description in the terms of racial stereotyping becomes complicated enough to make the reader see around and through the rhetoric of racial typing.

After a short while Anton Trendellsohn came down. To those who know the outward types of his race there could be no doubt that Anton Trendellsohn was a very Jew among Jews. He was certainly a handsome man, not now very young, having reached some year certainly in advance of thirty, and his face was full of intellect. He was slightly made, below the middle height, but was well made in every limb, with small feet and hands, and small ears, and a well-turned neck. He was very dark—dark as a man can be and yet show no sign of colour in his blood. No white man could be more dark and swarthy than Anton Trendellsohn. His eyes, however, which were quite black, were very bright. His jet-black hair, as it clustered round his ears, had in it something of a curl. Had it been allowed to grow, it would almost have hung in ringlets; but it was worn very short, as though its owner were jealous even of the curl. Anton Trendellsohn was decidedly a handsome man; but his eyes were somewhat too close together in his face, and the bridge of his aquiline nose was not sharply cut, as is mostly the case with such a nose on a Christian face. The olive oval face was without doubt the face of a Jew, and the mouth was greedy, and the teeth were perfect and bright, and the movement of the man's body was the movement of a Jew. But not the less on that account had he behaved with Christian forbearance to his Christian debtor, Josef Balatka, and with Christian chivalry to Balatka's daughter, till that chivalry had turned itself into love. (p. 11)

We are in the world not of Dickens but of Scott. Revisiting the possibilities glimpsed for a moment in *Ivanhoe*, we participate in their revision in terms made possible by nineteenth-century Jewish emancipation. From his privileged position within Anton's mind, Trollope's narrator tells us that it was impossible for him "to forswear the religion of his people. To go forth and be great in commerce by deserting his creed would have been nothing to him. His ambition did not desire wealth so much as the possession of wealth in Jewish hands, without those restrictions upon its enjoyment to which Jews under his own eye had ever been subjected. It would have delighted him to think that, by means of his work, there should no longer be a Jews' quarter in Prague, but that all Prague should be ennobled and civilised and made beautiful by the wealth of Jews" (p. 70). Trollope's Prague, as Joan Cohen notes, is "a mysterious place" that "seems dark and empty of people." Though Nina travels continually "between the Jewish quarter and her Christian home she seldom meets or even sees anyone." Given this division, the novel functions in the wish-fulfillment terms of a "fairy tale," where the "threatening landscape" is divided into "Jewish and Christian quarters — symbolically linked together by the bridge over the Moldau — which denotes the impossible gap which separates these religious and racial enemies."[14]

Trollope refuses to leave anything singular in this novel. Even the social construction of antisemitism is reinforced and doubled by showing how it poisons the relations not only of Jews and Christians but Jews and Jews: it figures centrally in the struggle between Nina and Rebecca for Anton's love — though it is also worth noting that when Nina, his beloved, is angry with him, she thinks of him in terms of the caricatured stereotype of the Jew. Still, it is fascinating to see a writer regarded as the author of mere Victorian entertainments hinting at the existence of that fierce subterranean phenomenon of Jewish self-hatred central to the explorations of contemporary writers such as Philip Roth and Rebecca Goldstein.

In Trollope's novel, Prague has a multiple presence. It is not only a feudal but an enlightened city, and both aspects complicate this tale of the conflict of money and love, which is characterized from the beginning as a question of interest both to Christians and Jews. Unlike Fagin, Anton Trendellsohn is not the only Jew in the novel and thus serves not as the lightning rod of difference but as an actor and agent in his own right. He exercises the right of citizenship, even though it is mostly for the purpose of private happiness, by contrast with Fagin's ability only to function as oppressed subject, or Deronda's larger political Zionism. One reason Trollope's fictional world here provides this commonality of interest is due to the social space of Prague — be it remembered still presided over by the Emperor Franz Joseph — including the all-important Charles Bridge, where the climactic incidents occur, which provides safe access for all the members of the different groups of this novel.

The aura of fear and terror lurking everywhere in *Oliver Twist*,[15] and carried by Fagin and Monks even into the house of the Maylies in the course of the attempted robbery, is absent in *Nina Balatka*. While the Jew is feared in Prague, the emotion is grounded in characters like Ziska, not only the cousin of Josef Balatka, Nina's father, but also Nina's potential suitor, and thus an implicit rival of Anton's. Nevertheless, Ziska, despite his association with feudal traditions, plays a facilitating role in the redeeming conclusion of the novel, which unites the lovers. This city, then, has a spectrum of possibilities, in which terror and Jew-hatred are only two of many, unlike the free-floating hostility circulating in Dickens's novel. And the multiple layers of Prague society as well as the city's open geography, by contrast with the medieval warrens of Oliver's London, make it possible for Anton to imagine a future in a universalist (read: Christian) world in which he does not have to cease to exist as a Jew. While Nina's story takes center stage, Anton's, unlike Fagin's, is narratable and sketched in its broad outlines even if not told in full detail.

Dreams of a high ambition had, from very early years, flitted across the mind of the younger Trendellsohn till they had nearly formed themselves into a settled purpose. He had heard of Jews in Vienna, in Paris, and in London, who were as true to their religion as any Jew of Prague, but who did not live immured in a Jews' quarter, like lepers separate and alone in some loathed corner of a city otherwise clean. These men went abroad into the world, as men, using the wealth with which their industry had been blessed, openly as the Christians used it. And they lived among Christians as one man should live with his fellow-men — on equal terms, giving and taking, honouring and honoured. As yet it was not so with the Jews of Prague, who were still bound to their old narrow streets, to their dark houses, to their mean modes of living, and who, worst of all, were still subject to the isolated ignominy of Judaism. In Prague a Jew was still a Pariah. (p. 69)

Trollope must have been aware of the Indian provenance of the word *Pariah*, and he understood its impact as a social construction. Its naturalization by racialist rhetoric had the effect of forcing the Jews into the social Darwinism of a world red in tooth and claw. Rather than focusing attention on the choices of politics, which kept the Jews oppressed, the naturalized Pariah image became a lightning rod to relieve the pressures of a reluctantly industrializing society. It is thus important to register the ways in which Anton's character combines a "universalizing commercialism with a preternatural 'romantic' racial particularism" — yet he also "restrains his racialized behaviour . . . acting as a 'Christian' in a 'dark' Jewish skin — and thereby anticipates Trollope's later models of 'forbearance' in the face of superior 'English' values." It may also be significant that Anton's initials are the same as Trollope's and "point to the stereotypical 'Jew' as an unconscious Trollopian self who, like his rigidly 'commercial' author, is an alien outsider needing to be accepted by a hostile society."[16] It is also important to note that racial stereotyping accepted the inheritance of religious caricature and made it a cultural resource, available for widespread deployment. In this sense, Trollope's exploration of Prague leads to Kafka's, Hannah Arendt's, and Philip Roth's.

Nina's interest in Anton's world makes her an anthropologist of the Jewish community, especially with regard to the celebration of its holidays — an effect that like most participant-observation leads the observer into eager and active immersion in the life of the subject of attention. In this way, the narrative point of view shifts from Christian to Jewish, carried from one sympathetic perspective to the other by the beloved. What it charts is not only individual perceptions but the general life of the community, which, it is worth noting, is central to Trollope's fictional strategies. Thus, when Ziska goes to find Anton in the synagogue on the day of a holiday celebration he is guided there by Rebecca, Nina's rival.

> "He is in the synagogue," said Ruth. "You will find him there if you will go in."
> "But they are at worship there," said Ziska, doubtingly.
> "They will be at worship all day, because it is our festival," said Rebecca, with her eyes fixed upon the ground; "but if you are a Christian they will not object to your going in. They like that Christians should see them. They are not ashamed."

The fullness of description, which like everything else in the novel is comparative, provides a focus for the erotic interest that takes its being in the elaboration of the Jewish service.

Ziska, looking into the girl's face, saw that she was very beautiful; and he saw also at once that she was exactly the opposite of Nina, though they were both of a height. Nina was fair, with grey eyes, and smooth brown hair which seemed to demand no special admiration, though it did in truth add greatly to the sweet delicacy of her face; and she was soft in her gait, and appeared to be yielding and flexible in all the motions of her body. You would think that if you were permitted to embrace her, the outlines of her body would form themselves to yours, as though she would in all things fit herself to him who might be blessed by her love. But Rebecca Loth was dark, with large dark-blue eyes and jet black tresses which spoke out loud to the beholder to their own loveliness. You could not fail to think of her hair and of her eyes, as though they were things almost separate from herself. And she stood like a queen, who knew herself to be all a queen, strong on her limbs, wanting no support, somewhat hard withal, with a repellant beauty that seemed to disdain while it courted admiration, and utterly rejected the idea of that caressing assistance which men always love to give, and which women often love to receive. . . . Such was Rebecca Loth the Jewess, and Ziska almost admitted to himself that she was more beautiful than Nina Balatka. (pp. 82–83)

Equally as important in this description is the way in which Trollope evades the stereotype of the Jewish woman as *la belle Juive*. Here she is emphatically not courtesan or prostitute, debased by her racialist mysteriousness into a sexual object to be forced into her sexual role and abasement.[17] She is emphatically not the screen on which the Christian division of women into Madonna or Whore can be projected and its implications acted out[18]—that powerful image hovering in the subtext of Balzac's *Comédie (In)Humaine* and extending to the Shylock-miser of *Eugenie Grandet*.

But the greatest triumph of *Nina Balatka* is the description of the service at the synagogue and the festival celebration, establishing its presence as a model of civilized and dignified behavior participated in by the entire community. Here we have the pleasure of difference of a realistic novel rather than the fear of Fagin as different—as other kind—that dominates the Gothic elements of *Oliver Twist*.[19]

The door was very low and narrow, and seemed to be choked up by men with short white surplices, but nevertheless he found himself inside, jammed among a crowd of Jews; and a sound of many voices, going together in a sing-song wail or dirge, met his ears. His first impulse was to take off his hat, but that was immediately replaced upon his head, he knew not by whom; and then he observed that all within the building were covered. His guide [Rebecca] did not follow him, but whispered to someone what it was that the stranger required. He could see that those inside the building were clothed in muslin shirts of different lengths, and that it was filled with men, all of whom had before them some sort of desk, from which they were reading, or rather wailing out their litany. Though this was the chief synagogue in Prague, and, as being the so-called oldest in Europe, is a building of some consequence, in the Jewish world, it was very small. There was no ceiling, and the high-pitched roof, which had once probably been coloured, and the walls, which had once certainly been white, were black with the dirt of ages. In the centre there was a cage, as it were, or iron grille, within which five or six old Jews were placed who seemed to wail louder than the others. Round the walls there was a row of men inside stationary desks, and outside them another row, before each of whom there was a small movable standing desk, on which there was a portion of the law of Moses.

Seen through Ziska's eyes the scene is diminished in value; nevertheless, given Trollope's comparative method, the reader sees around Ziska's perceptions to a fuller vision of a thriving communal life.

There seemed to be no possible way by which Ziska could advance, and he would have been glad to retreat had retreat been possible. But first one Jew and then another moved their desks for him, so that he was forced to advance, and some among them pointed to the spot where Anton Trendellsohn was standing. But as they pointed, and as they moved their desks to make a pathway, they still sang and wailed continuously, never ceasing for an instant in their long, loud melancholy song of prayer.

With Ziska we discover the structure of the service, who its leaders are, and how they function, all by means of the description provided by Trollope's narrator.

At the further end there seemed to be some altar, in front of which the High Priest wailed louder than all, louder even than the old men within the cage; and even he, the High Priest, was forced to move his desk to make way for Ziska. But, apparently without displeasure, he moved it with his left hand, while he swayed his right hand backwards and forwards as though regulating the melody of the wail. Beyond the High Priest Ziska saw Anton Trendellsohn, and close to the son he saw the old man whom he had met in the street, and whom he recognised as Anton's father. Old Trendellsohn seemed to take no notice of him, but Anton had watched him from his entrance, and was prepared to speak to him, though he did not discontinue his part in the dirge till the last moment. (pp. 84–85)

The account of the Synagogue service, presented in terms familiar to Ziska from his own religious tradition and its teachings about the Jews, is echoed and balanced in other scenes in Trollope's novel, where he represents Eastern European traditions of Catholic worship, including the appeal to saints for personal intercession and salvation.

What is at stake in Trollope's narrative, as in Dickens's and George Eliot's, is not only verisimilar representation and the demands of social and political justice—all those elements that are bound up in the acknowledgment of the Jewish right to citizenship—but the (re)presentation of bodily presence. Cruikshank's picture of the condemned Fagin is that of the bogey-man-devil with teeth chattering in fear; its negative after-image is of evil incarnate gnashing its teeth in Luciferian revenge; and leads us by a series of historical ironies to the Nazi caricature of the Jew. George Eliot's concluding image of Daniel Deronda, which has baffled many critics, is of a man discovering his Jewishness in realizing he is circumcised: he bears the mark of Abraham's covenant with God in the most intimate part of his flesh.[20] By contrast Trollope's Jews are men and women existing in the realistic space of sexual need, sociality, and economic struggle, though their representation is simultaneously conditioned by the orientation embodied in Ziska, who exoticizes the Jews, hears their prayer only in the orientalist mode of wailing and a dirge, and eroticizes the Jewish woman. In their multiplicity, Trollope's representations thus call to mind the differences be-tween the brutal musculature of Tom Buchanan in F. Scott Fitzgerald's novel and Jay Gatsby's bright easiness of spirit, which Nick memorializes in his elegiac romance. And like Fitzgerald's but unlike Dickens's, the im-pact of Trollope's novel is the result of a typological strategy that ensures the doubled representation of the Jew.

CHAPTER FIVE

Henry James and the Discourses of Antisemitism

JONATHAN FREEDMAN

I propose here to inquire into the relation between an author I very much admire, Henry James, and a social formation I very much distrust: that of antisemitism. But I do not propose to do so by staging an inquisition of Henry James the historical individual. If *I* were put to the question on this matter, I would state for the record three things: that James subscribed, reflexively, to a number of bigoted beliefs; that among these were beliefs we would and should label antisemitic; but that James's explicit antisemitic sentiments represent a garden-variety antisemitism at best. I would also add, however, that unremarkable as it might have been, James's response to the Jew was neither unnuanced nor insignificant. This response originated in James's struggle with a discursive current in the fin de siècle that conflated Jews, art, and social degeneration. James's reaction to this discourse was not antisemitic in any simple sense of the term; precisely because that figure embodied so many of the qualities he valued, the Jew became the vehicle through which James staged an encounter with his deepest anxieties about himself, his art, and the relation of both to his culture. But the result of this response was also problematic. The Jew was placed by James in a position as culturally familiar as it is socially untenable: that of the scapegoat who bears the burden of social deficiencies so that its accuser may deny his own. How James's structure of response came to be, how it related to that of his contemporaries, and how the current critic ought to respond to it, will be my subject here.

*

At a moment when the prejudices of the canonical figures of high Anglo-American modernism have been much discussed, it is odd that so little attention has been paid to those of Henry James.[1] One reason for this inattention is doubtless the fact that the subject has already been canvassed quite thoroughly — and the fact that, when it was, James proved to be extraordinarily lucky in his choice of enemies. The most rigorous inquisition of James's antisemitism was staged by Maxwell Geismar in 1965, and Geismar wrote in terms so hyperbolic that his inquiry could only elicit greater sympathy for its object:

> Quite logically (for this frightened, insecure, snobbish, and authoritarian temperament, that is) he substituted the later [Jewish] immigrants as a new scapegoat, demon and villain on his own "native scene.". . . Reaching backward, as for refuge, into the Victorian myths of his youth, James called upon the resources of Anglo-Saxon romance to combat this ominous and threatening menace to *his* American tradition. . . . But no modern St. George emerged in answer to Henry James's fervent appeal, unless it was the Germanic Hitler who used a more barbarous mythology, combined with all the skills of scientific-industrial technology, to quell the same alien presence.[2]

And while many Jamesians of this era were themselves Jewish — Leon Edel comes first to mind, but only as a representative of many others — few raised the question of James's antisemitic attitudes and comments.[3]

This non-response may tell us much about the multiple, conflicting loyalties of the first generation of Jews to enter mainstream American intellectual life. But it may also remind us that in this matter, as in so many others, James has been blessed in his choice of friends. And he continues to be remarkably lucky in this regard: Ross Posnock has brilliantly argued that James's labile representation of the alien, and the Jew in particular, in *The American Scene* represents his most profound response to the problem of modernity itself. Posnock suggests that James generates from his encounter with the Jew a new model of subjectivity that accommodates otherness without incorporating the Other and a politics of non-identity that valorizes the alien without plotting his extinction through assimilation into the American mold.[4]

As brilliant as Posnock's argument may be, it does have something of the air of special pleading — explaining away, for example, James's obvious deployment of antisemitic slurs in *The American Scene* with a certain degree of ingenuity that nevertheless stops one step short of the credible. I want here accordingly to reopen the question of James's antisemitism by taking a position resolutely in between those adopted by Geismar and Posnock: by arguing, that is, neither that James is to be reviled as a pernicious demonizer of the Jew as arch-alien (a position that can only be seriously held by selective quotation, at which Geismar was quite adept) nor that James is to be deemed a celebrator of the Jew as privileged Other (a more attractive view of James's enterprise, to be sure, but one that must necessarily downplay its less attractive elements). Rather, I want to suggest that James did indeed respond to the Jew with the complicated admixture of identification and rejection Posnock describes, but that this response grew out of a profound crisis experienced on both a psychic and a cultural level, and that it performed in its turn complex and problematic social work.

But before turning to this pattern explicitly, I want to look at the problems of assessing James's antisemitism by glancing at a crucial text: *The American Scene*. And with good reason: *The American Scene* presents James's most extensive and most explicit commentary on the presence of Jews in American life, climaxing with an encounter with what James terms "a Jewry that had burst all bounds" on the Lower East Side of New York.[5] Geismar, needless to say, concentrates on this moment with an undisguised glee, and Posnock spends his most ingenious efforts on parsing it; but there is much in this passage to give support to either position. To be sure, one's first reading of these passages inclines one to the view of James as a card-carrying antisemite. There is here, to give a brief taste of that antisemitism I termed above trivial, a bit of physiognomical tomfoolery, whose ugliness is not so much concealed by the circumlocutions of simile as it is revealed by the very casualness with which it is drawn into James's textual net: "It was as if we had been thus . . . ," James writes, "at the bottom of some vast sallow aquarium in which innumerable fish, of over-developed proboscis, were to bump together, for ever, amid heaped spoils of the sea" (p. 131). Such an effort at ethnic comedy recurs frequently throughout James's writing, as we shall see in more detail below—and its appearance here may remind us of why, of all the many studies of James that have proliferated in recent years, the one titled "The Homespun Humor of Henry James" has yet to appear. But it is important to note that such attitudes were a staple of late-nineteenth-century race theory as well: the "Jewish nose" became installed in this period in scientific as well as popular discourses as a prime marker of Jewish racial identity.[6] For example, American physical anthropologists hypothesized that the so-called "Jewish nose" was a classic example of a Lamarckian acquired trait—a mysterious piece of adaptive behavior that soon becomes genetically encoded; and some even speculated over the precise means by which that trait was acquired: American geneticist Robert Bennett Bean, to cite one influential example, suggested that "the Jewish nose" elongated and upturned because it was "the hereditary product of an habitual expression of indignation."[7]

To put James's text in this context is to begin to see the dimensions of the problem I am trying to address here. If James's piece of nasal stereotyping represents nothing more than a failed piece of ethnic humor, then it deserves to be noticed little if at all; but if it indicates his deployment of categorizations that render him complicit—or worse—with the dominant patterns of nineteenth-century race thinking, it suggests that we need to regard his responses to the Jew with no little degree of suspicion. And this latter tendency is heightened later in this same passage at that moment when James discusses that "intensity of Jewish aspect," which, according to James, "makes the individual Jew more of a concentrated person . . . than any other human, noted at random." "Or is it simply rather," James continues, "that the unsurpassed strength of the race permits of the chopping into myriads of fine fragments without loss of race-quality?" (p. 132).

This last note, the note of racial essentialism, is ominous indeed; and it may well incline us to move a good deal of the way toward Geismar's position, if not so far as to adopt his overheated rhetoric. One is reminded by language like this of Sartre's eloquent unveiling of the irrational "primitive conviction" that lies beneath the tissue of "intellectual principles" appealed to by the antisemite: "For the anti-Semite what makes the Jew is the presence in him of 'Jewishness', a Jewish principle analogous to phlogiston or the soporific virtue of opium. . . . Without the presence of this metaphysical essence, the activities ascribed to the Jew [by the antisemite] would be utterly incomprehensible."[8] And, perhaps more to the point, one is reminded of similar meditations on Jewish race-quality and the intellectual expression of antisemitic sentiment among Anglo-American intellectuals at the moment of *The American Scene*: eugenic theory.[9]

Both the gentry anti-immigration activists of the fin de siècle and their successors in the full-blown eugenics movement of the early years of the twentieth century claimed that Jews composed a homogeneous racial body whose racial identity was signified by their distinctive appearance—and whose entry into American society, if not forestalled, would lead to corruption of the native Anglo-Saxon stock:

The foal of a Percheron dam by a Percheron sire is, of course, a Percheron. . . . The children of Jews have their parents' prominent nose and other physical attributes. Like breeds like, and when the unlike mate together the progeny have some of the characteristics of both parents. It is beyond question that the vast infusion of southern European blood which is each year passing into American veins is certain to work marked changes in the physical appearance of Americans. It is reasonable to conclude that the future American will be shorter in stature, swarthier of skin, that his skull will be shorter and broader, that probably his nose will be more prominent than is the case to-day.[10]

And if one continues to pursue the analogy, disturbing parallels between James and his antisemitic contemporaries continue to present themselves. For, as the above quotation suggests, from their meditations on Jewish race-quality, it was not a far step for these thinkers to fantasize Jewish race conquest, both through "over-breeding" — that promiscuous over-production that has been held against every social out-group since Malthus — and through successful adaptation to the urban environment. And here, too, James's response to what he rather hyperbolically calls the "Jewish conquest of New York" is not entirely dissimilar from the reactions of his explicitly racist contemporaries (p. 131). Their language of immeasurable reproduction suffuses James's description, too: his dominant tropes here are those of a thoroughly urban population "swarming," "bursting all bounds," and — most tellingly — "multiplying." "Multiplication, multiplication of everything, was the dominant note," James writes; and then he continues: "[The] children swarmed above all — here was multiplication with a vengeance" (p. 131). And, to play with James's terms, the vengeance that these proliferating progeny quite literally embody is one that will ultimately be wrought on the civic life of the American nation. For while it is the sheer plentitude of humanity crowded into the Lower East Side that James the social observer notes, it is the "agency of future ravage" they threaten that James "the incurable man of letters" fears; this rapidly reproducing minority, James suggests, will transform utterly the English language and hence frustrate the already tenuous possibilities of a national culture informed by it (p. 138).[11]

James's responses to the Jew in *The American Scene*, then, possess disturbing analogies to the most offensive slurs that circulated through both elite gentry circles and the popular press of his time. But merely noting this similarity is not, in my view, sufficient; indeed, it is misleading in precisely the same way as are prejudices of all sorts — which are, after all, based on the false logic of metonymic associations passing themselves off as potent predications. For when one places these passages from *The American Scene* in the context of elite eugenic theorizing and anti-immigrant activism, one's prevailing impression is of James's relative mildness. One does not, that is to say, immediately focus on the prevailing or even latent racist tonalities of James's response to the Lower East Side — tonalities which, furthermore, seem mild indeed in comparison with the responses of James's avowedly racist and antisemitic contemporaries. Nor does one wish to overstress James's emphasis on the threat posed by the Jew to the purity of the English language; throughout the section there is also a countervailing sense of the organic vitality of Yiddish culture, the deadening effects of American mass culture on that formation, and the Jew as potential bearer of enlightenment in a stultifying American cultural scene. Indeed, James goes to some lengths to distinguish between the Lower East Side ghetto and the "dark, soul-stifling Ghettos of other remembered cities"; the former represents, he argues in a trope that tellingly resembles the most resonant figurations of an earlier New England elite, a shimmering city on a hill: "For what did it really all come to but that one had seen with one's eyes the New Jerusalem on earth? What less could it all have been, in its far-spreading light and its celestial serenity of multiplication?" (p. 133). In this "city of redemption," even the signifiers of degeneration are transvalued: "multiplication" itself functions, for this moment at least, as a trope of enlightenment and redemption, not one of cultural despair.

Moments like this might well incline us to shift closer to Posnock's position. They suggest that, while James here writes in fear of the proliferative energy of the alien in general and the Jew in particular, he simultaneously glosses those very qualities as signs of a thoroughly praiseworthy vitality. And it would thus seem that James's discourse is not susceptible to the charge of simple antisemitism that not only Geismar but also many cultural and intellectual historians have proffered against it.[12] But we ought not move too far in the direction of exoneration. What we witness here, I would suggest, is more than just a simple (or complex) case of ambivalence. Underneath the tense interplay between anti- and philosemitism evident in *The American Scene* lies what can only be described as a structuring, second-order antisemitism, a persistently problematic pattern of thinking and writing that installs the Jew in the position of the vexing other—and that is all the more problematic because it half-recognizes in that figure the shadowy double of the Jamesian artist or the things that he would value. It is this pattern of response that I want to designate as the discourse of Jamesian antisemitism, and whose implications and complications I propose to interrogate more fully below.

Both the overdetermined quality of and the problems with this pattern of thought can be best grasped by noting the uniqueness of the threat the Jew poses to James's value system. For in comparison to other representatives of "the alien"—the Italian workers James meets, the "Negro" and "Chinaman" whose "human value," along with that of the Italian, is, James chillingly writes, "the most easily produced"—his response to the Jew is uniquely intense (p. 128). "There is no swarming like that of Israel when once Israel has got a start," James writes at the opening of the Lower East Side rambles; similarly, there is no threat to American language, and hence national identity, like that of the Jew when once he enters into the national conversation: that figure, and that figure alone, speaks in what James portentously calls the "Accent of the Future" (pp. 131, 139). And to witness this response is to be led to an overwhelming, if simple, question: Why should the Jew function in this way for James? The simple (and not necessarily incorrect) answer is of course that such overdetermination is endemic to western representations of Jewry: from time immemorial, the Jew has been installed within western discourses as that figure onto whom feared and desired qualities are first projected and then decried. But, rather than focusing on the all-too-familiar thematics of scapegoating, I want to look more closely at the particular patterns of incorporation and expulsion evident throughout James's view of that figure, not only because of the greater precision of doing so but more importantly because of what it can tell us about the relation between James's portrayal of the Jew and his linked crisis of individual and cultural identity.

Perhaps it is best, in other words, to connect James's responses to the Jew with that role he names in this passage as the "incurable man of letters" (p. 138). I want to do so by taking that self-description quite literally; for, I want to suggest, the notion of the "incurability" of the man of letters signifies James's participation in a discourse that identified both high culture and the man of letters as irrevocably diseased — as, in fact, the bearer of a (again quite literal) social disease, the disease of cultural "degeneration." Indeed, in late-nineteenth-century debates on degeneration, all the terms we have been seeing in James's response to the Lower East Side are present in different, yet familiar, combinations. Jews, writers, overcrowded urban environments, anxieties over sexuality, fears about cultural identity: all these circulate throughout the fin-de-siècle debate centering on the origins and consequences of putative cultural "degeneration" — and all, except one, point the finger of degeneracy directly at James himself. That one — and it is the one that James, somewhat against his better instincts, seizes upon as his own candidate as a locus of cultural corruption — is none other than the Jew.

*

The nineteenth-century degeneration debate, like its recent incarnation, the late nineteen-eighties American controversy over "national decline," constituted an extraordinarily powerful controversy over a culturally resonant pseudo-question — one that involved medical authorities, cultural critics, and imaginative writers alike in protracted discursive struggle over the causes and consequences of the alleged deliquescence of that highly problematic entity, "western civilization."[13] While the debate had its origins largely in European writing of the middle of the nineteenth century, its specific relevance for James's responses to the discourses of antisemitism was brought into sharp focus by the fin-de-siècle vogue for Max Nordau's influential popularizing tome, *Degeneration*. For prior to Nordau, one major strain in that discourse identified the prime embodiment and agent of degeneration as the Jew. This is a current of thought one immediately associates with that supreme dialectician of decadence, Nietzsche, for whom Jews are at once more degenerate and more vital than their Christian successors:

Considered psychologically, the Jewish nation is a nation of the toughest vital energy which, placed in impossible circumstances, voluntarily, from the profoundest shrewdness in self-preservation, took the side of all *dècadence* instincts — *not* as being dominated by them but because it divined in them power by means of which it can prevail against "the world."[14]

But Nietzsche's meditations were not composed in a vacuum; rather, he is responding to and writing against many of the most powerful currents of his own social moment. As Sander Gilman observes, the Jew was located throughout nineteenth-century medical and evolutionary discourses as a pernicious atavism, a remnant of a past stage in history's Hegelian march toward the consummation of a thoroughly Christianized Spirit.[15] But the Jew was more than just an evolutionary relic. In that coupling of ontogenic and phylogenic logic that provided so much of the buttressing for late-nineteenth-century scientific racism, Jews — along with Africans, Asians, and the lower classes — were seen as the incarnation of those instincts that individuals and societies alike needed to outgrow; childish, primitive, and thoroughly inbred, the Jew embodied "a stage of sexual development which was understood as primitive and perverse and therefore degenerate" (Gilman, pp. 214–15).

And the Jew embodied another form of putative "degeneration" as well — mental enfeeblement or madness. Such propensities, it was claimed, resulted from Jewish endogamous marital practices — precisely those qualities, in other words, that also allegedly constituted Jews as a distinct and identifiable "race" in the first place. "Nervous illnesses of all types," according to the authoritative voice of Charcot, "are innumerably more frequent among Jews than among other groups," and he identifies the prime cause of such illnesses as the Jewish propensity for in-breeding (quoted in Gilman, p. 155).[16] Charcot's diagnosis was confirmed in a number of professional and discursive arenas. In the established professions of law and medicine and the newer ones of psychiatry, physical anthropology, and criminal anthropology, the image of the fatally inbred, sexually aberrant, and congenitally neurasthenic Jew rapidly became canonical.

The link between this strain of medicalizing and evolutionary discourse and the topos of cultural degeneracy was both powerful and paradoxical.

On the one hand, in-breeding was seen to result in weaker nervous systems and a lesser degree of sexual self-control, and a decline from the highest standards of physical well-being. But on the other hand, cultural degeneration is the result of *inter*breeding, assimilation—which is seen as conducing, in the most offensive terminology of the time, to a "mongrelization" of the races, a decline of stable racial identities, the destruction of the ethnic purity of the "Aryan" race, and thence the corruption of western culture.[17]

The force of this paradox, it might be noted here, was activated with particular intensity among the Anglo-American social elite, and the discursive burden of its double imperatives was largely borne by that increasingly demonized figure, the Eastern European immigrant. As in Nietzsche, the Jew was paradoxically located by Anglo-American race theorists as being either more degenerate or more vital than his gentile counterparts—and sometimes as being both at once. "In a community of rascals," wrote Paul Popenoe, editor of the house journal of the American Genetic Association, "the greatest rascal might be the fittest to survive. In the slums of the modern city the Jewish type, stringently selected through centuries of ghetto life, is particularly fit to survive, although it may not be the physical ideal of the anthropologist."[18] Indeed, in a paradox repeated throughout the discourses of these writers, the Jew was constructed as a figure whose very degradation betokened his extraordinary vitality—all the more so for a WASP elite obsessed, at the turn of the century, with its own falling birth rate in comparison with the robust reproduction of the *Ostjuden* and other southern European immigrants.[19]

And following directly from this paradox, linked to it by the bemusing metonymies of racism, was another double bind. As a result of the Jew's insistence on maintaining his "race and religious purity," it was claimed, the ameliorative influences of intermarriage and assimilation could not work to curb the potent purity of his racial vitality. Yet—to complete the chain of paradoxes that encircled the immigrant as thoroughly as the ghettos into which he was confined—the assimilation of the Jew by means of intermarriage was not, to say the least, a consummation devoutly to be wished. For the eugenicists, Jews' refusal to intermarry or intermingle (and these two quite separate issues mingled in their writings with a promiscuity all their own) only heightened the decline of the native stock when they did. The Jew "stubbornly resists absorption and assimilation by the peoples among whom he casts his lot," complains Henry Suskdorf on one page of his 1911 racist-eugenicist tract *Our Race Problems*, but then on another, he turns around and complains about the effects of precisely that possibility: "[The] strong current of inferior quality has set in from the unprogressive east and north-east of Europe. . . . This bodes no good for the American nation. If this rising flood will continue to pour into this country, and if this undesirable human element will continue to be absorbed and assimilated, American manhood and womanhood, and American civilization, will certainly deteriorate."[20] The only acceptable solution was to limit immigration — or worse; and it bears repetition at a moment when similar anxieties pervade our culture that the most extravagant fantasies of the nineteenth-century eugenicists anticipate the most nightmarish realities of twentieth-century history.[21]

In fin-de-siècle Europe, by contrast, the brunt of this discursive current was borne not by immigrants but rather by those figures who were then entering the mainstream of European high-cultural life: those assimilating Jewish intellectuals who were joining, at a time of resurgent social anti-semitism, precisely the professions that occupied themselves with denouncing Jews for promoting social degeneration. For this discursive current placed secular Jewish intellectuals in a position that could only be described as problematic. If they accepted the dominant terms of their own vocations, they would reinforce the antisemitic tendencies of their moment; but if they failed to accept these terms, they would consign themselves to the very marginality they were entering those professions to avoid. The response of these Jewish intellectuals was appropriately complex. While they tended to accept the terms of the degeneration debate and even its identification of the Jew as a prime source of degeneracy, many sought to shift the burden of degeneracy to other forms of causation and consequence: either to lower-class Eastern European Jews or to the immiserating and overcrowded living conditions under which they were forced to live. The most influential medical authority on degeneration, Italian criminologist (and Zionist) Cesare Lombroso argued that the Jewish struggle against persecution was responsible for high levels of mental illness; Lombroso identified degeneracy as well among such groups as Africans, prostitutes, criminals, and that entirely new social type, homosexuals.

This discursive task was also central to the most influential writer on the topic of degeneration, the writer who bundled together the medical and anthropological discourses on degeneration and packaged them for broad public consumption: Max Nordau. Nordau's activities were wide-ranging: originally trained as a doctor, he soon settled into a career as a journalist, a free-lance cultural critic, and a political activist. And it is in this last role, I believe, that his anti-degeneration polemics are most accurately to be read. It is true that, as one critic has written, "in the case of Nordau, politics were complex. He was after all not only a polemicist against decadent literature but also a leading figure in the Zionist movement."[22] But, I would suggest, this coalescence of anti-degenerate and Zionist rhetoric is simple: both necessarily involve an anti-antisemitic agenda. Like Lombroso, to whom

Degeneration is dedicated, Nordau's Zionist writings adopt much of the accepted linkage between Jews and forms of degeneracy: ghetto-dwelling Eastern European Jews and city-dwellers are shown to be afflicted with all the physical and mental symptoms of degeneration, and the salvation of the race was to be found in physical vigor and self-assertion embodied in an entirely new conception of Jewish identity that Nordau dubbed "the muscle Jew." But Nordau's massively influential tome continued the shift away from the identification of the Jew as degenerate to a broader definition of degeneracy—one that ultimately scapegoated other marginalized figures and groups as prime degenerates.

For Nordau expanded the notion of degeneration to include just about any and all deviations from just about any and all norms, often antithetically related to one another. Excitation and exhaustion; genius and idiocy; egomania and excessive susceptibility to suggestion; sexual indulgence and rejection of the body; criminality and aspirations to sainthood: all these incompatible qualities are to be read as signs of degeneration. And its causes are equally global; they are for Nordau nothing less than modernity itself. When the pressures of modern urban life impacted on the weakened nerves of the "cultivated classes"—those removed from the bracing life of manual labor and relentlessly exposed to the cultural productions of pessimism and gloom—the result was nothing less than a mass "derangement of the nervous system" leading to fatigue, exhaustion, boredom.[23] This derangement, perceptible on the very physical level of the brain cells and nerves, may have been caused by factors in the environment, but, Nordau continues, it soon came to be encoded on the very level of the genotype, passing on from one generation to the next in that parade of cultural declension Nordau calls "degeneration."

The efficacy of this move, from an anti-antisemitic point of view, is obvious. Nordau effectively redefined the degeneration debate by locating the effeteness of the elite and ultimately modernity itself, not the hyper-contagious Jews, as the source of cultural decline and social corruption. Indeed, it is a sign of both his intent and his effectiveness that Nordau was ultimately able to turn the discourse of degeneration against those who would use it to demonize the Jews—against the antisemites themselves. "German hysteria manifests itself in anti-Semitism, that most dangerous form of the persecution mania, in which the person believing himself persecuted, is capable of all crimes (the *persécuté persécuteur* of French mental therapeutics)" (p. 209). But Nordau did more as well. He also nominated a figure to replace the Jew as arch-degenerate: the avant-garde artist. Contemporary literature's preoccupation with morbid subject matter like crime, sexuality, slum conditions; its defiantly anti-bourgeois attitude; its evocation of decadence, gloom, pessimism, decay, malaise; the well-publicized non-normative sexualities of so many fin-de-siècle artists: all these provide

Nordau with evidence of the fundamental degeneracy of his culture. And—in a paradoxical move tellingly similar to that of those who read the degraded conditions in which Jews were forced to live as evidence of their innate racial inferiority—Nordau defined the artist not merely as the witness of degeneration but also as its source. Focusing first on the nonnormative sexuality and madness of actual fin-de-siècle artists and then sliding metonymically to their efforts at formal experimentation, Nordau argued over and over in this hyper-repetitive tome that the works of contemporary writers and artists functioned as the vector of "mental contagion" through which these "graphomaniacal fools and their imbecile or unscrupulous bodyguard of critics" were able to spread the "Black Death of degeneration and hysteria" throughout the social body. For Nordau, the only solution—which, luckily, is the inevitable one—is the eventual decomposition of degenerates themselves under the pressure of "anatomical necessity." "The feeble, the degenerate, will perish," Nordau prophesies. "The aberrations of art have no future. They will disappear when civilized humanity will have triumphed over its exhausted condition" (p. 233).

It would be tempting but misleading to treat the degeneration debate as a conflict between antisemites and Zionists proposing Jews and artists as competing candidates for agent of cultural decline. (For one thing, the two positions were far from incompatible, as the Nazi conflation of "degenerate" and "Jewish" art suggests.[24]) But what one can conclude about it with some degree of accuracy is that the particular spin Nordau wished to give the issue, the shifting of the burden of degeneration from the Jew to the socially and sexually marginalized artist, fell on receptive ears, particularly in Anglo-American middle-class, middlebrow culture. *Degeneration* was translated into English in 1895 and instantly became an object of popular enthusiasm and dinner-party discussion—a rough analogue would be the vogue surrounding Alan Bloom's venture into Straussian best-sellerdom, *The Closing of the American Mind*. William Dean Howells recorded in *Harper's* with characteristic sanity both the extensiveness of Nordau's popularity and the reasons for it:

The most interesting fact in regard to this book is that it has made any stir in the world [at all], and Dr. Nordau's success here, where a great many people are now reading his book, is another proof of the advantage of living in Europe. . . . If some ill-conditioned American had written his senseless and worthless book, we should scarcely have troubled ourselves to say that it was senseless and worthless, far less tried to prove it. But it comes to us with authority, coming across seas, and it comes from Germany, where if the critical thinking is somewhat slow, it is believed to be deep and thorough.[25]

For all his justified scorn, Howells reminds us that Nordau achieved a considerable degree of cultural authority—at least to those for whom the discourses he invoked were novel and unfamiliar. Howells also suggests that Nordau attained this authority because he used his patter of pseudo-knowledge to give a name (many names, in fact) to the anxieties that the middle-class public faced in all facets of social experience. But Nordau's fulminations also did more: despite his explicit intent (Nordau was a man of the utmost cultural sophistication), his work also lent a patina of respectability to the strains of anti-intellectualism, homophobia, and philistinism of that public — qualities never far from the surface in both American and British middle-class culture, and activated (then as now) precisely at moments of social dislocation and transformation. The time of Nordau, it is important to remember, was also that of the Oscar Wilde trial; and the press-driven revulsion at Wilde fed and fed into Nordau's reflections on the artist as agent of degeneration.

That current in the discourse of degeneration Nordau emblematized had an energizing effect on many contemporary artists and writers, many of whom labeled themselves as degenerates with an enthusiasm bordering on zeal. But this discursive tendency posed a serious threat to an eminent, if deeply depressed, fin-de-siècle writer named Henry James. To this (probably closeted) gay man and (undeniably) audaciously experimental writer, the cultural currency of the linkage between degeneration, stylistic hypertrophy, non-reproductive sexuality, and madness carried a powerful charge. The responses of his critics — many of whom, at that very moment, were lamenting the obscurity of his style and decrying his participation in "decadent" journals like *The Yellow Book* [26] — only served to heighten the association between what James felt to be the very ground of his psychic health and corruption, madness, and disease. This response is partially registered in James's private communications of this period, particularly in those letters following the *Guy Domville* affair, in which he lashes out at the insensitivity of the brutish, philistinish public and positions himself as a martyr to the cause of art. But it is in the stories of this period that James evidences his greatest defensiveness in the face of this cultural indictment, and to a certain extent, his internalization of its terms. Writers in these tales are aging, diseased, dying, or dead; their writing is cryptic, crabbed, incomprehensible, ignored; those readers who do take them up rapidly become obsessed monomaniacs. Authorship is connected with an inability or disinclination to enter modes of reproductive sexual relation — sometimes charmingly ("The Lesson of the Master"), sometimes problematically ("The Figure in the Carpet"); tellingly, these tales are contained in volumes with titles like *Terminations* and *Embarrassments*. The tendency reaches something of a climax with *The Sacred Fount*, which provides a virtual textbook of these topoi; the obsessive ravings of that novel's nameless narrator firmly link the very enterprise of fiction-making to madness, sexual eccentricity, and, ultimately, exhaustion and decrepitude. And at this very moment, James begins to use, with a cautious admixture of defensiveness and self-revelation, the language of degeneration itself to describe his art. Many of James's most famous assertions and ascriptions demand to be read in the light of the culturally resonant links between madness, non-normative sexualities, and the artist, and the vision of the artist as a carrier of the disease of degeneration. "The madness of art," "that queer monster, the artist": expressions like these suggest a James who finds himself culturally inscribed into a position of dementia and monstrosity even as — especially because — he turns those culturally resonant definitions of his office into a badge of authorial pride.

It is with this context in mind that we can best understand James's responses to the Jew in the early years of the twentieth century. For even as James turns his authorial attention to the discursive link between the artist and "the degenerate," insulting references to Jews appear in the fiction of this period with increasing frequency. And as they do so they begin to comport themselves to patterns that reach their fullest development in *The American Scene*. For the Jew enters the fiction of the 1890s as both character-type and figurative resource in a manner that can only be described as resolutely overdetermined: characters, sustained allusions, and offhand references alike all connect, in a manner one could label either compulsive or consistent, the Jew to art, but in ways that bear problematic consequences. There are, to be sure, the kinds of slurs one routinely expects in Anglo-American gentry discourse, frequently thematized as such — the unpleasant narrator of an 1888 story called "Glasses" makes a few nasty remarks about Jews at French resorts at precisely the moment when they were being excluded from American ones, for example. But other novels comport themselves to the pattern I have described above — and, significantly, these contain James's most resonant explorations of the problems and possibilities of art.

For example, in *The Tragic Muse* — written just one year after "Glasses" — James presents us with a figure, named Miriam Rooth, an actress whose preternatural dramatic abilities and human monstrousness both seem to be tied to her Jewish "blood." In this novel so thoroughly devoted to the accounting of the relation between art and its "life," Miriam remains the only truly dedicated and truly successful artist. And her success as a dramatic artist is linked, characters in the novel frequently believe, to her racial heritage, which gives her both the sense of beauty and the ability to manipulate appearances necessary to become a great dramatic actress. But the more successful she gets, the more alienated she becomes from her own Jewish identity; at the end of the novel, a great point is made about the fact that she has married her most non-Jewish manager: "A servant opened the door and was ushering in a lady. . . . 'Miss Rooth!' the man announced; but he was caught up by a gentleman who came next and who exclaimed, laughing and with a gesture gracefully corrective: 'No, no—no longer Miss Rooth!'"[27] This "gracefully corrective" gesture is meant to signify Miriam's new identity as a married woman—to announce that she is no longer *Miss* Rooth. But it more fully announces her metamorphosis from Jewess into some other racial identity—that she is no longer Miss *Rooth*. It announces what the rest of the book confirms: that Miriam has fully transformed herself into nothing less than "Miriam"—the English Rachel, the culturally apotheosized Tragic (and Comic) Muse of the London stage. And as such, she knows no ethnicity or race. She is merely—magnificently—herself; and in being so grandly herself, she becomes the very type of the artist.

But if Miriam's ascension to this exalted status involves an extinction or denial of her Jewish identity, it does not extinguish the text's concern with the dynamics of Jewishness. The persistence of the novel's concern with Jewish identity, its properties, and, most significantly, its acquisition, is signaled by a fascinating maneuver in the text in which another character takes on Jewish characteristics precisely as Miriam divests herself of her own. And given the novel's concern with artistic identity, it is particularly significant that this figure is none other than Miriam's (gentile) mother. For, while painting Miriam, Nick sees Mrs. Rooth with new eyes:

Mrs. Rooth's vague, polite, disappointed bent back and head made a subject, the subject of a sketch, in an instant: they gave such a sudden glimpse of the pictorial element of race. He found himself seeing the immemorial Jewess in her, holding up a candle in a crammed back shop. There was no candle indeed, and his studio was not crammed, and it had never occurred to him before that she was of Hebrew strain, except on the general theory, held with pertinacity by several clever people, that most of us are more or less so. The late Rudolf Roth had been, and his daughter was visibly her father's child; so that, flanked by such a pair, good Semitic reasons were surely not wanting to the mother. Receiving Miriam's little satiric shower without shaking her shoulders, she might at any rate have been the descendent of a tribe long persecuted. (p. 444)

In this resonant—and truly *weird*—passage, James initially seems to reinforce the link between the two discourses we have seen brought together with such problematic intensity—that of the racial identity of the artist and the racist discourse on the Jew—but on further examination, it becomes clear that he only does so in order to dismantle that connection. The work this passage performs is to disavow the very rhetoric of "blood" we have seen attached to Miriam's ancestry and Miriam's artistry alike. Jewish characteristics here become a matter not of racial origin (although that notion is not disavowed) but rather of custom and attitude — something that, it would seem, can be picked up merely by prolonged experience and exposure, something like a bad habit, or a cold. But whatever the weirdness of that move, it is clear that race here functions in such a way as to make Jewishness bear all the problems of art in order to leave the artist free to explore its possibilities.

Even more problematic along these lines is *The Golden Bowl*, each of whose plots are set in motion by Jewish vendors of antique goods: Gutterman-Seuss, who sells Adam the antique tiles he gives to his wife-to-be Charlotte as an engagement present; and the Italo-Jewish *antiquari*, who sells Charlotte the antique bowl she gives Maggie Verver as a wedding present. Here, the associations that persist in the rest of the writing of the 1890s are heightened: between the Jew, an old or antique species of art or artifice and hence a past or passing civilization, and a species of moral corruption. For each of these gifts is touched with a sexual taint: incest in the first case, since Adam is marrying the best friend of his daughter (and will make of the marriage only an opportunity to spend more time with Maggie); adultery in the second, since Charlotte is choosing the gift with the aid of her former lover, now Maggie's fiancé. Here again, in the figure of the Jew congeals all the things that James finds of greatest value: art, love, passion, cultural amplitude; but those things are there in a purely negative guise — so as to preserve, it would seem, the qualities that James values most intensely from the force of the antagonism directed against them by his culture.

One Jew in this novel, however, performs a redemptive, almost sacrificial act: the antique dealer returns to buy back the cracked golden bowl. But this act is glossed by the novel as being insufficient, and insufficient precisely because of the Jew's Jewishness. Here is the passage in which Maggie defends the Jew from Amerigo's instinctive antisemitic response, which translates from the Jamesian into the vernacular as: What's in it for him?

She gave a slow headshake — as if, no, after consideration, *that* way were an issue. "I can only think of him as kind, for he had nothing to gain. He had in fact only to lose. It was what he came to tell me — that he had asked too high a price, more than the object was really worth. There was a particular reason which he hadn't mentioned and which had made him consider and repent."

That reason was that four years earlier the Prince had "guessed the flaw" in the bowl and refused it as a gift from Charlotte. Maggie, however, does not want or ask for her money back — particularly after the shopman sees photographs of the Prince and Charlotte in the drawing room and tells Maggie of their ease with one another on the day of her and Amerigo's wedding. She receives, she tells the Prince, "nothing but an apology for empty hands and empty pocket; which was made me — as if it mattered a mite! — ever so frankly, ever so beautifully and touchingly."[28]

This passage is crucial both to James's representation of the Jew and to the plot of the novel as a whole; indeed, it reminds us of the indissoluble, if thoroughly subterranean, connection between the two. The antique dealer's "repentance" both controverts and confirms common antisemitic stereotypes — confirms, that is to say, precisely what it seems to controvert. The odd conversion of this Jew to a form of behavior identified by the text as Christian, or at least not-Jewish, in effect endorses the Prince's calumnies even as it redeems the *antiquari* from them. And, most importantly, it is absolutely central to the novel's emplotment. Not only does this conversion of the Jew, that is to say, make that plot happen, accomplish its central peripety; it also anticipates the similar conversion of the Jew's greatest antagonist — and most exact double: Amerigo. Just as the Jewish antique dealer undoes the slightly shady bargain he had made with Maggie by turning around and comporting himself to a higher — a non-Hebraic — standard of behavior, so too does Amerigo repent for a breach of faith and comport himself to a redeemed standard of behavior, one in which, far more than the antique dealer, he loses his own racial identity in order to take on that of Maggie. Indeed, the resemblance between the two goes farther, if somewhat paradoxically, to a significant differentiation. For the Jew's "repentance" here is, the text suggests, a slightly disingenuous one; since he claims to have "empty hands and empty pocket," it would seem, he makes good on his slightly shady business transaction only verbally, without any of the financial remuneration that, the text seems to imply, is the real ground of his concern. The Prince's repentance and restitution must and does go even farther, to a recasting of his very identity and pattern of behavior climaxed by his metamorphosis at the end of the novel into a fully engaged, if problematically so, husband to Maggie.

In both of these novels, Jews function in such a way as to incarnate possibilities James would wholeheartedly endorse, but in such ways as to collect taints that accrue to those possibilities — and to leave other characters free to explore them. Given this pattern and its implications for James's own career as an artist and a non-normatively emotional and sexual being, I want to return to the question with which I began this essay: How is the contemporary academic reader to interpret James's responses to Jews? I have been telling the narrative of that response in such a way as to stress both its marginality and its centrality to James's own literary and imaginative projects alike. The Jew, I have been suggesting, functions most fully for James not as a concrete figure or even as a stereotyped one, but as a receptacle: a figure onto which can be loaded all the sources of his inchoate anxieties and unacknowledged terrors. As such, my narrative is quite similar to the one Julia Kristeva has recently told of Céline: a narrative of expulsion, excorporation; of what she calls "abjection":

There looms, within abjection, one of those violent, dark revolts of being, directed against a threat that seems to emanate from an exorbitant outside or inside, ejected beyond the scope of the possible, the tolerable, the horrible. It lies there, quite close, but it cannot be assimilated. It beseeches, worries, and fascinates desire which, nevertheless, does not allow itself to be seduced. . . . Unflaggingly, like an inescapable boomerang, a vortex of summons and repulsion places the one haunted by it literally beside himself.[29]

I turn to Kristeva at this moment because the quality of her language is, to the Jamesian, uncannily familiar. I can think of no better words, for example, to describe James's habitual problematic in the more compelled writing of this period—in the ghost stories, for example, or the odd fables of artistic practice like *The Sacred Fount*. But there is more than linguistic affinity to note here. Like Kristeva's Céline, James seems more than usually "haunted" and "beside himself" when confronted with the figure of the Jew; and his own responses to the Jew do indeed at times seem to comport themselves to the pattern Kristeva traces: "The image of the Jew will concentrate negated love become hatred for Mastery on the one hand; and on the other and jointly, desire for what mastery cuts out: weakness, the joying substance, sex tinged with femininity and death" (p. 180).

Indeed, Kristeva's analysis suggests a possible juncture between the psychoanalytic and the cultural hermeneutic we have been looking at in James's treatment of the Jew. Briefly to sketch such a narrative suggested by this juncture requires little effort: James's own, heavily culturally overdetermined aspirations for "mastery"—his projection of himself as consummate high-culture authority of the Art of the Novel—involved a process by which he was forced to repress with particular vigor all the messy, fluid formations of his own psyche; and this self-limitation, we might further speculate, became all the more powerful when that material was brought to the surface by the degeneration debate. James, we might continue to argue, responded to this psychic roadblock with the classic defense of negation (of entertaining as the forbidden or the denied the wishes or desires subject to the vicissitudes of repression). Inflating the power of the artist-Jew, James connects that figure to all the things in his own sexual and emotional makeup that he is forced to deny himself, but at the same time constructs that figure as one connected to filth, degeneration, decay. James thereby explores his desires even in the act of renouncing them—and suffuses them, in that act of renunciation, with the very qualities he feels compelled to expel from himself. Hence the curious effect by which the Jew is at once bound to and distanced from James himself—a boundary problem that is constitutive of antisemitic discourses: "The Jew becomes the feminine exalted to the point of mastery, the ambivalent, the border where exact limits between same and other, subject and object, and even beyond these, between inside and outside, and disappearing — hence an Object of fear and fascination" (p. 184).

The model of Jamesian antisemitism is neat — perhaps too neat. For one thing, placing James against Céline (even Kristeva's Céline) reminds us of how much more sympathetic James allows himself to be to the qualities he would expel than was Céline. And, perhaps more importantly, this juxtaposition reminds us of how much more open to the process of self-inquiry and self-renovation he was than were most of his fellow artistic antisemites, such as Céline — or, more relevantly, James's contemporary and friend, the French writer and rabid antisemite, Paul Bourget; or — most relevantly of all perhaps — those gentry colleagues and contemporaries who helped effectuate the rise of the scientific discourse on race and the eugenics movement at the very time James was writing. James was, to put the matter simply, saner — more open and more generous on every level — than were figures like these; although, admittedly, on the subject of Jews, Henry was undeniably less generous than brother William, a committed Dreyfusard and an outspoken opponent of the rise of discrimination at the turn of the century.

Again, then, considering James under the sign of his antisemitism leads us to a measured, and somewhat ambiguous, response. But here, too, the very pattern of similarity and difference with Kristeva's model can help us position James's attitudes with a greater degree of precision. Kristeva writes at one of her more dazzling and problematic moments — dazzling because it is so dialectically appropriate, problematic because it might seem to excuse antisemitic discourses — of the recuperative, cathartic function of the process of writing in and about abjection. The very putting into language of the responses to the abject "call[s] for a softening of the super-ego. Writing them imagines an ability to imagine the abject, that is, to see oneself in its place and to thrust it aside only by means of the displacements of verbal play." But, she continues, "it is only after his death, eventually, that the writer of abjection will escape his condition of waste, reject, abject" (p. 16).

For James, however, this process of encountering the Jew in all of that figure's uncanny similarity to and defensively drawn difference from himself performs the very psychic "softening" Kristeva writes about. Thus to turn one last time to the passage from *The American Scene* that has served as our touchstone throughout this inquiry, what's perhaps most interesting about it is not only the lability of James's affect — his swinging from one polar extreme, that of slurring references to Jewish noses, to another, that of an idealization of the Jew as the privileged figure in an America governed by a homogenizing mass culture — but rather the *rhythms* of his response. We watch James shifting about, testing, contesting, interrogating, and remaking his own responses to these Jews — emerging, in the end, with a response in which James the alien outsider from the American Scene measures through the difference between the Jew and America the difference that difference itself will make. It is true that James's attitude at this moment is ambiguous — far more ambiguous than Posnock is willing to admit; his final, and powerfully uncanny, image is that of the Jewish café whose

> fostered decencies and unprecedented accents took on thus, for the brooding critic, a likeness to that terrible modernized and civilized room in the Tower of London, haunted by the shade of Guy Fawkes, which had more than once formed part of the critic's taking tea there. In this chamber of the present urbanities, the wretched man had been stretched on the rack and the critic's ear (how else should it have been a critic's?) could still always catch, in pauses of talk, the faint groan of his ghost. (p. 139)

But whatever else one may say about this passage, it brings to bear on James's relation with the Jew a powerfully moving reversal of the pattern we have seen Kristeva describing in Céline. In this passage it is not the Jew, but rather James, who reveals himself as the abject — and he so reveals himself in the very language of degeneration he had earlier used to position the Jew as arch-degenerate. It is James, rather than the Jew, who is revealed at this moment to be intrinsically connected to the past and passing values of art; he is the one who is set aside from the currents of modern, bustling New York; he is the one who is associated with ghosts, and who alone is capable of hearing their groan of pain. Indeed, the famously loose Jamesian syntax here links the critic irrevocably to the ghost he alone is capable of perceiving; although the two are distinct enough early in the passage, by its end they appear nearly indistinguishable, linked indissolubly to one another by pronominal ambiguity.

In this passage, then, James the "incurable man of letters" positions himself as the irrevocably ghostly critic, the eternal outsider in the rapidly transforming world of culture — as that which is excrescetial, unnecessary, waste, in the bustling world of the modern metropolis; and the age-old, if not eternal, Jew is positioned as the very embodiment of modernity. But what is most remarkable about this moment, it seems to me, is that James does not mourn — too much — this position; rather, he depicts it with a ruefulness and irony that allows both the Jew and James himself a certain degree of independence from the qualities associated with each other while seeing the ways in which they might be arranged in a loosely contiguous relation with one another. In this representational structure, in other words, the critic and the Jew serve not as metonymies masking as identities — the basic linguistic structure, as we have seen above, of racist discourse — but rather as metaphors in which both retain a certain independence from each other: whose tenors and vehicles gloss each other but are free of any but the most general injunction to accomplish the work of definition.

The passage — and, indeed, James's entire intercourse with the Jew throughout the period we have been discussing — can be understood, as Beverly Haviland has suggested of James's responses to the African Americans he encounters in the South, as a process of hermeneutic self-inquiry and re-vision.[30] I would like to conclude on a slightly different note by suggesting that what we are witnessing in the pulsions and compulsions of James's response to the Jew may be seen, rather, as something akin to the psychoanalytic process of working through — a process in which the sheer otherness of the Jew presents James with the chance to articulate and represent those conflicts within himself coming under cultural pressure at precisely this moment. Such a process may indeed, as I suggested early in this essay, resemble the mechanism of scapegoating; at times, it certainly serves that function in James's career. But the shift in James's tone in *The American Scene* from abjection to appreciation, from demonization to a measured form of deference: these qualities, it seems to me, indicate a process of psychic loosening, of decathexis, of psychic reworking undertaken on both a conscious and an unconscious level. "To worry or to smile, such is the choice when we are assailed by the strange; our decision depends on how familiar we are with our own ghosts," Kristeva writes elsewhere of the contemporary European's enactment of the highly Jamesian scenario of encountering an alien other in one's newly strange homeland.[31] James's response to the Jew represents, I am arguing, the process by which he moves from worrying to, if not smiling, at least accepting; and he makes that process work by confronting his own ghosts — or at least his own potential ghostliness.

And perhaps it is this response that might guide the contemporary academic, as she or he decides whether to worry or to smile over James's response. That is, just as James's labile response to the Jew enacts a kind of working through by means of a response to an abjected figure, so too the academy's treatment of James's antisemitism can be seen as a process of coming to terms with the problematic of modern antisemitism itself. From a period of repression — the period when James's antisemitism was the dirty little secret of academic Jamesianism of the 1940s and 1950s — through the response of Geismar, who abjects James as fully as James abjects the Jew, through Posnock's recuperative reading, James has served as an emblem of the Anglo-American academy's response to the scandal of fin-de-siècle and modernist antisemitism — a scandal affiliated with the rise, in the late nineteenth century, of scientific racism, eugenics, and anti-immigrant hysteria and one that threatens to return along with those pernicious forces at our own fin-de-siècle moment.[32] To face this scandal in a way that registers without demonizing the vicissitudes, specificities, and problematics of the various authors who contributed to it — whether enthusiastically (like Céline), ambivalently (like James), or somewhere in between (like Wharton, Cather, Eliot, Pound): this is the task to which, it seems to me, the encounter of the contemporary academic with James and the discourses of antisemitism might profitably next lead. It is certainly one in which James's wrestlings with the Jew might guide us — for good *and* for ill — even as we interrogate with the utmost of care his recognitions and responses.

CHAPTER SIX

The Imaginary Jew:
T. S. Eliot and Ezra Pound

MAUD ELLMANN

> These tears are shaken from the wrath-bearing tree.
> — T. S. Eliot, "Gerontion"

T. S. Eliot and Ezra Pound, like Coleridge and Wordsworth, tend to be coupled in literary history and hence to be regarded as accomplices. There are many similarities between them: both rejected the "huge looseness" of the United States, together with its liberal individualism, and fled to Europe in pursuit of pastures old. Both adopted a radical conservatism which, in Pound's case, led to fascism; yet both wrote poetry whose experimentalism poses a puzzling contrast to their political authoritarianism. The most damning resemblance, however, is the antisemitism revealed by both in varying intensities. While Eliot denied the presence of antisemitism in his poetry and attempted to conceal its symptoms in his prose, Pound's prejudices grew increasingly fanatic, culminating in his fascist broadcasts for Rome Radio during World War II.[1] Although he was arrested for treason and incarcerated in a mental hospital, Pound did not repent his ways until 1967, when he reportedly expressed regret for what he lamely termed the "suburban prejudice" of antisemitism.[2] His last years, however, were spent in utter silence, which suggests a more profound and harrowing remorse, of the kind expressed in his last fragments of *The Cantos*: "Let the Gods forgive what I / have made."[3]

Compared to Pound's obsessive vitriol, Eliot's scattered and equivocal discourtesies against the Jews scarcely merit the charge of antisemitism. However, George Steiner has pointed out that "Eliot's uglier touches tend to occur at the heart of very good poetry (which is *not* the case of Pound)."[4] Pound, when seized with hatred, degenerates into obscenity; yet the "uglier touches" in *The Cantos* rarely violate the incandescent lyric passages. *The Cantos* would have benefited from the "caesarian Operation" Pound performed upon *The Waste Land*—removing, among other infelicities, its impalatable passages of antisemitism—but Eliot's early poems would never have survived such cuts.[5] For their aesthetic power depends upon the wrath that bore such figures as the syphilitic Jew, "Spawned in some estaminet of Antwerp," who "squats on the windowsill" in "Gerontion" (1917); or "Rachel *née* Rabinovich," who "Tears at the grapes with murderous paws" in "Sweeney among the Nightingales" (1920); or the ghastly image in "Burbank with a Baedecker; Bleistein with a Cigar" (1920), in which "the rats" are yoked together with "the Jew" as fellow vermin of the underworld:

> The rats are underneath the piles.
> The Jew is underneath the lot.[6]

This image, which resembles Pound's scatalogical Hell Cantos, also resembles Nazi propaganda films, where juxtaposition is similarly used to insinuate a kinship between rats and Jews. Yet animal imagery is such a commonplace in Jew-baiting and other forms of racist rhetoric that it is strange that Eliot succumbed to the cliché, even if he approved the sentiment. So strange is it that Christopher Ricks has convinced himself that Eliot, at moments like these, is satirizing the *vox populis*, rather than expressing his own views. According to Ricks, even a poem as offensive on first reading as "Burbank with a Beidecker; Bleistein with a Cigar" dissolves into a "multiplicity of partial dramatisations," in which the poet cannot be conclusively identified with any of the poem's points of view.[7]

Another notorious passage occurs in "A Cooking Egg," where Eliot writes:

> The red-eyed scavengers are creeping
> From Kentish Town and Golder's Green.
> (*Collected Poems*, p. 45)

These lines probably refer to a popular mythology that Jews were particularly susceptible to eye disease.[8] In the hearings of the 1903 Royal Commission on Alien Immigration, Dr. F. A. C. Tyrell contended that trachoma, a disease of the eyes, was "very largely a disease of race. . . . the Jewish people are peculiarly prone to trachoma." From this standpoint, he was anxious about admitting them into British society. However, other doctors disagreed, arguing that the disease was prevalent in overcrowded districts, "whether occupied by aliens or Christians," being particularly "common among the poor Irish."[9] Either way, eye disease was perceived as an effect of overcrowding and therefore as a malady of urban life. In this respect the English myth of Jewish eye disease resembles the German myth of Jewish flatfootedness, an ailment likewise attributed to "citification." Since the nineteenth century, as Sander Gilman has observed, Jews had been regarded as the embodiments of urban civilization, and their supposed flatfootedness imputed to their sinister work as merchants. At the same time, the malformed foot—like the evil eye to which the image of the "red-eyed scavengers" alludes—also harks back to medieval representations of the devil.[10]

These passages, and others like them in the work of Eliot and Pound, cast doubt on the redemptive power traditionally ascribed to art: its capacity to cure life's ills, absolve its sins, correct its errors, or sublimate its passions.[11] At their worst moments, Eliot and Pound confront us with an art mired in paranoia and delusion, infernal and beyond reprieve. But it is important to remember that Eliot repeatedly denied his antisemitism, regarding the accusation as "a terrible slander on a man."[12] Some of his denials took the form of doctoring his prose: the different editions of *Notes Towards the Definition of Culture*, for example, reveal an attempt to clarify, if not to withdraw, his previous reservations about Jews. The first edition of 1948 contained the following statement:

In certain historical conditions, a fierce exclusiveness may be a necessary condition for the preservation of a culture: the Old Testament bears witness to this.

A footnote continued:

Since the diaspora, and the scattering of Jews amongst peoples holding the Christian Faith, it may have been unfortunate both for these peoples and for the Jews themselves, that the culture-contact between them has had to be within those neutral zones of culture in which religion could be ignored: and the effect may have been to strengthen the illusion that there can be culture without religion.[13]

In the 1962 edition, however, Eliot revised the first part of this footnote to read as follows:

It seems to me highly desirable that there should be close culture-contact between devout and practising Christians and devout and practising Jews. Much culture-contact in the past has been within those neutral zones of culture in which religion can be ignored, and between Jews and Gentiles both more or less emancipated from their religious traditions. (p. 70)[14]

The first footnote holds the Jewish diaspora responsible for both the Jews' and the Christians' lapse from orthodoxy, whereas the second exonerates the Jews for this dilution of tradition. In the revised edition, we are told that only "emancipated" Jews or Christians need be kept apart; "devout" practitioners of either faith may be trusted to withstand the adulterating influence of "culture-contact" with the other. Unpleasant as it is, the second footnote cannot be accused of antisemitism, but merely of a general distrust of laxity.

Even with its original footnote, *Notes Towards the Definition of Culture* caused Eliot less trouble than the previous work, *After Strange Gods* (1934), which he withdrew from print after its first edition. Later he explained to Pound: "'After Strange Gods' is not a good book. Intemperate and unjust, and expresses emotional state of its author rather than critical judgment.... I let 'After Strange Gods' go out of print."[15] It was in this work that Eliot made his notorious pronouncement that "any large number of free-thinking Jews" is "undesirable" in Christian society.[16] By quoting this passage out of context, however, critics have tended to overlook the ambiguities in which it is embedded, especially its intertextual preliminaries. Eliot begins by defining his concept of *tradition*:

Tradition is not solely, or even primarily, the maintenance of certain dogmatic beliefs; these beliefs have come to take their living form in the course of the formation of a tradition. What I mean by tradition involves all those habitual actions, habits, and customs, from the most significant religious rite to our conventional way of greeting a stranger, which represent the blood kinship of "the same people living in the same place."[17]

Curiously, Eliot's quotation, "the same people living in the same place," derives from the Cyclops episode of James Joyce's *Ulysses*, in which Leopold Bloom, the Jewish hero, is attempting to define the word *nation* to a bunch of drunken Irish antisemites:

Bloom was talking and talking with John Wyse and he quite excited with his dunducketymudcoloured mug on him and his old plumeyes rolling about.

— Persecution, says he, all the history of the world is full of it. Perpetuating national hatred among nations.

— But do you know what a nation means? says John Wyse.

— Yes, says Bloom.

— What is it? says John Wyse.

— A nation? says Bloom. A nation is the same people living in the same place.

— By God, then, says Ned, laughing, if that's so I'm a nation for I'm living in the same place for the past five years.

So of course everyone had the laugh at Bloom and says he, trying to muck out of it:

— Or also living in different places.

— That covers my case, says Joe.

— What is your nation if I may ask? says the citizen.

— Ireland, says Bloom. I was born here. Ireland.[18]

In this hilarious exchange, Joyce seems to be anticipating Hannah Arendt's argument that antisemitism is the consequence of modern nationalism.[19] If the nation is defined by sameness, as Bloom ventures (or by "blood kinship," as Eliot amplifies), the Jews are bound to be perceived as foreign bodies at the heart of consanguinity. Bloom, however, claims his Irishness on grounds of birthplace — "I was born here. Ireland" — while he later claims his Jewishness on grounds of "race": "And I belong to a race too, says Bloom, that is hated and persecuted" (*Ulysses*, p. 273). In *After Strange Gods*, Eliot advocates cultural homogeneity, enshrined in his concept of tradition, which is defined as the tendency to sameness in communities; yet he undercuts this argument by quoting Bloom — the most free-thinking of Jews — in words that Joyce has already consigned to the ridiculous: "the same people living in the same place."

In 1940 Eliot had an exchange of letters with J. V. Healy, who complained of Pound's antisemitism and also alluded to Eliot's tendencies in this direction. Eliot replied sharply, "As for Mr. Pound, I have already made it clear that I do not associate myself with any of his opinions about Jews. I am no longer in a position to communicate with him."[20] Previously, Eliot had challenged Healy to provide evidence for his allegation; Healy had replied by pointing out the passage on free-thinking Jews from *After Strange Gods*:[21]

The population should be homogeneous; where two or more cultures exist in the same place they are likely either to be fiercely self-conscious or both to become adulterate. What is still more important is unity of religious background; and reasons of race and religion combine to make any large number of free-thinking Jews undesirable. There must be a proper balance between urban and rural, industrial and agricultural development. And a spirit of excessive tolerance is to be deprecated. (p. 19)

Eliot defended this passage by insisting that he was objecting to "free-thinking," rather than to Jews per se: "It should be obvious that I think a large number of free-thinkers of any race to be undesirable, and the free-thinking Jews are only a special case." Healy replied: "Assuming that you meant what you now claim to mean, it still strikes me as unfortunate that you should pick on Jews (free-thinkers or not) at a time they were being hounded and tortured."[22] At this point Eliot took umbrage and the correspondence ended acrimoniously. Nonetheless, Eliot probably regretted his remark about free-thinking Jews, since his friend John Hayward, in his edition of Eliot's *Selected Prose* (1953), cut short the excerpt from *After Strange Gods* to end two sentences before the offending passage.[23] To describe this editing as white-washing would be extreme, but the passage looks a good deal less "intemperate and unjust" (in Eliot's words) thanks to its abbreviation.

In 1957, Eliot was again accused of "unambiguous signs of anti-semitism," this time by an anonymous reviewer in the *Times Literary Supplement*, who evaded Eliot's subsequent demands for chapter and verse.[24] Christopher Logue replied instead, citing as evidence the passages from Eliot's early poetry discussed above; an editorial from *The Criterion* where Eliot commended the policy statement of *The British Lion*, a fascist publication; and of course, the notorious passage from *After Strange Gods*.[25] In his reply, Eliot demonstrated that Logue, through selective quotation, had misrepresented his editorial in *The Criterion*; but he offered no defenses of his other works, only pointing out that Logue had missed two further passages regularly arrayed against him, including the 1948 footnote in *Notes Towards the Definition of Culture*. It seems that Eliot had finally wearied of self-exculpation.

"Between the conception / And the creation . . . / Falls the Shadow."[26] The contrast between Eliot's intentions toward the Jews and the aspersions that he cast upon them makes one wonder what shadow fell between conception and creation, what unconscious forces tempted him into a prejudice he earnestly disowned. William Empson offers the brilliant suggestion that the "Jew" in Eliot's writing is a stand in for his Unitarian father:

Eliot wanted to grouse about his father, and lambasted some imaginary Jews instead. . . . Unitarians describe themselves as Christians but deny that Jesus was God, whereas Eliot was beginning to feel a strong drag towards a return to the worship of the tortured victim. . . . Now if you are hating a purse-proud business man who denies that Jesus is God, into what stereotype does he best fit? He is a Jew, of course.[27]

The value of Empson's reading is its specificity: rather than accusing, he attempts to penetrate the singularity of Eliot's ambivalence. Without this attention to textual and biographical detail, the critic, in exposing antisemitism, always runs the risk of witch-hunting, of re-enacting the paranoia of the antisemite toward the Jew. What was it that troubled Eliot so much about the Jews that he compromised his reputation as a moralist to snub them? Part of the answer may be found in his correspondence with Healy, where Eliot (confirming Empson's suspicions) insists that the Jewish religion, "shorn of its traditional practices, observances and Messianism . . . tends to become a mild and colourless form of Unitarianism." To justify his misgivings about "free-thinking Jews," he argues that the "Jew who is separated from his religious faith is much more deracinated thereby than the descendant of Christians, and it is this deracination that I think dangerous and tending to irresponsibility."[28] Taking Eliot at his word, the remainder of this essay argues that the fear of "deracination" or displacement is the wellspring of much of the antisemitism to be found in Eliot as well as Pound. For both writers, Jewishness comes to stand for the deracinating,

mongrelizing, disembodying effects of writing; and the imaginary Jew becomes the mirror image of the poet himself, his diabolical *semblable*.[29]

*

In his essay "The Music of Poetry" (1942), Eliot compares the relations between words in language to the relations between classes in society:

Ugly words are . . . words not fitted for the company in which they find themselves;
there are words which are ugly because of rawness or because of antiquation; there
are words which are ugly because of foreignness or ill-breeding (e.g. *television*): but
I do not believe that any word well-established in its own language is either beautiful or ugly. . . . Not all words are equally rich and well-connected: it is part of the
business of the poet to dispose the richer among the poorer, at the right points.[30]

This image presents poetic and political ideals as interchangeable: just as
a government enforces rank and precedence, so the poet must regulate
the pecking order of his words. Immigration should also be controlled, for
verbal foreigners, like verbal upstarts, disturb the rooted traditions of the
tongue. The poet's task, Eliot claims, is to use "the right word *in the right
place*, the rightness depending upon both the explicit intention and an in-
definite radiation of sound and sense."[31] What goes for language goes for
people, too, who are best advised to stay where they were born. In *Notes
Towards the Definition of Culture*, Eliot argues that "it would appear to be
for the best that the great majority of human beings should go on living *in
the place* in which they were born" (p. 52, my emphasis). Though he permits some cultural diversity in so-called "satellite" communities, he insists
that these subserve a central "orthodoxy," whose role is to maintain the purity of Christian doctrine. Any restlessness within these satellites endangers
their integrity, unbalancing the delicate economy of difference. As Terry
Eagleton remarks, "When the human beings begin to move, Eliot's structures begin to crumble."[32]

For Eliot believes the boundaries of *meaning* to depend upon the boundaries of the speech community. In the epigraph to *Notes Towards the Definition of Culture*, he cites the definition of definition from the *Oxford English
Dictionary*: "DEFINITION: I. The setting of bounds; limitation (rare). . . ."
To define, then, is to confine, to delimit, to put things in their places and to
keep them there. *Displacement*, on the contrary, erodes the bounds of
definition, creating social and semantic turmoil. The fear of such displacement, whether of deracinated peoples or uprooted words, resurfaces
throughout Eliot's literary and cultural criticism. In his famous discussion
of "dissociation of sensibility," for instance, he accuses Milton of allowing
sound to take the place of sense, thus forsaking meaning for mellifluence.
According to Eliot, "Language in a healthy state presents the object, is so
close to the object that the two are identified." In Milton, however, the

pleasure "arises from the *noise*": from a language that refuses to subordinate itself to objects, delighting in the "mazes" of its own sonority. By dissolving meaning into music, Milton bequeathed a fallen language to generations of poets in his wake. Eliot argues that Swinburne's writing, centuries later, exhibits the same deviance: "It is the word which gives [Swinburne] the thrill, not the object."[33]

Once word and object are dissociated, the author's personality assumes the limelight, with catastrophic consequences for his poetry. In an essay of 1919, Eliot objects to poems that "make you conscious of having been written by somebody" — and it is the *writtenness*, as much as the *somebody*, that irks him.[34] He implies that the author's personality breaks forth when word and object break asunder, when language refuses to defer to what it means. Ideally, words should efface themselves before their referents, as should the somebody who wrote them down. Eliot's famous theory of "impersonality" was devised, at least in part, to counteract displacement, specifically the displacement of the meaning by the word, but also the displacement of the old by the new, the tradition by the individual, the poem by the poet. He introduced the theory in his famous essay "Tradition and the Individual Talent" (1919), where he condemns the Romantic cult of originality, arguing that the values of tradition have been overshadowed by the greed for novelty. He argues that the writer who seeks novelty "*in the wrong place*" merely "discovers the perverse" (*Selected Essays*, p. 21). Instead, the modern writer should cultivate impersonality, sacrificing individual for universal values: only by undergoing this "extinction" in his art can he hope to gain distinction in eternity, purified of self-indulgent idiosyncracies.

In the early 1930s, Eliot renews this crusade, inveighing against "the whole movement of several centuries towards the aggrandisement and exploitation of personality." In its "proper place," he argues, personality may not be damnable; but now that the eternal values of the Church have surrendered to the vagaries of liberal individualism, the author's personality has grown increasingly obstreperous: "It seems to me that the eminent novelists who are nearly contemporary to us, have been more concerned than their predecessors — consciously or not — to impose upon their readers their own *personal view of life*" (*After Strange Gods*, p. 53). Their personalities are therefore *out of place*, having exceeded their permitted bounds; and this displacement is responsible not only for the cult of personality but for every other form of modern "heresy." In *After Strange Gods*, Eliot draws a distinction between "blasphemy," which he admires, and "heresy," which he deplores, arguing that "no one can possibly blaspheme . . . unless he profoundly believes in that which he profanes" (p. 52). This implies that blasphemy is a backhanded form of faith; like the psychoanalytic patient, who denies desires so that they may surface into consciousness ("No, I *don't* want to kill my father!"), the blasphemer, by denying religion, affirms that it is worth the trouble of repudiating. Eliot may have borrowed this idea of blasphemy from *A Rebours* (1884), where Huysmans argues: "Since sacrilege depends on the existence of a religion, it cannot be deliberately and effectively committed except by a believer, for a man would derive no satisfaction whatever from profaning a faith that was unimportant or unknown to him."[35] Heresy, on the contrary, seeks faith *in the wrong place*, fetishizing substitutes and simulacra, and thus creates "strange gods"—like Yeats's ghosts, or Pound's Confucius, or Lawrence's dark deities of Mexico—which threaten to dislodge the long-established icons of the West (p. 41).

According to Eliot, Matthew Arnold instigated modern heresy by substituting literature for faith: "Literature, or Culture tended with Arnold to *usurp the place of* religion" (*Selected Essays*, p. 424, my emphasis). As a result of this displacement, religious writings are now appreciated solely for "literary merit," and religious rituals for entertainment value, having been deprived of "the beliefs with which their history has been involved."[36] Arnold, Eliot claims, "discovered a new formula: poetry is not religion, but it is a capital substitute for religion—not invalid port, which may lend itself to hypocrisy, but coffee without caffeine, or tea without tannin" (*Use of Poetry*, p. 26). In Arnold's philosophy, poetry supplants belief in the same way that the sound of Milton's verse supplants its sense. In either case, the fetishism of the signifier, of the written or acoustic substance of the word, takes the place of eternal truths, substituting form for content, sound for meaning, rite for faith.

For Eliot, the only way that poets can resist the spread of "heresy" is to return to speech: "every evolution in poetry is apt to be, and often to announce itself to be a return to common speech" (*On Poetry*, p. 31). Speech, because it necessarily involves "one person talking to another," presupposes a community of speakers, and thus confirms the "vital connection between the individual and the race" (*On Poetry*, p. 31; *After Strange Gods*, p. 48). Writing, as opposed to speech, is a solitary, even narcissistic, activity: we write, as we read, alone in silence. Eliot bemoans the fact that "most poetry is written to be read in solitude" (*On Poetry*, p. 17). Disparaging "such individual benefit from poetry," he pleads for "something that it does collectively for us, as a society." An oral literature, such as the poetic drama he struggled to revive, might reunite what he describes as "that mysterious social personality which we call our 'culture'" (pp. 18, 23). If the writer spoke directly to his audience, he would be obliged to honor their collective values instead of flattering his reader's private predilections and his own. Writing, on the contrary, entails the dangerous privacy in which the cult of personality expands, while the author, as a social servant, disappears from view.

It is these anxieties about displacement that give rise to Eliot's imaginary figure of the Jew. At one level the free-thinking Jew stands for the heresy of liberal individualism, epitomized by Unitarianism, that Eliot deplores. Having been raised as a Unitarian himself, his wish to segregate the Jews conceals another wish to cordon off his own free-thinking past. The Jews, for Eliot, represent the adulteration of traditions severed from their living speech and native soil. Yet Eliot himself is doubly displaced, being exiled from a land of exiles, and thus suspiciously resembles those deracinated Jews who endanger his ideal of rootedness. His struggle to transplant himself to England, by dispossessing his American past ("History is now and England"[37]), requires him to disavow his own affinity with the wandering Jew.

At a deeper level, though, Eliot's distrust of Jews corresponds to his distrust of writing. Sooner or later, written words are destined to desert the place of their origination; like Jews, they refuse to remain in the place where they were born. The wandering of words, like the wandering of peoples, erodes the boundaries of the speech community; and Eliot's attempts to control the movements of nomadic Jews correspond to his desire to delimit the dissemination of the written word. Constantly disowning or revising his past writings — especially his remarks about the Jews — Eliot had reason to resent the errancy of written words, their independence from the will of their creator. At the same time, though, his poetry exploits this very errancy, uprooting words from other authors, texts, and nations: "great poets steal." *The Waste Land*, for example, performs a textual diaspora in which the writings of the past deracinate themselves and recombine with words of other ages, languages, and authors, in a limitless process of miscegenation. Thus Eliot, by banishing free-thinking Jews from his utopia, was attempting to banish from himself the forces of displacement exemplified in both his life and his art.

*

Most of Eliot's expressions of antisemitism occur in his early writings of the 1920s, at a time when such remarks were fashionable. As Leonard Woolf, himself a Jew, observed, "I think T. S. Eliot was antisemitic in the sort of vague way which is not uncommon. He would have denied it quite genuinely."[38] In the 1930s, however, Eliot as editor of *The Criterion* warned Pound that he would terminate their correspondence unless the latter desisted in his Jew-baiting. It seems that Eliot was forced to act upon this threat, judging by his letter to Healy of 1940: "I am no longer in a position to communicate with [Pound]." In the 1930s, therefore, Eliot decisively repudiated antisemitism, though he may have persisted in it without knowing it; but this is an altogether different prejudice from Pound's maniacal crusade against the Jews.

Robert Casillo has distinguished four stages in Pound's career of anti-semitism: the first, when he absorbed in childhood the fashionable preju-dices of suburban Philadelphia; the second, when he returned to America in 1910–11 and grew alarmed, like Henry James, by the multitudes of re-cent Jewish immigrants: "There is no swarming like that of Israel once Is-rael has got a start."[39] The third stage occurred in the late 1920s through the 1930s, when Pound, obsessed with economics, seized upon the quaint idea of "usury" as the key to the decline of the West. During this stage Pound also borrowed from Tadeusz Zielinski the idea that Christianity originated in the Dionysian mysteries ("Christ follows Dionysus / Phallic and ambrosial") but was later corrupted by the Judaic tradition, which pro-duced the flesh-hating austerities of Protestantism.[40] Only in the 1930s, though, did Pound reach the fourth stage of blaming the Jews for all the sins of usury. In his fascist broadcasts for Rome Radio, his antisemitism, like the Nazis', took a racial rather than religious form, in which he vilified the Jews as excrement, disease, and vermin.[41] It is tempting to dismiss these broadcasts as the ravings of a lunatic, except that the views expressed in them were held so widely at the time that madness had become the norm, and reason the anomaly. The fact that the neo-fascist party in Italy, which made important gains in the 1994 elections, decorated its headquar-ters with the sayings of Ezra Pound shows that we cannot afford either to forget or to extenuate his diatribes against the Jews.

To vilify him in return, however, is to collude in his pursuit of scape-goats and to overlook the complex sources of his antisemitism. Pound's prejudice, like Eliot's, makes sense only in the context of a whole entangle-ment of phobias, in which the dread of Jews features as a symptom rather than a cause. The next section of this essay investigates the ingenuity of Pound's delusion, the rigor of its blindness to itself, by unraveling the meanings impacted in his personal mythology of usury. Usury means ex-cessive interest rates, but Pound capitalizes on the word itself until it en-compasses all forms of exorbitance—especially writing, which he comes to regard as a usurious excess or excrement of speech. In Pound's work, an-tithesis begets antithesis: usury is opposed to economic health in the same way that writing is opposed to speech, or space to time, or excrement to semen. To track down this contagion of antitheses, it is useful to begin with his analysis of music in *Antheil and the Treatise on Harmony* (1927). Pound opens this work with the complaint that "the element most grossly omitted from treatises on harmony up to the present is the element of TIME."[42] He believes that the essence of music is measure, which origi-nates in "the age-lasting rhythms of the craft, cloth-clapping, weaving, spinning, milking, reaping" (p. 88). These crafts obey the living rhythms of nature rather than the deathly ticking of the metronome.

The early students of harmony were so accustomed to think of music as something with a strong lateral or horizontal motion that they never imagined any one, ANY ONE could be stupid enough to think of it as static; it never entered their heads that people would make music like steam ascending from a morass. (p. 11)

This "steam," Pound thinks, disfigures rhythm. Wagner, for example, "produced a sort of pea soup, and . . . Debussy distilled it into a heavy mist, which the post-Debussians have desiccated into a heavy dust cloud" (p. 40). It is chords, according to Pound, which are responsible for turning music into swamp gas; being "spatial," chords coagulate the moving energies of rhythm. For this reason Pound compares the analysis of chords to studying "the circulation of the blood from corpses exclusively" (p. 23). Like Henri Bergson, who believed that the fundamental error of western thought was to misconceive of time in terms of space, so Pound believes that everything went wrong in music when space usurped the precedence of time.

"Clogs are spatial," Pound announces to Louis Zukofsky in a letter of 1936, dated "anno XIV" in deference to the fascist calendar. Here Pound is referring to the "clog" of usury; but it is through such metaphors that his early, aesthetic antipathy to space insinuates itself into his later economic theory. "Monetary reform occurs in TIME," he writes: the same element of time that inheres in music. When this "YELLYment of TIME" prevails in the economy, money moves with unimpeded rhythm. "Whereas clogs (as the German railway signs tells [sic] us, are SPATIAL. raumlich)."[43] Space produces clogs and constipation on the one hand, incontinence and foetor on the other, resulting in a kind of sphincteral collapse of the economy.

Usury, Pound argues, arose in the same era in which space crept into music and corrupted it: by "1200 / or after 1221," at the latest, "it ALL went to rot."[44] Usury spatializes money in the same way that writing spatializes speech, through an operation Pound describes as "satanic transubstantiation":

Only spoken poetry and unwritten music are composed without any material basis, nor do they become "materialised."

The usurers, in their obscene and pitch-dark century, created this satanic transubstantiation, their Black Mass of money, and in so doing deceived Brooks Adams himself, who was fighting for the peasant and humanity against the monopolists.

". . . Money alone is capable of being transmuted immediately into any form of activity."—This is the idiom of the black myth![45]

Since spoken poetry and unwritten music exist only in time, they cannot be "materialised," and hence cannot be bought or sold. The same "majestic rhythm" that articulates their movement should ideally regulate the flow of cash.[46] Pound believes that money should be treated as a "ticket," because tickets are "timed," and the "timing of budgets" is crucial to economic rhythm.[47] Instead, money has degenerated into a fetish, which hoards the very energies it should unleash. The usurers, in their "obscene and pitch-dark century," spatialized money, which henceforth petrifies and putrifies.

Just as money hoards the powers of production, so writing hoards the energies of speech and music. Once committed to the page, poetry and music undergo "satanic transubstantiation," for they stagnate in space when they should flow in time. According to this logic, writing, insofar as it is spatial, represents the "usury" of speech: for writing clogs the moving energies of speech in the same way that usury obstructs the rhythms of exchange. In Pound's mythology, usury not only blocks financial circulation but also infiltrates the body, deranging its interior economy. In the Hell Cantos, where Pound invents his own inferno for the usurers, the human body is turned inside-out and back-to-front:

> Standing bare-bum.
> Faces smeared on their rumps,
>   wide eye on flat buttock,
> Bush hanging for beard.
>   Addressing crowds through their arse-holes,
> Addressing the multitudes in the ooze. . . .
>
>   (XIV 61)

In this Bosch-like vision, the anus takes the place of mouth and genitals at once and, in defiance of Pound's principle of "clear demarcation," substitutes its "ooze" for speech and sperm. For usury has seized "Control of the outlets" (CIV 738): be they the outlets of the market, the organs of the news, or even the orifices of the human body. In 1921, Pound proposed the extraordinary theory that the world began with a cosmic ejaculation, whose spermatic force still circulates through art and nature, dispensing incarnation as it moves. The brain itself, he postulated, is a clot of genital fluid, restless to enflesh a second cosmos.[48] The Hell Cantos, however, show how usury derides this spermatic thrust ("phallic and ambrosial") and substitutes the anus's perverse fecundity: "a continual bum-belch/distributing its productions" (XV 65).

This bum-belch is a non-origin, which parodies the very notion of a source. To purify the currencies of words or flesh or finance, Pound believes that it is necessary to return to sources, be they the classics, time, the mint, the phallus, or the sun. But usury is money "created out of nothing," as Pound quotes wrathfully from Paterson, the founder of the Bank of England.[49] It corresponds to the attempt in discourse "to lift zero by its own bootstraps."[50] Having no origin, it also has no destination, and thus defies the very principle of teleology. Wherever usury's influence has spread, foul aftergrowths engorge their origins. Thus Pound, following Dante, condemns usurers and sodomites to the same circle of his inferno, because both seek wealth or pleasure "without regard to production" (XLV 230n), and thus without regard to ends. "By great wisdom sodomy and usury were seen coupled together," Pound writes, for both are enemies of generation.[51] *The Cantos* constantly lament the "*coitu inluminatio*" which has been supplanted by these usurious excesses (e.g., LXXIV 435). In a healthy economy, "any note will by paid"; "the deposits," Pound repeats, "will be satisfied" (LXXXVI 564; XXXVIII 190). But neither sodomy nor the "buggaring bank" is ever satisfied or cashed into production (LXXVII 468). Instead, both fester in the sty of the between. Teeming in darkness, they create an excremental universe, exuberant as the spermatic one they imitate.

It is this *betweenness* that worries Pound more than any of the other crimes of usury, because it undermines the temporal order. "Entering all things," usury *defers*. It comes *between* the stonecutter and the stone, "*between* the young bride and her bride-groom": [52]

> between the usurer and any man who
> wants to go a good job
> (perenne)
> without regard to production —
> a charge
> for the use of money or credit.
> (LXXXVII 569)

This passage suggests that any form of interest interrupts production, breeding difference and delay where coitus and generation should occur. Elsewhere, however, Pound insists that even interest had an origin in nature before it was corrupted into usury; for nothing can come of nothing, no matter what the wretched Paterson might say. "The idea of Interest existed before the invention of metal coin," he argues. "And there is MUCH more justification for collecting interest on a loan of seed, on a loan of she-goats and buck-goats, than on a loan of non-breeding, non-breedable metal."[53] He insists that money should "represent something . . . such, namely AS rams and ewes."[54] But usury inflates the sign out of all proportion to the signified, so that money stands for nothing but its own unnatural fecundity. "Money is now the NOTHING you get for SOMETHING before you can get ANYTHING," wrote Frederick Soddy, an economist whom Pound admired despite his name.[55]

"Money is an articulation," Pound wrote in 1951. "Prosody is an articulation of the sound of a poem. Money an arti/of/say NAtional money is articulation of total purchasing power of the nation."[56] It is by means of money that nations articulate their power; by means of prosody that poems budget their expenditure of sound. So close is this analogy between the flow of money and the flow of words that Pound believes the purification of one economy will magically decontaminate the other. Economic "mess" is both the cause and consequence of "muddling and muddying terminology" (*Guide to Kulchur*, p. 31):

MESSES of cliche supplied by Iouce and the restuvum to maintain the iggurance spewed out by the OOzevelt Anschauung.
AND the OOze was possible because writers did not keep the language clean.[57]

This rant, though it appears in a letter of 1954, shows Pound to be arrested in the widespread antisemitism of the 1930s, when the New Deal was frequently maligned as the "Jew Deal" (Pound also calls it the "spew deal"). During this period, the American upper classes, fanatically opposed to Roosevelt, accused the president of being mad, unprincipled, dishonest, alcoholic, syphilitic, Communist—and sometimes, Jewish; many referred to him derisively as "Rosenvelt," although his ancestry, in fact, was Dutch.[58] In the letter quoted above, Pound blames the ooze of Roosevelt (and the ooze of usury) on writers who failed to purify the dialect of the tribe. But elsewhere he blames the fall of language on the rise of usury. In *Guide to Kulchur*, he argues that the "infamy which controls English and U.S. finance has made printing a midden, a filth, a mere smear" (p. 184). "Gold bugs against ANY order," the usurocracy inscribes the currencies of money and language alike with its excremental signature, its "smear" (LXXXVII 572).

It is through this smear that usury disseminates itself through history, manifesting itself wherever monuments and records are destroyed. If the world was created by an ejaculation, hell's bum-belch is busy decreating it by blotting out its history. "My generation was brought up ham ignorant of economics," Pound frets in a radio broadcast. "History was taught with OMISSIONS of the most vital facts. Every page our generation read was overshadowed by usury" (*Radio Speeches*, p. 339). It is by "destroying the symbols," he declares, that Usura spreads her empire of forgetfulness, and she even keeps herself under erasure. An "octopus," she disappears behind her ink, behind the filth to which she has reduced the printed word (see XXIX 145). The Jews, Pound thinks, are doubly implicated in the crime of usury, for they not only practice it but they refuse to represent or even name their God. Their taboo against the graven image colludes with that compulsion to undefine, erase, unname, unrepresent that Pound identifies with usury. Indeed, the term *semitic* in Pound's writing actually comes to *mean* erasure, particularly the erasure of history: "Time blacked out with the rubber" (VII 25). However, he does not restrict this accusation to the Jews, but extends it to the Protestants whom he regards as their descendants. Protestantism, for Pound, is nothing more than "jewdianity . . . renewed jewdianity, reJEWed whichianity"; it conspires with Judaism "semitically to obliterate values, to efface grades and graduations."[59] When Canto C declares that usury is "beyond race and against race" (798), this is because the semitic is ultimately doomed to obliterate *itself* by destroying boundaries and embastardizing breeds.

Of all usury's assaults on definition, the last and consummate is its erasure of the proper name. In Canto XCVI, Pound despairs of finding anyone "whom the ooze cannot blacken," because "the stench of the profit motive has covered their names" (XCVI 662). No name is proof against this ooze, this smear, this "semitic" process of obliteration. What is more, the law of libel forces Pound himself to collude in the erasure of the name, for many of the Semites he would like to damn sneak through *The Cantos* under pseudonyms. "That ass Nataanovitch," for instance:

> Or some better known -ovitch
> whose name we must respect because of the
> law of libel   (XXXV 172)

Pound attacks the law of libel in his *Guide to Kulchur*: "The purpose of law is to eliminate crime not to incubate it and cause it to pullulate" (p. 186). This law flouts Pound's first principle of language and economics: "to call things by their right names — in the market" (XXXIV 168; cf. *Selected Prose*, p. 333). Whereas "clear definition" purges the economy, withdrawing names from circulation only helps to breed the crimes they signify. Like usury, they pullulate in darkness.

Unnamed and unnaming, smearing names with their semitic ooze, the Jews defy the very principle of definition. Yet Pound, in spite of his crusade for clarity, inculpates himself in this semitic process of erasure. In his typescripts, he uses the £-sign to delete his errors, thus transforming his own name into a wandering obliteration. His first name, too, becomes a synonym for erasure. When he first read *Ulysses*, he disapproved of Bloom's cloacal pleasures, writing coyly to Joyce: "I don't arsk you to erase. . . ."[60] It is of course the arse that Pound would like to ask Joyce to erase; but Joyce noticed that "arse," "erase," and Ezra are virtually anagrams for one another. In *Finnegans Wake*, Ezra is spelt with an "s" ("Esra"), thus exposing its proximity to "arse," "erase," and even "usura."[61] These puns suggest that Pound (£) himself is the usurious currency; while Ezra (Esra) is the other face of the same coin, the hinter-face that belches into hell ("Faces smeared on their rumps / Addressing the multitudes in the ooze"). As regards his identification with the Jews, Pound himself is disarmingly candid: in *Guide to Kulchur*, he acknowledges his own "nomadic" temperament and adds that "it is not for me to rebuke brother Semite for a similar disposition."[62] It seems that there is more than a fraternal bond between the poet and the race—"beyond race and against race"—that he abominates: for the semitic principle is enshrined in his own name: Ezra the prophet, Ezra the wanderer, Ezra the pound. And if, as *The Cantos* say, "there is / no end to the journey" (LXX 477), how could Ez defeat ooze, or Esra erase Usura?

*

John Berryman, in an essay called "The Imaginary Jew" (1945), describes an occasion of his youth when he was accused of being Jewish by a drunken Irishman in Central Park. "You talk like a Jew," the drunk insisted.

> "What does that mean?" Some part of me wanted to laugh. "How does a Jew talk?"
> "They talk like you, buddy."
> "That's a fine argument! But if I'm not a Jew, my talk only—"
> "You probably are a Jew. You look like a Jew."
> "I *look* like a Jew? Listen," I swung around with despair to a man standing next to me, "do I look like a Jew? It doesn't matter whether I do or not—a Jew is as good as anybody and better than this son of a bitch—" I was not exactly excited, I was trying to adapt my language as my need for the crowd, and my sudden respect for its judgment, possessed me. . . .
> "You look like a Jew. You talk like a Jew. You *are* a Jew," I heard the Irishman say. . . .
> "I'm *not* a Jew," I told him. "I might be, but I'm not. You have no bloody reason to think so, and you can't make a Jew by simply repeating like an idiot that I am."
> "Don't deny it, son," said [a] red-faced man, "stand up to him. . . ."
> "Jesus, the Jew is excited," said the Irishman.

The argument continues, violent and ridiculous, long into the hot summer night. In the days afterwards, however, Berryman comes to the conclusion that his persecutors were right: he *is* a Jew.

> The imaginary Jew I was was as real as the imaginary Jew hunted down, on other nights and days, in a real Jew. Every murderer strikes the mirror, the lash of the torturer falls on the mirror and cuts the real image, and the real and the imaginary blood flow down together.[63]

This essay, too, has traced the imaginary Jew back to the mirror in which Eliot and Pound gazed unknowingly into their own souls. Both reviled in the Jew what they feared and cherished in themselves: their exile from their homeland and their diaspora among the texts that bear their names. Pound projected onto the imaginary Jew the anal fantasies and phobias enciphered in his name—a persecutor he could never overcome. His anti-semitism, like Eliot's, is founded on identification, and his writings represent a lifelong struggle to exorcise his unknown self.

Freud argues that the psychic mechanism of identification originates in fantasies of cannibalism, whose aim is to possess the object unconditionally. For this reason, identification is "ambivalent from the very first," since eating can preserve the object only at the cost of its destruction: "The object that we long for and prize is assimilated by eating and is in that way annihilated as such." However, in the case of mourning, the object, once incorporated, preys upon the ego in return, until the latter is "totally impoverished."[64] The work of mourning thus consists of the struggle to devour, but also to disgorge, the things we love.

This theory casts some light on Pound, who is consumed with what he hates, forever struggling to eliminate his own obsession in the form of scatological abracadabras. Both Pound and Eliot reveal the dangers of identification, of this consuming love in which the object has to be destroyed. These dangers also lurk in any politics based upon identification, whether of the right or of the left. To identify oneself as male or female, white or black, gentile or Jew is always to produce a hated double: it is to repeat the error of Eliot and Pound, who projected their own darkness upon the Jews. To avoid this error, we must look beyond the pieties of identity politics to rediscover the radical singularity of human experience. The mirror of identification must be broken if the real and the imaginary bloodshed is to cease.

CHAPTER SEVEN

A Nightmare of History: Ireland's Jews and Joyce's 'Ulysses'

MARILYN REIZBAUM

One of Stephen Dedalus's most quotable lines from *Ulysses* — "History . . . is a nightmare from which I am trying to awake" — is perhaps a line even more appropriate for Leopold Bloom. And indeed, Stephen says it in response to Mr. Deasy's antisemitic pronouncements in Nestor:

He raised his forefinger and beat the air oddly before his voice spoke.

— Mark my words, Mr Dedalus, he said. England is in the hands of the jews. In all the highest places: her finance, her press. And they are the signs of a nation's decay. Wherever they gather they eat up the nation's vital strength. I have seen it coming these years. As sure as we are standing here the jew merchants are already at their work of destruction. Old England is dying. . . .

— A merchant, Stephen said, is one who buys cheap and sells dear, jew or gentile, is he not?

— They sinned against the light, Mr Deasy said gravely. And you can see the darkness in their eyes. And that is why they are wanderers on the earth to this day.

On the steps of the Paris Stock Exchange the goldskinned men quoting prices on their gemmed fingers. Gabbles of geese. They swarmed loud, uncouth about the temple, their heads thickplotting under maladroit silk hats. Not theirs: these clothes, this speech, these gestures. Their full slow eyes belied the words, the gestures eager and unoffending, but knew the rancours massed about them and knew their zeal was vain. Vain patience to heap and hoard. Time surely would scatter all. A hoard heaped by the roadside: plundered and passing on. Their eyes knew the years of wandering and, patient, knew the dishonours of their flesh.

—Who has not? Stephen said.

—What do you mean? Mr Deasy asked.

He came forward a pace and stood by the table. His underjaw fell sideways open uncertainly. Is this old wisdom? He waits to hear from me.

—History, Stephen said, is a nightmare from which I am trying to awake. (2.345–77)[1]

Mr. Deasy's sentiments echo not only the general attitudes toward Jews, but what was then a present and ongoing controversy over antisemitic occurrences in Limerick. His words constitute an amalgam of statements made by such Fenians as Arthur Griffith and Buck Mulligan's presumed original, Oliver St. John Gogarty, who wrote in the party newspaper, *Sinn Fein*: "I don't hate the English, for the simple reason that I have never met the embodiment of certain British virtues that are self-avowed, because the avower, was a hypocrite in every case. I can smell a Jew, though, and in Ireland there's something rotten."[2] While both the Limerick riots and Fenians' comments testify to a certain Irish antisemitism, they represent slightly different sorts of antisemitism, not peculiarly Irish, and Joyce capitalizes on both in *Ulysses*. Deasy ends the Nestor chapter with a kind of riddle:

Mr Deasy halted, breathing hard and swallowing his breath.

—I just wanted to say, he said. Ireland, they say, has the honour of being the only country which never persecuted the jews. Do you know that? No. And do you know why?

He frowned sternly on the bright air.

—Why sir? Stephen asked, beginning to smile.

—Because she never let them in, Mr Deasy said solemnly.

A coughball of laughter leaped from his throat dragging after it a rattling chain of phlegm. He turned back quickly, coughing, laughing, his lifted arms waving to the air.

—She never let them in, he cried again through his laughter as he stamped on gaitered feet over the gravel path. That's why. (2.436–44)

Deasy here is unwittingly both confirming and exploding a favorite myth held by the Irish. The Irish maintained then (and many still do) that they were never persecutors of the Jews; yet, as Bloom might put it, at the very moment they were being "plundered, insulted, persecuted" in Limerick and in the Irish press. Ironically, Deasy explodes the myth by pointing to the relative absence of Jews in Irish society—they can't oppress them if they are not there. The irony is underscored by the ball-and-chain image used to describe Deasy's wheezing cough, a sign of internal disorder in Deasy, apposite to what is in Deasy's mind the "internal disorder" caused by the Jews. He thinks of the Jews as "signs of a nation's decay" after having discoursed on the subject of foot-and-mouth disease, a form of which (foot-in), needless to say, he suffers from. He worries that if the disease is not cured, there will be an embargo on Irish cattle, a kind of assault on Irish commerce, since he suggests that these cattle are prevented from receiving available (Austrian) cures. This leads him to think of "intrigue," and "backstairs influence" (2.343–44), and associatively to the stereotype of Jew as financial "wheeler-dealer." Just as the ball-and-chain image ironically responds to the shackling of Jews, so too the embargo on Irish cattle that might be diseased corresponds to Deasy's notion that Jews should be prevented from entering Ireland and bringing with them "diseases" that "eat up the nation's vital strength." What Deasy does not see is the doubleness in his own point of view. While he is willing to see the Jews as helpmates to the oppressors of the Irish, he cannot see them as oppressed themselves, as symbolically like the cattle, which are in turn symbolically like the Irish. (This is even more ironic since Deasy, as Unionist, aligns himself, on the one hand, with the oppressor of his own people.) This duality (myopia and double vision) in the Irish point of view—toward Jews and regarding the status of the Irish themselves as an oppressed group—is again demonstrated, as we shall see, in the person and work of Arthur Griffith, and by Stephen Dedalus, despite what seems to be at this moment in Nestor his defense of Jews against Deasy's slur. Joyce is not merely documenting Irish antisemitism but creating a set of metaphoric identifications from certain historical apperceptions of Jews and Judaism.

While Deasy's reference to "never letting them in" seems confusing, as something that should perhaps be read as a metaphor for Jewish exclusion from Irish society, the facts are that in 1871 the Jewish population in all of Ireland was 285, in 1881, 453; by the year 1904, the estimate was 3,371, most of them residing in Dublin (2,200).[3] The sudden influx at the turn of the century resulted from a wave of immigration, primarily from Russia, where Jewish persecution had become acute. Until that time Ireland never had had to let Jews in, and with their sudden appearance in greater numbers came the attitudes toward Jews that were prevalent on the continent.

The myth of Irish tolerance is certainly one of Joyce's themes. As Dominic Manganiello has observed, "Joyce's indictment of Irish nationalism covered not only its provincialism but its arrant prejudice as well" (Manganiello, p. 131).[4] In the months preceding June 1904, the Limerick boycotts against the Jews of that city stirred up the press and the intolerance of the Irish. Articles concerning the affair appeared in the *All-Ireland Review*, *Freeman's Journal*, the *United Irishman*, *Irish Times*, and other publications. Bloom alludes to it in Cyclops and in Eumaeus, and Molly makes a rather cryptic reference to it and Arthur Griffith's part in it in Penelope.

On January 12, 1904, a boycott against the Jews of Limerick was incited by Father John Creagh, who in a sermon condemned the Jews as usurers and invoked the myth of ritual murder—blood libel.[5] In a follow-up sermon, he enjoined his listeners to boycott the Jews—to stop doing business with them and to forget all former business arrangements.[6] The Irish would not have been surprised by Creagh's assessment of their Jewish neighbors, since as Louis Hyman, among others, tells us, the image of the Jew as "parasite" was already established in the communities in which Jews lived (Hyman, pp. 160–61). Furthermore, Father Creagh was not a maverick among his Catholic counterparts. There is evidence that the Catholic establishment was in large part wary of the Jew/outsider, and it often openly expressed antisemitic views to the effect that Jews were immoral, undesirables.[7] Joyce is likely to have known the Catholic establishment's attitude toward the Jews, making the parallel he draws between Charles Stuart Parnell and Bloom more pointed than it might seem.[8] To complicate matters further, the Protestant community supported the Jews throughout the trouble, making their "national" position doubly untenable (Hyman, p. 124). Not only was the Jewish community of Limerick essentially destroyed, but Jews were hounded and attacked in the streets. One such attacker was quoted as saying, "They are bad devils, they have persecuted the country and I intend to do for them," thereby demonstrating his schooling in the "catechism of anti-Semitism."[9]

Arthur Griffith, leader of Sinn Fein and editor of the *United Irishman*, took up Creagh's cause, supporting both his sentiments and his call for action against the Jews. Griffith publicized his antisemitism in his articles on the Boer Wars, in which he aligned the Jews with the "Imperialist English."[10] In an article in the *United Irishman* of September 23, 1899, Griffith held that "the Three Evil Influences of the century were the Pirate, the Freemason and the Jew." (Bloom, of course, is also a presumed Mason.)[11] He goes on in the article to attack the Jews for being united against the Transvaal Republic and therefore in league with the English, and for being "wild, savage, filthy forms" who detest soap and water; he takes the French establishment's side against Dreyfus, and accuses the Jews of supporting only those causes that serve their interests. Joyce certainly knew Griffith (and his work), for not only were Griffith and Gogarty friends, but apparently he was a regular visitor at the Martello tower (Manganiello, p. 135).

It is perhaps from Griffith that Joyce first heard the peculiar split in sentiment toward the Jew. Griffith believed (at least initially) that the Zionist Jew, in representing the Jewish people, was to be applauded, for Zionism was equated with nationalism, a cause that the leader of Sinn Fein would support; on the other hand, the Jew's image in Ireland or in any other country (South Africa–Transvaal, for example) was that of the parasitic outsider, who exploited in order to survive. This corresponds to the historical split in perception of the Jews as at once a noble, ancient people, but unacceptable as individuals in modern society:[12]

The Jews of great Britain and Ireland have united as is their wont, to crush the Christian who dares to block their path or point them out for what they are — nine-tenths of them — usurers and parasites. In this category we do not include the Zionist minority of the Jews, who include those honest and patriotic Jews who desire the re-establishment of the Hebrew nation in Palestine — the last thing on earth the majority desires. Attack a Jew — other than a Zionist Jew — and all Jewry comes to his assistance. Thus, when France condemned a Jew, Captain Dreyfus, to perpetual imprisonment for high treason, all Jewry combined to ruin France. . . . Precisely the same tactics are being followed in regard to Father Creagh of Limerick. . . . "The Cry of Outraged Israel" rings in the land. The old women of both sexes are moved to tears at the thought of the Irish workingman of Limerick removing his custom from the persecuted Jew to his countryman the Irish shopkeeper, and the Reverend Mr. Hallowes thinks the castle is failing in its duty in not locking up those who advocate "boycotting the Jews" — that is, supporting the Christian. . . . In all countries and in all Christian ages the Jew has been a usurer and a grinder of the poor. The influence he has recently acquired in this country is a matter of the most serious concern of the people. . . . The Jew in Ireland is in every respect an economic evil. (*United Irishman*, April 23, 1904)

Griffith may have been one of the most vociferous of attackers, but the sentiments expressed in the above passage were shared and voiced by many others.[13] And while there were those of the establishment who defended the Jews, even they, in the course of their defense, would often engage in the rhetoric of antisemitism: for example, Standish Hayes O'Grady, at that time the editor of the *All-Ireland Review*, could write in one editorial that "those Limerick Jews seem to be a very harmless body, neither money-lenders nor extortioners," and that their attackers "believe, on the contrary, that the Limerick Jews cannot differ much from Jews everywhere else" (Magalaner, p. 1221).

Arthur Griffith is employed in *Ulysses* essentially as a symbol of one branch of Irish nationalism. But Joyce's notions about the movement and the man are clearly less than laudatory. He sees the movement as exclusive, as supportive of measures and methods that make it potentially no less destructive than British imperialism, and no more acceptable than the Parliamentarians, who saw separation from England as undesirable, inherently contradictory in its aims.[14] It purports to unite Ireland under the banner of the exclusion of those whom it does not deem properly Irish; unity is sought through disunity. Joyce makes this observation in "Ireland, Island of Saints and Sages," which he delivered to a Triestine audience in 1907:

Recently, when an Irish member of Parliament was making a speech to the voters on the night before an election, he boasted that he was one of the ancient race and rebuked his opponent for being the descendant of a Cromwellian settler. His rebuke provoked a general laugh in the press, for, to tell the truth, to exclude from the present nation all who are descended from foreign families would be impossible, and to deny the name of patriot to all those who are not of Irish stock would be to deny it to almost all the heroes of the modern movement — Lord Edward Fitzgerald, Robert Emmet, Theobold Wolfe Tone and Napper Tandy, leaders of the uprising of 1798, Thomas Davis and John Mitchel, leaders of the Young Ireland movement, Isaac Butt, Joseph Biggar, the inventor of parliamentary obstructionism, many of the anticlerical Fenians, and, finally, Charles Stuart Parnell, who was perhaps the most formidable man that ever led the Irish, but in whose veins there was not even a drop of Celtic blood.[15]

Bloom may be included under this rubric of exclusion, as would Jews generally.

Griffith is first mentioned in Proteus. Stephen thinks of him as one who wishes to claim him as one of his "yokefellows": "Of Ireland, the Dalcassians, of hopes, conspiracies, of Arthur Griffith now. To yoke me as his yokefellow, our crimes our common cause. You're your father's son. I know the voice" (3.227–32). Stephen refers to the "crimes" perpetrated through the common cause, among them the discrimination against loyal Irishmen not of Celtic stock. After all, this passage comes shortly after Stephen's talk with Deasy in which the Jews have been made accountable for the troubles of Ireland, and only two lines later in this same passage Edouard Drumont,[16] nineteenth-century French journalist and notorious antisemite, is mentioned. Both Griffith and Drumont used their respective publications to promote antisemitism; Joyce's response to Griffith's antisemitism and journalistic "ethics" was emphatic: "What I object to most of all in his paper is that it is educating the people of Ireland on the old pap of racial hatred whereas anyone can see that if the Irish question exists, it exists for the Irish proletariat chiefly" (*Letters* II, p. 167). The last two lines of the passage from Proteus — "You're your father's son. I know the voice." — as well as alluding to the similarity between Ulysses' and Telemachus's voices, echo the lines from *Leah the Forsaken* that first appear in Lotus Eaters, wherein the blind Jewish patriarchal figure, Abraham, recognizes the voice of the apostate son ("I hear the voice of Nathan who left his father to die of grief") (5.204–6).[17] Stephen is being racially identified; the implication is that if he is his father's son, of Simon Dedalus, then he is Irish-Catholic and must meet his calling. Of course, the reader is being prepared, primed, perhaps baited for a father-son alliance between Stephen and Bloom, a preparation that is effectively achieved here through the allusion to *Leah*. Further, Stephen may be equated with that apostate son who wishes to abandon his background (non-serviam), who is, in this case, suspicious of the cause for Irish nationalism, whose aims he sees as narrow and confining.

Later, in Penelope, Molly thinks "Poldy not Irish enough," which leads directly into a reference to Griffith:

and he was going about with some of the Sinner Fein lately or whatever they call themselves talking his usual trash and nonsense he says that little man he showed me without the neck is very intelligent the coming man Griffiths he well he doesnt look it thats all I can say still it must have been him he knew there was a boycott (18.383–87)

We laugh at Molly's epithet for the Fenians — "Sinner Fein" — and the way in which she cuts Griffith down to size, as it were. They sin against her husband by thinking Bloom "not Irish enough," while Bloom fervently supports the cause. Ironically, when Bloom rejects Zionism for himself — "nothing doing" — in favor of Irish nationality, if not nationalism — "I was born in Ireland" — he becomes a pariah in the eyes of those like Arthur Griffith, and in any case doubted, as in Cyclops, where his Irishness is challenged, his Jewishness confirmed. Even more ironic in this context is the suggestion in Cyclops that Bloom gave Griffith the idea for Sinn Fein (12.1573–75). On the one hand, Joyce uses this anachronism (Sinn Fein was first named at the end of 1904) to establish the differences between the Fenians who believed in violence (Citizen) and those moderates who sought home rule through passive resistance (Griffith and, in this context, Bloom) (Manganiello, p. 123). But beyond this, Griffith's idea that Ireland should be commercially independent is being attributed to Bloom, "the robbing bagman," as a tactic imaginable only of and by a Jew (12.1581).

Manganiello's comment on Joyce's attitude toward Sinn Fein works to illuminate the relationship between Griffith and Bloom presented by the text:

For Joyce militant patriotism represented the twin symptom, with the Church militant, of the same disease. He objected to the application of the principle of physical force to any phase of national life. The practice of Fenianism had taken hold of Ireland, and it is in this context that Joyce makes "fenian" the symbol of the "Cyclops" chapter. It is the Sinn Féin philosophy, employing violent rhetoric, proclaiming "We'll put force against force" (329; 427), that Joyce is primarily attacking. That is why the Citizen, a Sinn Féin Fenian, is hostile to Bloom even though Bloom is purported to have given Griffith the idea for the Hungarian Policy. Griffith's moderate objectives are not adequate for the Citizen, who desires complete separation from England by force. Confusion as to the object of Joyce's satire has led many critics to argue that he is denouncing the Sinn Féin movement outright. But Joyce is exposing the dangers of militant nationalism which extreme Sinn Feiners were advocating. (Manganiello, pp. 137–38)

Griffith devised what was known as the Hungarian Policy (derived from his "The Resurrection of Hungary"), in order to promote the path of passive resistance in the parallel with the Magyars' strategy against Austria; yet he advocated the use of force against the Jews of Limerick. Molly seems to be implicating him as a participant in the boycott against the Jews when she says "it must have been him he knew there was a boycott." Any suggestion of an alliance between him and Bloom seems ironic. The Citizen may in part be hostile to Bloom because of Bloom's philosophy of nationalism, but finally, it is the perception of him as a Jew, rather than his affinities in this regard, which makes him unacceptable to either side.

The parallel that Griffith makes between the Irish and the Hungarians—one which may in large part account novelistically for Bloom's Hungarian background[18]—reminds us of the parallel that was being drawn between the Hebrews and the Irish in their resistance to conquest (the ancient Hebrews against the Egyptians as in Aeolus; see note 26), and in their desire to establish a homeland (the modern Zionists). These are parallels Griffith probably could have accommodated within his paradoxical attitudes toward Jews. These two parallels are collapsed together in Circe in the scene in which Bloom is proclaimed the King of Ireland (15.1540–1632). Joyce parodies Griffith's "Resurrection of Hungary" in this scene in which Bloom pledges, as had Emperor Franz Joseph, his commitment to independent nationhood.[19] It is significant, however, that Bloom speaks Hebrew here instead of Irish, which would be more in keeping with Griffith's depiction of the coronation scene in which Franz Joseph is speaking in Hungarian rather than German. Griffith's point in having Franz Joseph speak Hungarian is that Ireland should be an "Irish-tongued nation," while Joyce, as Manganiello suggests, seems to be dramatizing his negative position on the Irish-language question by having Bloom speak in another language (Manganiello, p. 122). Beyond this, by having Bloom speak in Hebrew, Joyce seems to be not only pointing to the "otherness" of this particular King of Ireland but also asserting another parallel between the Zionists and the Irish—the move to make Hebrew a spoken rather than a "holy" language.

While in one section of Circe Bloom is raised up to the level of king, even if only parodically, in the trial section we see him as persecuted, falsely accused, in the parallel with Parnell. The instrument of persecution is the notorious judge, Sir Frederick Falkiner (15.1158–80). While Griffith used the pen, it is well known that Falkiner used the law as a weapon against Jews. Although the scene in Circe is a kind of burlesque mock trial whose purpose, it seems, is to play on the notion of betrayal (Parnell, Judas Iscariot, Jacob and Esau, etc.), it is significant that Joyce chooses Falkiner to preside over this and other cases involving Jews, displacing historical fact with metaphorical accuracy.[20] Falkiner denied being antisemitic, but he would hand down excessive sentences to Jews (Hyman, p. 163). Joseph Montefiore, then president of the London Committee of Deputies of the British Jews (1902), exhorted Falkiner to "correct the unfavorable impression which your words as reported have conveyed," and Falkiner responded with a disclaimer.[21] Joyce seems in any case to have been aware of Falkiner's "notoriety" among the Jews (see also 8.1151–61; 12.1084–1110).

In the context of the Ireland of 1904, then, it is no wonder that Stephen would be predisposed to the rhetoric of antisemitism. When in Ithaca Bloom sings the first two lines of "Ha-tikvah" (*The Hope*, the Israeli national anthem), Stephen responds with "The Ballad of Harry Hughes," an antisemitic verse that evokes the myth of ritual murder (17.761–831). Yet, while he resorts to antisemitic remarks when faced with Bloom personally, in Nestor, for example, he identifies with the Jews as a wandering people, and as so-called "sinners against the light" (see pp. 102–3). Stephen returns to the idea of the Jew as moneylender when in Scylla and Charybdis he argues for an affinity between the character, Shylock, and author, Shakespeare:

—And the sense of property, Stephen said. He drew Shylock out of his own long pocket. The son of a maltjobber and money lender he was himself a cornjobber and moneylender with ten tods of corns hoarded in the famine riots. (2.741–44)

Stephen's sentiments overall reflect a paradoxical (Irish) attitude toward the Jew. Like Deasy and Griffith, he is unaware of his own double vision; he is able to defend the Jews, as in Nestor, to identify with them as mythical characters, and then to feel "a strange kind of flesh of a different man approach him" (16.1722–23), when in Eumaeus Bloom offers him his arm for support. Those Bloom supports typically see him as other, viewing him with a kind of cultural myopia. And all seems to hinge on Bloom's Jewishness, which functions, at least in part, as a metaphor for the "nightmare of history."

This particular aspect of the nightmare and its resonances within the Irish setting are vividly dramatized in the Cyclops chapter of *Ulysses* in the encounter between Bloom and the (at least) visually impaired Citizen. Their exchange becomes a clash of types, both textual and historical, framed or insinuated by the running parody of the clash of Titans in Irish mythology. Where before this chapter and later in the novel Bloom disavows his Jewishness with characteristic partiality, here he lays claim to it with the same partiality; the rhetorical gesture of avowal is adjusted by the historical evidence. "Christ was a jew like me," says Bloom in the famous line, immediately then referencing as exemplary the figures of Mendelssohn, Karl Marx, and Spinoza, along with Christ in this list of converts, heretics, apostates, either proclaimed or self-proclaimed. In fact, though this may seem ironic, they are all Jews like Bloom, at once Jews and non-Jews. As with Deasy's shifting positionality, even Bloom and the Citizen come into focus on the same side—culturally dispossessed and possessed, as it were, both shifting and, at least, perceived as, shifty. In keeping with the dominant motif of sexual and national betrayal, associatively and playfully iterated in this cluster of chapters — Sirens, Cyclops, Nausicaa — through the symbol of the cuckoo, you might say the chapter is "textually cuckoo." Nothing is traditionally at home here, neither the characters nor the forms; place is displace(d).

Although Joyce may not yet have conceived of Bloom in 1904, the use of cultural stereotypes to embody the principle of the outsider is evident in the Jews who appear briefly in *Dubliners*. While the stereotypes of Jews in *Dubliners* are continuous with those in *Ulysses*, Joyce's conception and use of them, as we shall see, differs markedly in the latter. Jews or Jew-*ish* figures appear or are mentioned in "An Encounter," "A Little Cloud," "Counterparts," and "Grace," and serve largely as convenient representations of qualities that become for Joyce closely associated with Jews and/or Jewishness. The most outstanding of these literary tags is a quality of otherness, often represented in Joyce criticism as "the exotic," which by its forbidden nature becomes at once attractive, desirable, and emblematic of corruption or decadence. Many of the characters in *Dubliners* long for that which is exotic by their standards — the oriental bazaar in "Araby" whose glamour is illusory; the "English" "actress" in "Counterparts" whom Farrington elevates into a symbol of his frustrated desires; Eveline's sailor Frank, who holds out to her the mysteries of love and South America. In *Dubliners*, these symbols of the exotic or of otherness are more crudely projections of and/or tunnels for the characters' needs and desires — truly objects in view.

In "An Encounter," the two boys set out on their adventure across the Liffey on a ferryboat, "paying our toll to be transported in the company of two labourers and a little Jew with a bag." They are in "other" company. In this curious passing reference, Joyce seems to be presenting the immigrant Jew, bag in hand, in the landscape of the Dublin of 1904, something to be encountered by the boys on their "exotic" and "dangerous" adventure.

As in the case of the green-eyed man whom the boys meet at the Pigeon House, that which appears as exotic in the stories often has a sexual component. What is exoticized is at once eroticized, calling up the historical alignment of race and sex in the figuration of the Other. Though they become inextricably linked, they clash in the fantasy lives of these viewers; what has been romanticized through race is disturbed by the sexual, as is the symbolic domain of Araby, for example (see note 23).

Jewish women who appear or are mentioned are exotic types, who are at once idealized and degraded by those who view them. In "A Little Cloud," Gallaher, who has acquired a quality of exoticism/otherness in Little Chandler's eyes, is played off against the stereotypes of the rich and unsavory Jew. When Little Chandler tries to hold up his wife as a possession which Gallaher does not have, Gallaher tops him, as it were, by talking about "thousands of Germans and Jews, rotten with money, that'd be only too glad . . ." (p. 81). Gallaher rejects that which Little Chandler holds forth as a superior possession — true love — for "the woman and the cash." In an economy of exchange (a kind of male trafficking) in which the Jewish woman becomes an object of barter, Gallaher degrades romance, while Little Chandler by nature seeks to idealize it; he fantasizes about Jewish women not as rich but as distinctly "other," certainly from his wife: "He thought of what Gallaher had said about rich Jewesses. Those dark Oriental eyes, he thought, how full they are of passion, of voluptuous longing! . . . Why had he married the eyes of a photograph?" (p. 83).[22] It is only a short trip from that imagining to the remorse and shame that he so resonantly feels at the end of the story. Both subject and object are guilty as sin.

The image of the rich and exotic Jewish woman is repeated and actually makes an appearance in "Counterparts" through the figure of Miss Delacour:

Miss Delacour was a middle-aged woman of Jewish appearance. Mr Alleyne was said to be sweet on her or on her money. She came to the office often and stayed a long time when she came. She was sitting beside his desk now in an aroma of perfumes, smoothing the handle of her umbrella and nodding the great black feather in her hat. (p. 90)

She is yet another "thing" which Alleyne "has" and Farrington does not, something which he tries to recreate through the idealized image of the English "actress" later in the story. Again, the image is implicitly sexual. The suggestion both here and with Gallaher's Jewish women is that they grant sexual favors: Miss Delacour stays a long time and strokes the handle of her umbrella; Gallaher's rich Jewesses would "be only too glad." But their "impulses" are elliptical, at best suggestive. These images of the exotic woman provide what is perhaps the outline for what would eventually become Molly Bloom, in whom we read an intrinsic relationship between race and sex.[23]

By the time we get to "Grace," the Jew has become firmly entrenched in the stereotype of the moneylender/shyster, another (con)figuration of the Jew within the symbology of otherness, no longer just an exotic part of the landscape. Mr. Kernan, the "fallen" drunk, reveals to his friends Messrs. Power, Cunningham, and McCoy, that one of his drinking companions was a Mr. Harford. Cunningham takes exception to Harford on moral grounds in a way that is illuminating both with regard to the story's confused morality and for our understanding of a detail in *Ulysses*.

Mr Harford sometimes formed one of a little detachment which left the city shortly after noon on Sunday with the purpose of arriving as soon as possible at some public-house on the outskirts of the city where its members duly qualified themselves as *bona-fide* travellers. But his fellow-travellers had never consented to overlook his origin. He had begun life as an obscure financier by lending small sums of money to workmen at usurious interest. Later on he had become the partner of a very fat short gentleman, Mr Goldberg, of the Liffey Loan Bank. Though he had never embraced more than the Jewish ethical code his fellow-Catholics, whenever they had smarted in person or by proxy under his exactions, spoke of him bitterly as an Irish Jew and an illiterate and saw divine disapproval of usury made manifest through the person of his idiot son. At other times they remembered his good points. (p. 159)

Harford is clearly a prototype for Reuben J. Dodd in *Ulysses* who is Jew-*ish*, considered a Jew because he fits the stereotype.[24] Furthermore, Bloom is in the company of these same men in the Hades chapter of *Ulysses* when he is associated, by Cunningham in particular, with Dodd (6.240–95). There is part of the historical backdrop for Bloom's arrival mise-en-scène. Jews came to Ireland as both known and unknown entities — known through the stereotypes that "travelled" with them and thereby made unknowable.

It emerges from this examination of the image of the Jew in the Irish milieu that the Jews were preeminently scapegoats in a country of scapegoats. Ironically, the Jews' arrival in Ireland provided some Irish with a convenient scapegoat, a displacement from their own marginality, as a nation of scapegoats themselves, mistreated and misrepresented, perhaps they were impelled to perpetuate the myth of Irish tolerance. As Michael Davitt, Irish nationalist leader in 1904, wrote in a response to the Limerick boycott: "The Jews have never done any injury to Ireland. Like our own race they have endured a persecution, the records of which will forever remain a reproach to the 'Christian' nations of Europe. Ireland has no share in this black record. Our country has this proud distinction . . . of never having resorted to the un-Christian and barbarous treatment of an unfortunate people" (*Freeman's Journal*, Jan. 18, 1904). His words are echoed by Deasy, and like Deasy he was capable of paradoxical thinking about Jews.[25] While analogies were drawn between the two peoples in the press, and in political speeches (Taylor),[26] and even in scholarly research (Vallancey);[27] every effort was being made in the Church and in the community to ostracize Jews, to establish them as other.[28] This paradox is at the heart of Joyce's depiction of Bloom. What Joyce learned about Jews in Ireland was only to be confirmed and extended on the continent where, as we know and as will be dramatized further in Joyce's work, this kind of paradoxical thinking was well developed beyond that which the Irish were capable of in 1904. The very term *Jew* was so loaded, so laden with myth and type, so charged, that applying it in any respect to the hero(es) of the novel would provide the work with a resonance of metaphor, symbol, and theme. The nightmare of history is one in which similarity and difference cannot be reconciled and from which Joyce's novel emerges.

CHAPTER EIGHT

Dorothy Richardson and the Jew

JACQUELINE ROSE

What happens if you substitute the language of assimilation and exclusion for the more familiar feminist vocabulary of belonging and refusal? If the vexed issue of woman's sexual and aesthetic participation in modern culture is rewritten in terms of her relation to nationhood and state? It has become commonplace to point out that the project of writing *otherwise* for women arises at the time of, and is inseparable from, the emergence of high modernist writing. Most often, the fact is used to throw doubt on, or indicate the limits of, the political emancipation or radical potential of such writing. But to point to the marriage of feminist experiment to high modernist culture as a sign of political failure may, oddly, involve overlooking some of the other more striking points of political contact at work. It cannot be a coincidence that early modernist experimentation parallels, even as it can be seen as critiquing, the emerging nation-state in which Hannah Arendt identifies the birth of modern antisemitism.[1]

To start with an obvious example, one of the best known, of this link between feminism and the issue of nationhood—Virginia Woolf in *Three Guineas*: "The law of England denies us, and let us hope will long continue to deny us, the full stigma of nationality"; or again, "in fact, as a woman, I have no country. As a woman I want no country. As a woman my country is the whole world."[2] The link is present much earlier, however. Not this time in a text by a woman writer, but in Henry James, at the heart of

The Portrait of a Lady, where it appears not as affirmation or freedom for women, but as curse. In a famous and much commented dialogue, Madame Merle says to Isabel Archer: "A woman, it seems to me, has no natural place anywhere; wherever she finds herself she has to remain on the surface and, more or less, to crawl."[3] Later in the same discussion, Madame Merle will argue that a person is nothing outside the accoutrements, attachments, and objects that tie her to the world. Fiercely, and against Madame Merle's degrading vision, Isabel insists on the independence and inviolability of selfhood—free of all trappings, Isabel will not crawl but walk tall. She fails, but when we meet her, or what I see as a version of her, again, the grounds of the opposition have shifted. In this essay, I want to suggest that in *Pilgrimage*, Dorothy Richardson rewrites that dialogue between Isabel Archer and Madame Merle as a battle—a battle that constantly threatens to turn into an identification—between the woman, her ethos of independence or non-belonging, and the plea for nationhood of the Jew.[4]

Before going into this in more detail, the argument needs to be placed in context. A fair amount has been written about the presence of antisemitism in modernist writing, especially with reference to T. S. Eliot and Ezra Pound; much less about the antisemitism of women modernist writers.[5] This may be another version of a problem that has recently become familiar to feminism—the limits to its earlier celebration of women writers, the point where feminism has had to acknowledge the other agendas and blind spots of oppression which that celebration apparently had to ignore. If the feminist reads the woman modernist for a lift into freedom, the presence of antisemitism in such a writer brings her (reader *and* writer) brutally back to ground. May Sinclair's *Mary Olivier—A Life* is a psychoanalytically fueled tale of one woman's escape from pre-oedipality into self-determination (thus avoiding the tragic destiny of the heroine of *Life and Death of Harriet Frean*).[6] At the end of the novel, in an episode where Mary Olivier is savoring the joys of literary London in the presence of her lover, this passage appears, seemingly out of the blue:

It came to her at queer times, in queer ways. After that horrible dinner at the Dining Club when the secretary woman put her as far as possible from Richard, next to the little Jew financier who smelt of wine. . . . His tongue slid between one overhanging and one dropping jaw, in and out like a shuttle. She tried not to hate him. (p. 374)

There are other instances—from Woolf's *The Years*, from Stevie Smith, from Djuna Barnes (not *Nightwood*, which I read as a critique of antisemitism, but from the *Ladies Almanack*: "When but five, she lamented Mid-prayers, that the girls in the Bible were both earth-hushed and Jew-touched forever and ever").[7] None of them is quite as unequivocal as the moment from Sinclair. But they all raise the same question: What is the relation between the feminist modernist project—whether that project is defined as the affirmation of autonomy and selfhood *or* as the dissolution of all selfhood into writing (both, to put it most crudely, forms of escape)—and this castigating-caricatured representation of that *other* outsider, the Jew?

In *Pilgrimage*, the central character, Miriam Henderson, is caught between two lovers both of whom she finally rejects: Hypo Wilson, unmistakably now if not unmistakably then a representation of H. G. Wells, and Michael Shatov, modeled on the Russian Jewish émigré Benjamin Grad. She becomes pregnant by the first and miscarries before detaching herself from him; she in any case repudiates what she sees as his ecstatic appropriation of her future through her unborn child. She refuses the marriage proposal of the second, but ensures his posterity by effectively arranging his marriage to her passionate, importunate woman friend, Amabel (it is a way of getting rid of both of them at once). The thirteen volumes of *Pilgrimage*—the last of which was not published until 1967, after Richardson's death—end with her picking up Michael Shatov and Amabel's child. In *Pilgrimage*, therefore, the issue of posterity and begetting, insofar as it is played out between Hypo (H. G. Wells) Wilson and Michael (Benjamin Grad) Shatov, gives us the woman sexually suspended, so to speak, between antisemite and Jew.

In this context, the presence-absence of H. G. Wells in the text can be taken as doubly symptomatic. First, the difficulty of representing Wells can be seen as one of the subtexts of *Pilgrimage* insofar as Richardson presents Hypo Wilson with all the details of Wells's intellectual identity as writer, scientific utopian, Fabian critic, but with no hint of his extended engagement with the question of the Jew—the question which via Shatov is simultaneously working itself out elsewhere across the pages of her novel (his relationship to Jewishness appears therefore to be one of the suppressed contents of the text). Second, that subtext is in turn representative of a form of "semitic" discourse, to use Bryan Cheyette's expression, more representative of this period of English literature than has until recently been acknowledged, which in Wells's case gradually hardens after the First World War into the more recognizable tropes of unequivocal antisemitism.[8] The following passage from Wells represents, therefore, not just that part of him which Richardson removes from the figure of Hypo Wilson, but also a much larger component of the political moment in which she writes:

It might have been supposed that a people so widely dispersed would have developed a cosmopolitan mentality and formed a convenient linking organisation for many world purposes, but their special culture of isolation was so intense that this they neither did nor seemed anxious to attempt.[9]

Note how this takes the form of a reproach against the Jew for too much isolated belonging (a type of oxymoron meaning the wrong kind of belonging, that is, belonging to nobody but the Jews), for not being cosmopolitan enough. What Wells objected to was the failure of the Jew to realize his historic destiny as the model for emancipated world identity. It was only one step from here to Wells's comments during the Second World War — cited by Mass Observation (a social-anthropological research program), by Foreign Office and diplomatic officials — that the Jews had provoked antisemitism and that any treatment of them as a special category would be to replicate the Nazi ideology of which they were now the victims.[10] Wells's comment provides one half of a paradox which haunts accusations against the Jews — reproached for being a "nation within a nation,"[11] they were also accused of being the embodiment of cosmopolitan — that is, infinitely mobile, infinitely corruptible — capital. "The merchant is the citizen of no country" (Benjamin Kidd citing Adam Smith in 1908); in *The Modern Jew* of 1899, Arnold White expressed the antisemitic version: "Cosmopolitan finance is only another word for Jewish finance."[12] According to this vision, the Jew was only ever parasitic — chameleon-like — on the community to which it became attached: "Although the only true cosmopolitan people in the world, with the exception of the Gitanos, they reflect, like the chameleon, the texture and the tint of the rock on which they rest."[13] Compare Madame Merle again: "We're mere parasites crawling over the surface."[14]

Supra-national or micro-national, what is crucial is that in neither case does the Jew (or woman) *belong*. The Jew therefore turns up on both sides of the divide which Kidd, whom Richardson read and admired, saw as emblematic of modernity:

It was insisted that the ideal condition of the world for the maximum production of wealth, and therefore, it was said, for international peace and progress, was one in which the exchanges of both labour and capital would be . . . absolutely untrammelled by considerations of nationalism. . . . No change which has taken place in the world in our time is more striking than the assertion of what has been called the passion of nationalism against the cosmopolitan political ideals of the early Victorian period.[15]

To the question of whether or not the Jew can belong, Richardson will propose her own particular, and complex, reply. Through the figure of Michael Shatov, she will provide the backdrop, from the side of the Jews, of the issue to which Wells's writings offer one representative response. Richardson met Benjamin Grad in 1896 in the middle of the decade which followed the period of highest Eastern European Jewish immigration into the country. This wave of immigration was characterized by its poverty — relatively and strikingly in relation to the already established Jewish community, which viewed it with anything but pleasure and often opposed it outright (the establishment of autonomous hebrots in the East End were seen by West End Jews as separatist — precisely a nation within a nation) — and by the fact that it introduced into British Jewry socialism, trade unionism, and Zionism.[16] By the 1890s, socialism in the Jewish community had declined, and social democratic trade unionism and Zionist nationalism were ascendant. More than one commentator sees this development as a split between assimilation and separatism in itself — socialism either absorbed into mainstream English trade unionism or carried off the map of England and Europe altogether by the nationalist vision.[17] In 1892, *Die Vekker* (*The Awakening*), the new journal of the Jewish Socialist movement, exhorted its brethren:

Do not stand apart from your English comrades, do not form a separate city within a city in which to live. Discard your Asiatic customs which you have brought with you from Russia. Cast away your wild tongue and learn the language of the land in which you live. Unite in unions. But, better yet, where possible enter English unions.[18]

The rise in anti-alien sentiment accompanying these developments then culminated in the Anti-Alien bill of 1905.

One of the difficulties, and interests, for the reader of *Pilgrimage* is the double or even treble time scale of the work — historical, referential time (the events from Richardson's life on which the novel is closely but tranformatively based); the time of the narrator (Miriam Henderson always present inside her experience but only emerging as writer at the end of the thirteen-volume work); the time of writing (the phases in which Richardson often painfully and laboriously completed her text). Running across the different instances of her life and identity, these moments are no less striking, in terms of continuities and disjunctions, in relation to the history of the Jews: from the second wave of Jewish immigration into England at the end of the nineteenth century to the rise of Hitler to power. *Pilgrimage* clearly takes its reference from Bunyan; as Jean Radford has pointed out, the title also carries the symbolic burden of the journey involved, over more than a quarter of a century, in the writing of the work.[19] But in its less familiar meaning of "to live among strangers," it also calls up the unfolding Jewish history shadowing her novel as she wrote (note already that Richardson has given her heroine, Miriam, a Jewish name).

If we cut, then, from the turn of the century to 1932–34, Richardson is writing — with anxiety and deferral — *Clear Horizon*, the last volume of her book to appear in her lifetime (a "complete" edition of *Pilgrimage*, one which she would be furious with for presenting itself *as* complete since she had not finished it, was issued by her publishers, J. M. Dent, in 1938). It is the volume that includes her separation from Hypo Wilson and the first stage of her attempt to bring her relationship with Shatov to an end.[20] To the rise of Hitler, clear by this time, Richardson responds, one might say, with a crisis of writing — which is to imply not that the events in Germany are the cause of her difficulty, but that they are present running in and out across the boundaries of her text. Why else, we might ask, as she struggles to complete *Clear Horizon*, would she interrupt the progress of her novel with two translations — Josef Kastein's *The Jews in Germany* and Robert Neumann's novel *Mammon (die Macht)* — both so deeply implicated in the Jewish history she both lives and transcribes?[21]

Kastein's book is a plea for Zionism, an appeal to the Jews to retrieve their historic destiny: "An act of consciousness: the desired, and in terms of will, realised return to the Jewish community . . . the genuine avowal of Jewhood as nationality and of Judaism as a totality in itself" (p. 121). Ascendant antisemitism is for him necessary — the argument will appear almost verbatim in the words of Shatov — in order to provoke the insight among Jews which will lead to the founding of the Jewish nation: "It required pressure from without to produce a recognition of the stronger formative force existing in the bonds of nationality" (p. 147).

Neumann's *Mammon* could be seen, on the other hand, as the countertext to Kastein. The novel centers on an assimilated Jewish lawyer, Albert Rosen, who becomes the legal facilitator behind an alliance, based on forged Russian currency, between an exiled Georgian prince and German nationalists to retrieve his lands from the Bolsheviks: "A Prince of our race," states the President of the Society for Promoting German Nationalism, "driven from his possessions by a Communism financed by international Jewry, demands our hospitality. He shall have it. His wealth will forward our aims" (p. 80). Why a Jew should support such a project, identify with such aims, is not clear, except as a statement of the ultimate assimilation, the furthest self-betrayal of his Jewishness. Rosen is in fact Rosenbaum; he has a brother from whom he is alienated by the fact that his brother, unlike himself, has failed to erase the most tangible traces of his Jewish identity:

Dr. B. Rosen, teacher at the University and specialist in Gynaecology, lives amidst the din of a business district at the point where it is impinged upon by the Jewish suburb. His brother notes with vexation that his name plate is the same as last year, is scarcely smaller than that of a provision-merchant's on the next floor, and bears under the name of B. Rosen, University Professor, another name, in poorer lettering and between tastelessly scrollful brackets: Dr. Benedict Rosenbaum — a name that two years ago ceased to be that of the doctor. (p. 30)

Richardson translates these two books at the same time as she attempts to complete the part of her novel that brings Miriam's relationship to Wilson and Shatov to some kind of resolution. She writes out ("gets into writing" and "expels") the Zionist in her novel as she translates him, the antisemite as she introduces into English one of his most offensive representations. In 1934, she also has a nervous breakdown which is attributed by her biographer Gloria Fromm to the combined pressures of overwork and poverty. Nothing achieved, nothing concrete; too little substance, too many words—a historically traumatic cacophony of writing—in the head. All this forms the background, although it involves stretching the term way beyond its most straightforward meaning of backdrop, context, and support, to Miriam Henderson's engagement with the Jew in *Pilgrimage*.

The main confrontations with Michael Shatov take place in *Deadlock*, published in 1921.[22] In two conversations, Shatov and Miriam Henderson split—take up their positions—over the issue of individuality versus the race:

> "I would call myself rather one who believes in the *race*."
> "*What* race? The race is nothing without individuals."
> "What is an individual without the race?"
> "An individual, with a consciousness; or a soul, whatever you like to call it. The race, apart from individuals, is nothing at all.". . .
> "The race is *certainly* more sacred than the individual."
> "Very well then: I know what I think. If the sacred race plays tricks on conscious human beings, using them for its own sacred purposes and giving them an unreal sense of mattering, I don't care a button for the race, and I'd rather kill myself than serve its purposes. Besides, the instincts of self-preservation and reproduction are *not* the only human motives. They are not human at all." (pp. 150–52)

In this dialogue, Shatov occupies the place of Madame Merle—the individual is meaningless without his attachments or form of belonging in the world: "You are wrong; what you call the shape affects every individual in spite of himself" (p. 169). Miriam occupies that of Isabel Archer, insisting on an individualism which rests in consciousness but which also in this case goes beyond it, is partly sacralized, since one of its possible meanings is the "soul." Miriam hovers between these two meanings. Only through the second can she counter Shatov's "sacred" vision of the race; only by retaining the domain of consciousness can she hold on to individuality as a woman's potential agency and being in the world. One could argue that, with reference to Judaism, this is at once a false antagonism and a *dialogue des sourds*. Thus Kastein will insist that it is through his commitment to national identity that the Jew will establish his "productive *individual* existence *as* a Jew" (emphasis mine); just as he will stress that the enlightenment concept of freedom as untrammeled agency has no meaning for Jewry which sees free-

dom as *willing* submission to authority (it thus ceases, in the enlightenment sense, to be both freedom and coercion at the same time).[23] For
Miriam who, as we will see, is much closer to Shatov than might at first appear, enlightenment can also be a dirty word: he was "in a state of decadence and of the enlightenment that accompanies it."[24]

But by lining up Shatov and Miriam in this way, Richardson also runs
her dialogue into another opposition being formulated at this time. She as-
signs to the Jew the prerogative of what Freud will refer to as species being,
when, in a famous moment, he describes the subordination of polymor-
phous bisexuality to genital reproductive sex as "a victory of the race over
the individual"; "The sexual instinct is now subordinated to the reproductive function; it becomes, so to say, altruistic."[25] Later, when he comes
to formulate it as such, this drive of the race to its own future, over the
pleasures, hearts, and minds of the individuals who bear its purpose unconsciously, will come to be designated, or receive its strongest parallel-
cum-analogy, in the concept of the drive to death (*Beyond the Pleasure Principle* appears in the same year as *Deadlock*).[26] Miriam, one could say, has got
the point, therefore, when she says she will kill herself rather than submit
to this version of the sacred — she has understood the relation of this future
to death. Hence her reproach to Hypo Wilson and Shatov both: "In Hypo
there was no sense of eternity; nor in Michael, except for the race, an endless succession of people made in God's image, all dead or dying."[27] This
future, destiny, history she reads in Michael's face: "The heavy white lids
came down over his eyes and for a moment his face, with its slumbering
vitality, at once venerable and insolent, was like a death-mask, a Jewish
death-mask."[28]

It is another paradox of antisemitism at this time that the Jew could be
seen at once to represent a fierce Darwinian individualism struggling only
for itself *and* a racial exclusivity which will not, which refuses to, mingle its
blood. In her section on the Jewish community in Booth's *Life and Labour
of the People of London*, Beatrice Potter accuses the Jew of lacking all "social
morality" and describes him as the embodiment of Ricardo's economic
man.[29] In a letter to Theodor Herzl, Israel Zangwill states that it is "a positive duty to marry out."[30] Arnold White, antisemite author of *The Modern
Jew*, writes: "If the Jews will consent to be absorbed and to mingle their
blood with ours, all will be well."[31] None of this gets in the way of that
other form of antisemitism, for which the main threat is the "leavening" of
British aristocracy with Jewish blood (separation and penetration as the
flip sides of the same racist paranoia).

There is therefore a crucial issue here about futurity. To whom — man or
woman, Jew or gentile — does the future belong? What does it mean when
a woman refuses to play her part in the reproduction of the species? By

having Miriam refuse to be a Jewish woman and mother, Richardson might seem merely to be adding a powerful intensifier to the feminist issue of women's right to control or even refuse their reproductive role. She is also demonstrating how this feminist agenda came partly in response to a eugenic theory of motherhood which stressed the importance of fertility for the future of the — best of the British — race (Claire Buck has shown just how central this was to the emancipatory project — emancipation from the woman's body into writing — of May Sinclair).[32]

But by calling this version of maternal sacrificial-cum-racial destiny Jewish, Dorothy Richardson also runs Miriam's emancipation straight into some of the most vicious anti-Jewish representations of her time. Ironically, then, Shatov appeals to an ideology of racial exclusion which anti-semitism reflected, appropriated, came at least halfway to meet; while Miriam rejects motherhood as race destiny, rejects eugenics, but in the language of antisemitism. The Jew as pure racial destiny — almost, one might say, jumping historically, as selfish gene. Again, Kastein will insist that this is to misunderstand fundamentally the Jewish conception of continuity: "The world's conception of the being and the value of race does not correspond with the Jew's conception of these things. For the Jew, the concept of the race does not begin with the production of species, but rather with the recognition that over a long period a people has represented a certain attitude of mind."[33] Echoing Otto Weininger, Richardson opposes Jewish to non-Jewish as nature to culture, race to individual, each time staking out — as Jean Radford has demonstrated — the second term for herself.[34] It is the moment at which, for all the historical reference she packs into her novel, she misses what might be described, for the Jew, as the whole historical point: racial destiny, not as biology or species, but as tradition, shared history, the claim for a socially realizable form of life.

Thus even Beatrice Potter will acknowledge the connection between this concept of a possible future and the "three thousand years" of persecution which have gone into the making of the East End Jew, whose religious rituals are there to secure the future, not of another world, but as historic prospect and destiny.[35] Writing on *Kristallnacht*, Kastein comments: "Since the events of last year, these things [Jewish over-hasty assimilation] belong to the past, and . . . must in all circumstances be banished into that past, where, for the Jew, they will always remain present. This dismissal must be accomplished by every Jew who to-day is determined to come level with his destiny and to shape it by taking his place once more within the stream of his own history."[36] Note how close this idea of a past still moving in the present — a past running ahead of its time — is to Dorothy Richardson's own, very specific, temporality of writing: "For both of them

[Richardson and Proust] the past was a world to which they went forward rather than back, thus making of it a future that would one day be present."[37]

As it takes shape between Miriam and Shatov, this quarrel about the future has another political resonance. The opposition between racial and individual destiny reappears in Benjamin Kidd, as the grounds of his argument for socialism: "The history of the world is not simply a history of the struggle for life. It is to an ever-increasing degree a history of the struggle for the life of the future."[38] Not individualism for now, but socialism for tomorrow. Miriam says to Shatov: "Are you a socialist? Do you believe in the opinions of mediocre majorities?" "Why this adjective?" he replies, "Why mediocre? No, I would call myself rather someone who believes in the *race*."[39] It is at the very least a problem for feminism that Miriam's affirmation rides the back of this repudiation of socialist and Jewish conceptions of destiny at one and the same time. The point is related to, but different from, the famous argument about *Jane Eyre*: does the emancipation of the bourgeois woman require the self-immolation of the Creole?[40]

The second key dialogue between Shatov and Miriam takes place when he returns from his first visit to English Jews:

"It is sad for me, this first meeting with English Jews."
"Perhaps you can make Zionists of them."
"That is absolutely impossible. . . . It is useless to talk to these people whose first pride is that they are *British*. . . . What they do not see is that they are not, and never can be, British; that the British do not accept them as such."
". . . The Jews are free in England."
"They are free; to the honour of England in all history. But they are nevertheless Jews and not Englishmen. . . . The toleration for Jews, moreover, will last only as long as the English remain in ignorance of the immense and increasing power and influence of the Jew in this country. Once that is generally recognised, even England will have its anti-Semitic movement."
"*Never*. England can assimilate anything.". . .
"No nation can assimilate the Jew. . . . Remember that British Jewry is perpetually and increasingly reinforced by immigration from those countries where Jews are segregated and ever more terribly persecuted. . . . The time for the closing of this last door is approaching."
"I don't believe England will ever do it. How can they? Where will the Jews go? It's impossible to think of. It will be the end of England if we begin that sort of thing."
"It may be the beginning of Jewish nationality. Ah, at least this visit has reawakened all the Zionist in me." (pp. 166–68)

This conversation is prophetic in that the episode takes place before the passage of the Anti-Alien Bill and the rise of British Zionism; it also anticipates not only Kastein on the productive link between antisemitism and Zionism but also Arnold White on the power of the British Jews:

The Jewish community in England, though not numerically strong, control so large a portion of the financial and journalistic power of the country that any Ministry undertaking a joust against the consolidated strength of the Jews would be infallibly unhorsed.[41]

But it is also, of course, not prophetic, because it is being *written* in 1921, long after the developments it predicts have taken place (the Balfour Declaration is made in 1917). In the figure of Michael Shatov, Dorothy Richardson has effectively condensed a set of sometimes evolving, sometimes antagonistic, moments in the history of the Jewish immigrant of the second wave (Potter says the Polish and Russian Jew "represents to some extent the concentrated essence of Jewish virtue and Jewish vice; for he has, in his individual experience, epitomised the history of his race in the Christian world").[42] In the East End of London, Zionism will start to flourish in the early years of the century among groups of those "who were not cosmopolitan socialists yet were alienated by the forms of immigrant religious life." (According to Lloyd Gartner, Herzl was given an almost-Messianic reception when he delivered his first public address on political Zionism in Whitechapel in 1896.)[43] According to Geoffrey Alderman, the children of the early Jewish socialists also, via the Labour party, became Zionists in turn.[44] Cosmopolitan socialist, Zionist, Russian émigré, Shatov hovers between — he lives in the same Bloomsbury boarding house as Miriam — the Jewish communities of East and West. Perhaps it is because of his borderline identity that he tries, in seeking to marry a non-Jewish woman, to take on what he himself defines as a marginal and untypical historical role: "No nation can assimilate the Jews." "What about intermarriage." "That is the minority" (p. 167).

Read the dialogue about Zionism through the preceding one (they occur in the same chapter of *Deadlock*), and the opposition of assimilation versus Zionism becomes overlaid with the proto-feminist opposition between the individual and the race. Feminism against nationalism sounds better, perhaps, than woman against Jew, but Richardson's text does not allow the reader to disentangle the terms. With whom does the Jewish woman reader identify at a moment like this? Shatov's historical analysis is, as it were, correct (he anticipates what will happen to British Jews). And however critically this reader might view the subsequent history of Zionism, especially its founding precondition in relation to the Palestinians, it is impossible not to recognize the grounded particularity of his desire, while Miriam's arguments against Zionism, her too-easy belief in assimilation, even in the name of liberal tolerance, back onto — the previous dialogue is there to remind us — some of the most familiar tropes of antisemitism. Assigning this position to Miriam, Richardson also reverses her own support for Zionism (the radical MP Josiah Wedgewood attributed to Richardson and Alan Odle his first knowledge of Zionism as a creed).[45] This is Wells on Zionism in the continuation of the quote discussed before:

After the World War the orthodox Jews played but a poor part in the early attempts to formulate the Modern State, being far more preoccupied with a dream called Zionism. . . . Only a psycho-analyst could begin to tell for what they wanted this Zionist state. It emphasized their traditional wilful separation from the main body of mankind. It irritated the world against them, subtly and incurably.[46]

The case for assimilation — "England can assimilate anything" — wears many colors and takes many forms: the liberal form of tolerance-cum-intolerance (acceptance on condition of shedding Jewish identity), the demand of the antisemite, the delusion and/or desire of the British Jew.

What Richardson offers us through Miriam Henderson could then be seen as a cameo, for feminism, of the clash between a liberal plea for individual rights and the particularities of cultures and nations, a type of vision in advance of how difficult it will become theoretically and politically to square the circle between these apparently antagonistic priorities and terms. To this problem, which stretches back and forward across the history of Europe, Miriam's position — and claim for herself — as a woman, adds a particular complexity. For, as a woman, Miriam Henderson is presented to us as distanced, alien, estranged in herself, as something, we might say, of a Jew. Like being a Jew, being a woman can also be described as a state of non- or partial participation in the available or dominant cultures. Curse and privilege, this unsettled self-positioning, as Woolf expressed it, can become alternately exclusion from, or belonging to, all possible worlds: "As a woman I want no country. As a woman, my country is the whole world."[47]

Even more, Richardson's involvement in Quakerism — an involvement repeated by Miriam in the last volume of *Pilgrimage* — allows her to stretch out, almost infinitely expand the boundaries of, this vision of woman on the edge of time. In her 1914 book on Quakerism, Richardson cites these words from Fox: "Be a stranger unto all. . . . forsake all, both young and old, and keep out of all"[48] (she also edited a selection from his works). Her account of his developing belief is remarkably close to the description in the central volumes of *Pilgrimage* of the young Miriam Henderson at the scientific and Fabian meetings she attended in London: "He went to hear the great preachers of the day in London and elsewhere, but found no light in them"; he refused to "be put off any longer with 'notions,' mere doctrines, derivative testimonies obscuring the immediate communication of life to the man himself" (pp. 6, 9). "The God of the Quakers," writes Richardson, is "no literary obsession coming to meet them along the pages of history, no traditional immensity" (p. 11). Compare this comment from Miriam (it is one of many similar comments): "It was history, literature, the way of stating records, stories, the whole method of statement of things from the beginning that was on a false foundation."[49]

This is the other meaning of *Deadlock* (deadlocked by false reason and tradition), against which Miriam offers — anticipating another famous theoretical moment — her own rereading of Descartes: "Descartes should have said, 'I am aware that there *is* something, therefore I am'" (p. 171). If this is individualism, it is also therefore a woman's refusal of that *cogito* in which so much recent theory has identified the worst of patriarchal self-knowing and law. Miriam's individualism thus takes the form of the woman's willing self-subordination (compare Kastein) — against the traditional immensities — to what one influential strand of feminist literary theory has come to describe as something *other*, something else.

It would be possible, therefore, to rewrite this division between Miriam and Shatov in aesthetic terms. In the penultimate volume of *Pilgrimage*, Miriam repeats her critique of Shatov: "The Russian in him believed it, knew, in spite of his Jewish philosophy, something of the unfathomable depths in each individual, unique and irreplaceable"; but "the Jew in him"

so far saw Amabel only as charmingly qualified to fulfil what he still regarded as the larger aspect, the only continuing aspect of himself, his destiny as part of his "race," the abstraction he and his like so strangely conceived as alive, immortal, sacred, and at the same time as consisting of dead and dying particles.[50]

Then she makes the link to the forms of language: "Are all the blind alleys and insufficiencies of masculine thought created by their way of thinking in propositions, using inapplicable metaphors. . . . Are all coherent words, in varying measure, evidence of failure?" (p. 427). Despite that reference to metaphor, it is propositional logic that is being criticized here — it is in fact the falsity of Shatov's statement, "The whole, Miriam, is greater than the parts," his view of race and nation as transcending individualism, that is at stake ("That had sounded unanswerable. But now I see the catch in the metaphor" [p. 427].)[51] Coherence, sequence, continuity, teleology — all these insignia of patriarchal language and culture, these aesthetic markers to which so much of modernist experimentation by women, although not only by women, comes as the response, are handed over to the Jewish conception of destiny. The fact that this is the case marks the limit, calls a halt, I would suggest, to any too-easy metaphoric or troped identification between forms of outsideness, between — in this case — woman and Jew.

But if Shatov is the voice of logic, he is not yet the written text. Later in the same chapter, Miriam will comment on his impatience with writing:

"Would Amabel succeed where she had failed, make him realise how prejudicial to his British career was his impatience with the written word?" (p. 429). His future, and that of the Jews, might be said to hang on whether he can transmute his spoken desire into writing, give to the history in which he hopes to participate the requisite forms of textual authority. And insofar as Miriam's whole journey in *Pilgrimage* is in some sense into writing, we might say that this is the point of the most powerful identification-differentiation between the woman — Miriam *and* Richardson — and the Jew.

At the very least, in the battles between them, it is not clear — not finally decided — who is right:

There was no one alive who could decide, in this strange difference, where lay right and wrong. Why should it be right to have no sense of nationality? Why should it be wrong to feel this as something whose violation would be a base betrayal? Much more than that. Something that could not be. Not merely difficult and sacrificial and yet possible. Simply impossible.[52]

*

In *The Origins of Totalitarianism*, Hannah Arendt describes total domination as the drive to "fabricate something that does not exist, namely, a kind of human species resembling other animal species whose only 'freedom' would consist in 'preserving the species.'"[53] For Arendt, such a vision is only possible in a society where species-being has already been degraded by being relegated to the domain of private labor, has already lost its link to public, civic participation and activity in the world. In *The Human Condition*, she wrote: "None of the higher capacities of man was any longer necessary to connect individual life with the life of the species; individual life became part of the life process, and to labor, to assure the continuity of one's own life and the life of the family was all that was needed."[54] (It is striking just how close this description comes to Beatrice Potter's reproach — lack of social participation, pure and private commitment to their descendants — against the East End Jews.)

In the recent article from which the last quotation is taken, Mary Dietz observes that feminism has its own particular relationship to the developments that Arendt describes. For if, on the one hand, women could be said to have carried the burden in the domestic sphere of that relegation of species-being to the world of private concerns, it is also the case that for one form of feminism it is exactly women's privileged connection to this human dimension which should now be revalorized or celebrated by women in turn. For this feminism, the public sphere — the world of civic participation — is irredeemably corrupt, and women take their political bearings and identity through the distance they strike from that world (the

world, among other things, of nationhood and state). For another feminism, however, that move is contaminated by the very identification—of
woman and species-being—on which it relies. Miriam's project, one might
say, shares this critique, and in doing so comes down on this side of feminist history.

What *Pilgrimage* demonstrates, however—as we watch Miriam moving
more and more into a form of spiritual self-containment—is the way this
second path can lead to the end of any form of active political being, of participation in public life. Rewriting the title of Elizabeth Young-Bruehl's biography of Hannah Arendt, we could say—as Arendt herself says—that
it requires the loss (not love) of the world.[55] Arendt can be—has been—
criticized for the specific form of civic life she returns to (what would such
forms of civic participation look like for women today?).[56] Yet *Pilgrimage*
could be said to show the price, the historic refusals—what has to be rejected for the woman, but not just for her—of relinquishing the domain of
public existence *even in the name* of feminist self-determination and freedom. To exist *otherwise*, free of all worldly entrapment, is to exist free of the
insignia of nations and cultures as they struggle for dialogue and differentiation, for cooperation and space. Exit is not neutral. It can be an inadver-
tent form of collusion with what is playing itself out on the other side. Perhaps, then, it is only in relation to other histories—Jewish history would
be one example—that feminism will find a way out of the disabling opposition between civic- and species-being, between public and private worlds.

CHAPTER NINE

"The Milk of Our Mother's Kindness Has Ceased to Flow": Virginia Woolf, Stevie Smith, and the Representation of the Jew

PHYLLIS LASSNER

Among the constantly shifting boundaries of canon formation, perhaps no other text so represents the intersection of gender, modernism, and anti-militarism as Virginia Woolf's *Three Guineas*. In its experiments with genre and form, it constructs a history and theory of fascism through a feminist pacifist polemic. Invoking the figure of Antigone as muse of women's war resistance, *Three Guineas* argues that the history of continuous conflict is evident in the ethos of the patriarchal family and state. Written at the moment World War II is about to begin, even its timing has revolutionary appeal. *Three Guineas* impugns myths of a united nation's victory over the external enemy by exposing as an internal danger England's failure to integrate women into its political economy. Woolf's method interrogates the very logic of a nation's polity as she calls for internal insurrection rather than debates on geopolitical solutions. In a shifting voice that reflects its decentering text, the narrator entreats, parodies, rages, and finally even challenges the oratory of her esteemed contemporary, Churchill. But instead of calling for self-sacrifice in a nation proud of its isolation, Woolf calls for a Society of Outsiders who disclaim the very idea of nationhood.

Three Guineas' self-reflexive, self-questioning form serves as a model by which to question Woolf's ideological assumptions as well as other texts by British women writing about World War II. Nowhere is this more paradigmatic than in her taxonomy of outsider/insurrectionists. "Fighting together" against the "monster Tyrant, Dictator" who "is making distinctions not merely between the sexes, but between the races" are women and Jews (pp. 102–3). In the late 1930s, this linkage is not gratuitous. Woolf's linkage of women and Jews as victims of fascist oppression forms a text that demands explication if we are to understand the consequences of her approach to the formation of fascism. As Jane Marcus has written, *"Three Guineas* was Virginia Woolf's attempt to articulate a unified intellectual position that would connect" the separate battles against the oppressive discourses and structures of "capitalism, imperialism, anti-feminism, and patriarchal culture," the sum of which Woolf constructs as the origins of fascism.[1] In turn, Woolf's text can be read as a critical method by which to examine the representation of Jews in novels of the 1930s and 1940s by British women writers. Adopting her own method of seeking correspondences, I will compare Woolf with the representation of the Jew, women, and fascism in texts also of the 1930s by Stevie Smith. Of different minds about the origins of fascism and the destiny of the Jew, they also inscribe different consequences for their rhetorical strategies.

Marcus explains the self-questioning method of *Three Guineas* as "a nonaggressive feminist/pacifist polemic of 'correspondence'. . . suggesting agreement and [a] harmonious . . . community formed by letter-writing . . . answerable to each other as well as to her" (p. 147). Taking Woolf at her word, one must assume that harmony is achieved only if she too is answerable, not only to her correspondents but to the precepts of her "anti-authoritative," non-aggressive intentions (p. 147). That Woolf took this warrant seriously is evidenced by her responses to those who wrote to her about *Three Guineas*.[2] As Brenda Silver shows, many readers were persuaded by Woolf's rhetoric and her extensive notes and quotations, and indeed, were inspired by Woolf's faith in the written word at a time when the Nazis were twisting words into lessons of hate.[3] Others criticized her denial that women can be militaristic or wish to be politically active. Lady Rhondda writes that she cannot join Woolf's Outsiders' Society if she is to activate her own antiwar views as editor of *Time and Tide* (Silver, p. 263). Complicating the issue of whether and how to take moral responsibility for war is such a desire to be involved; this could be at the personal level of "looking after people rather than [being] . . . looked after" or, as the pacifist Naomi Mitichison considered, one might engage in "revolutionary actions arising from 'intolerable situations' that one shares with one's 'fellow-beings'" (Silver, pp. 263, 264). Such an intolerable situation could be envisaged in the Nazi drive to power and Europe's defensive rearmament, events that made it impossible for other correspondents to "stand aside indifferently . . . when bombs are killing their families and destroying their homes" (Silver, p. 267).

Woolf responded to both compliments and criticisms in letters, in her reading notebooks and diaries, in her essay "Thoughts on Peace in an Air Raid," written to an American audience in 1940, and by implication, in her last, posthumously published novel, *Between the Acts*. Because *Three Guineas* is her response not only to the immediate events leading up to World War II but to what she saw as continuous male aggression, we can see all of her writing in the thirties as a plea to "attack Hitler in England" by responding to his "savage howl" with a call for "the emancipation of man."[4] "Thoughts on Peace in an Air Raid" asks women to reject the "desire to dominate and enslave" that produces "subconscious Hitlerism," just as the "talk of white feathers," she reminds Shena Simon on January 22, 1940, sharpened "the spur of the fighting cock" in World War I.[5] Woolf's images in these writings coincide with her method of dramatizing ideas in *Three Guineas* and thus invite us to see correspondences between its arguments and those figured in her other writing that confronts "the whole iniquity of dictatorship, whether in Oxford or Cambridge, in Whitehall or in Germany, in Italy or in Spain."[6] The symbolic weight of images that achieved political force in *A Room of One's Own* and would shape her fiction emerged in *Three Guineas* as a political rhetoric counterattacking not only the institutional fascism of the patriarchal family but the oratorical power of Mussolini and Hitler.

Part of Woolf's imagistic method is to counter the names of villains with those of victims. Naming Jews as victims of fascism establishes her knowledge not only of Jewish persecution in Nazi Germany but, since she is also critiquing Britain's home-grown fascism, of British antisemitism. In fact, Marcus tells us that Woolf "called herself a Jew," and Woolf herself records in her diaries and letters that she and her Jewish husband planned to commit suicide if the Nazis invaded, because they would both be arrested. However the Woolfs may have disagreed about the inherent roots of fascism, they certainly concurred about its consequences.[7]

In 1932 Woolf sketched a portrait of "The Great Jeweller," included in her list of "Caricatures," and later developed it into a short story, "The Duchess and the Jeweller." This is not a work that has received any critical attention, although Woolf herself felt "a moment of the old rapture" when copying the story (*Diary*, vol. 5, p. 107). Her "rapture" is clear testament to Woolf's creative drive, for she had to revise the story twice before it was published in *Harper's Bazaar* (London, April 1938; New York, May 1938). The revisions, however, were not her idea but were demanded by her New York agent "on grounds that it was 'a psychological study of a Jew' and thus, because of widespread racial prejudice in America, unacceptable to his (unnamed client)" (*Diary*, vol. 5, p. 107).

The jeweller in question, Oliver Bacon, has worked himself up from "sell[ing] stolen dogs on Sunday" in the alleyways of Whitechapel to become owner of a Mayfair shop famous from Germany to America (p. 249). Being "the richest jeweller in England," however, only marks him as socially vulnerable, for the presence of his most prestigious client, the Duchess of Lambourne, in "the dark little shop in the street off Bond Street" only calls attention to his inability to escape "the dark alley" he left behind (pp. 249, 250). Having decided, against his practical judgment, to save the Duchess from her gambling debts and buy her suspect pearls, he is defeated by her promise of a weekend at her country estate. He has been seduced by the vision of her daughter Diana into buying what turn out in the end to be fake pearls. In fact, the successful jeweller is cut down by the very symbols he attaches to the Duchess's prestige: "the swords and spears of Agincourt" which still aggressively defend Britain's imperial sovereignty (p. 253). In a web of ironies, the world of the Duchess, which is the guarantor of Oliver Bacon's success, remains intact because of his presence as hidden protector. Whenever he buys the Duchess's jewels, he underwrites the power that keeps her estate safe from the likes of him. At the end, the Duchess's duplicity joins forces with Bacon's self-delusion, and he is refigured once again as "a little boy in the alley" (p. 253).

The repetitions which produce the tale's comic ironies take on a different pallor if we examine the published text against the earlier drafts. To be sure, earlier markers of the jeweller's Jewish identity are removed. His original name, Theorodoric, then changed to Isidore Oliver, is, in the published version, ambiguous. Mispronunciations such as "pet" for "bet" are deleted as are references to "crowds of Jewesses."[8] Such changes, however, do not expunge the published story of earlier resonances, for as Susan Dick reports, "In revising the story for publication, VW removed all *direct* references to the fact that the jeweller is a Jew, along with *some* of the details associated with stereotypes of the Jew."[9] Those details and references that remain shape a different kind of irony when read in relation to those Woolf deleted. For example, the published portrait focuses on features that have stereotyped Jews throughout western literature, but in terms that call attention to that stereotype while denying its presence.[10] The narrator introduces us to Oliver Bacon by his "nose, which was long and flexible, like an elephant's trunk" and which

seemed to say by its curious quiver at the nostrils (but it seemed as if the whole nose quivered, not only the nostrils) that he was not satisfied yet; still smelt something under the ground a little further off. Imagine a giant hog in a pasture rich with truffles; after unearthing this truffle and that, still it smells a bigger, a blacker truffle under the ground further off. So Oliver snuffed always in the rich earth of Mayfair another truffle, a blacker, a bigger further off. (p. 249)

The very length and twists of this passage resemble the nose it describes, and thus represent Oliver Bacon as the feature most bound to concern

Woolf's New York publisher. In addition to their suggestiveness, the sheer number of words Woolf must use to recast the Jewish nose implicates her synecdoche in a suspicious gesture that both elides his Jewish identity and disparages it. While Bacon is a name for both Jews and non-Jews, and thus seemingly innocuous, its link to the hog's character — gluttonous and unclean — leads us on a regrettable course, especially as the place where Oliver learns his craft, the alleyways of East End Whitechapel, is known by Londoners to be a native habitat of the Jew. This is also true of the location of his first shop, Hatton Garden, which Joseph Bannister's 1907 work *England Under the Jews* calls a "London nosery."[11] To depict Oliver Bacon as having "dabbled his fingers in ropes of tripe" would seem to reinforce his surname as a sign of non-Jewish character, but since the Jewish identity is present for her English readers, albeit obscured from Americans, the image indicts the Jew nonetheless as desecrating his own tradition, particularly as the ropes of tripe suggest the ropes of pearls which the venal nature of "the hog" cannot resist. As it highlights itself, the repeated and extended imagery that shapes the jeweller's nose and character invokes the revision process, which only highlights the absent antecedents that had been found offensive.

Woolf's two-faced imagery of the jeweller is ironized even more acutely by that which shapes his career. The "wily astute little boy . . . sells stolen dogs on Sunday," an apprenticeship which Woolf creates as a parable of the jeweller's rise to the purlieus of Mayfair by landing him in a shop, not on Bond Street, but "off" (pp. 249, 250). Travestying the Christian sabbath condemns Oliver Bacon to a limbo he is made to deserve. That this is the pale of Jewish jewellers is shown by Margery Allingham's story of the thirties, "The Hat Trick," in which a socialite reports buying a curio "from old Wolfgarten in one of those cute little streets off Bond Street [who] gave me his solemn word by everything he feels to be holy that it's quite u-nique."[12] Based on this Jewish geography, it is no wonder that the Duchess brings her fake pearls to Bacon's establishment and not one appointed to do business with the king; she simply knows where to bring a shady deal. Oliver is neither a fence, like Fagin or Mr. Benjamin in Trollope's *The Eustace Diamonds*, or even a Mr. Carat in Maria Edgeworth's "The Good Aunt," who buys the aunt's jewels when she needs money but is exposed as a criminal. But as Anne A. Naman points out, these are models for "associating the figure of the Jewish jeweller with criminal deviations from that profession," which thus plays to the audience's acceptance of Jewish characteristics adding up to sleazy characters (p. 119).

These models become even more arresting when we see how much Oliver Bacon and the Duchess share with Trollope's Mr. Benjamin and Lizzie Eustace. Like the Victorian pair, who take advantage of each other's vulnerability and desire, the Duchess and the jeweller "were friends, yet enemies . . . ; each cheated the other, each needed the other, each feared the other, each felt this and knew this every time they touched hands" (p. 251). Although Woolf pities the jeweller for being taken in by his desire for the golden Diana and her world, and satirizes the Duchess as bloated with "prestige, arrogance, and pomp," clearly "the daughter of a hundred Earls" (p. 251) is less at risk at any time than is any Jew in 1938. Woolf accedes to the demand that she not "offend" readers by encoding her "psychological portrait of the Jew" in a dangerous game, one which pits the "wily" Jew against readers who, if they play by Woolf's rules, might share her triumphant last word.[13] For other readers, and this would include other correspondents to *Three Guineas*, such a rhetorical strategy questions Woolf's solidarity with those who are "shut out . . . because you are Jews" and therefore questions her call to fight "the tyranny of the Fascist state" and reject one's own "desire to dominate and enslave."[14]

I single out 1938 because it was the year of publication of "The Duchess and the Jeweller" and *Three Guineas* and coincides with Woolf's diary entries: "Jews persecuted, only just over the Channel" and "The Jews obsess [Leonard's mother]" (*Diary*, vol. 5, pp. 189, 191). Mrs. Woolf was not alone in her obsession, for her son too was "obsessed with" newspaper reports and photographs of "wholesale torture" and saw this persecution as part of a program of "liquidation of tens of thousands of persons, classified . . . for destruction."[15] Given the depth of his concern — although Virginia refers only to that of her mother-in-law — it is not farfetched to see Leonard figured in *Three Guineas* as one of the "outsiders" she would save.[16] He could also be one of the pamphlet's correspondents; his political activism aligns him with the man to whom *Three Guineas* responds and with those who wrote to her later.[17] As we have seen, although a number of these responses survive, Virginia's diary refers only vaguely to Leonard's doubts about *Three Guineas* (vol. 5, pp. 118, 126, 127, 133, 141).[18] We do not have his specific questions, but we can reasonably assume that although the Woolfs had agreed on international peace plans after World War I, by the 1930s, when Leonard was deeply anxious about the threat to Jews of a unique German fascism, his historically specific and pragmatic approach to geopolitics would be incompatible with Virginia's transhistorical, pancultural call to emancipate men's political consciousness.[19]

Such disagreement could have influenced Leonard's dislike of Virginia's 1936 novel, *The Years*, a reaction which made her feel not only "pessimistic, but . . . [that] these are disgusting, racking . . . days" (*Diary*, vol. 5, p. 22). Freema Gottlieb speculates that their differences could easily have centered on a passage which "savour[s] of the genteel antisemitism which afflicted Chamberlain's England in the years immediately preceding the Second World War" ("Leonard Woolf," p. 28). The passage begins with North reading a poem to Sara, which is interrupted by the sound of the Jew, Abrahamson, taking a bath. As ritualistic as the bath itself, North and Sara keep repeating the words "The Jew," and with no intervening thought, express their joint disgust at the "line of grease" and hair they picture the Jew leaving.[20] Their direct discourse affirms the view that Woolf represents her character's prejudices rather than her own, and that juxtaposing Sara as a "shabby scapegoat" to the "scapegoats" of *Three Guineas* not only presages the Holocaust, but "transform[s] their diaspora into a conspiracy for 'Justice and Liberty'" (Marcus, *VW*, p. 42).

Two lines of the poem North is reading (Marvell's "The Garden") are printed in the novel and serve as both context and gloss on the passage in question: "Society is all but rude — / To this delicious solitude. . . ." (*Years*, p. 365). If what North and Sara say about the Jew implicates them in the "rude" society of their "polluted" diaspora (p. 366), what of the narrator/author who has safely absented herself from the characters' direct discourse? North helps us to locate the narrative voice. He reflects that Sara's words refer to her poverty, but her "excitement . . . had created yet another person; another semblance, which one must solidify into one whole" (p. 368). Typical of Woolf's dialectic form, uniting disparate entities into a symbolic bond, the vision here joins the hunchback Sara and the Jew, just as *Three Guineas* joins women and Jews into a Society of Outsiders. Unfortunately, the critical distance which is at stake here collapses with this union, for the very history invoked by the novel's references to dates, the suffragist movement, and the two world wars, distinguishes between the plights of women and Jews as definitively as the novel relates their fates. As Zwerdling argues, because Woolf was so distraught over the coming war and the fragmentation of personal and political relations, she could no longer construct a vision of providential union. Instead, she engages in "antiromantic deflation, the deliberate juxtaposition of beautiful and sordid" in order to represent the "sinister implications . . . of a return from civilization to barbarism" (pp. 315, 306).

The last section of *The Years*, "Present Day," invokes a significant intersection on that "return" — the time when Woolf was writing *The Years* and when North and Sara share their revulsion at the Jew. This is a time, as we now know, when Woolf was aware that ambivalence toward Jews endangered them as never before, and yet she risks a moral ambiguity that is never clarified. Why, one must ask, are there no images other than that of the Jew to represent the "sordid"? Abiding by Woolf's own vision, the question remains: Where does she position herself as "outsider" when, on the one hand, there is no positive identification with that other outsider, the Jew, and no narrative distance from the "sinister implications" of his portrait?

That Virginia Woolf was capable of "genteel antisemitism" has been well documented. Looking back at her feelings about marrying Leonard, she wrote to Ethel Smyth: "How I hated marrying a Jew . . . how I hated their nasal voices & their oriental jewellry and their noses and their wattles" (Aug. 20, 1930).[21] She added, however, "What a snob I was: for they have immense vitality and I think I like that quality best of all." Allowing for Woolf's personal ambivalence, the question remains one of literary representation and its impact on readers, especially those concerned with her moral and political vision. How do we explain her failure to unify the one vision she never abandoned — that between her art and politics — in short, her failure to integrate her avowed sympathy for the plight of oppressed Jews with her representation of them? The answer lies, I believe, in Woolf's constructions of history, which, while uniquely her own, invest as well in tenets of a modernist aesthetic. If *The Years* is filled with historic moments and mimesis, it is also, as Jane Marcus shows, infused with "mythical motif," allusive of Sophocles' *Antigone*, Wagner's *Ring of the Nibelung*, and Jane Harrison's studies of matriarchal myth (*Languages*, pp. 36–37). Working "as Gotterdammerung," the novel interprets history as apocalypse, and becomes a chronicle of purgation and regeneration (p. 57).

Nowhere is the effect of this mythic history more apparent than in the scene in question where the graphic particulars of plumbing mock a mythic figure — the Jew — Abrahamson, the father and son of Jewish history and myth. In the "sordid" history of how two characters in England between the wars perceive the Jew, the modernist moment fails to distinguish between "genteel anti-semitism," Nazi racial policy, the plight of an impoverished and handicapped woman, and that of a Jew in 1936. The combination of mythic drama and political novel allows elements of each to bleed into the other so that the pungent critique of patriarchal fascism elides the difference between the disenfranchisement of the daughters of educated men and the Jew endangered by a historic moment. This is a moment that may be continuous with earlier persecutions, but within the scope of Woolf's voracious newspaper reading and historical imagination could be recognized as unique.[22]

Woolf's last novel, *Between the Acts*, written when war had already broken out, combines a sense of history as both continuous and riddled with crisis, the effect of which is a confrontation and denial of history.[23] As enacted by the pageant, the characters' dialogue and reflections, and the imagery, history in this novel points to 1939 as a juncture in the continuum of English time from its primordial roots through cultural efflorescence and barbaric regressions. That 1939 marks a downward trend is evinced by a moment of startling violence, when Giles Oliver stomps to death a snake in the throes of strangling on a toad it cannot swallow. All too similar to a stormtrooper, Giles epitomizes the masculine aggression that Woolf felt was responsible for the return to war. Zwerdling argues convincingly that "Giles's behavior is . . . very close to the Fascist threat he fears . . . a good indigenous example of the ethos Woolf had seen in the first days of Italian Fascism" (p. 308). But Giles is unexceptional in the history of England, for the seemingly idyllic village that spawned him suffers from disharmony and xenophobia, as attested to by Miss La Trobe and the Manresas. If Miss La Trobe suffers the indifference of her audience, and Mrs. Manresa is derided as vulgar energy, it is the absent Ralph Manresa who is made to suffer from the text's own ironies. Represented as the construction of village gossip, Ralph is only known as "a Jew, got up to look the very spit and image of the landed gentry, supplied from directing City companies — that was certain — tons of money" (*Between the Acts*, p. 40).

The alien Jew in this novel is the creation of a home-grown fascism which in its anonymous indirect voice is distinct from that of the author and narrator. The quintessential outsider, he is represented only by his garish car and wife, figured, therefore, as an absence, not only from the ancestral country home and the pageant, but from the saga of English history. The Jew's absence and the images which paradoxically mark his presence dramatize the novel's theory of that history as disjunctive; indeed, it is consistent with mocking the Olivers for being two-hundred-year-old newcomers to Pointz Hall, or oppressive, as in Isa Oliver's constrained life. Unlike the Olivers, however, who are pictured at the end of the novel as integrated into the ebb and flow of their national and personal histories, the Jew's position in the novel remains disjunctive and oppressive. Even more extreme than his position in English history, Woolf's novel acknowledges the Jew's rescue as necessary but can't tolerate his difference. The villagers express sympathy: "And what about the Jews? The refugees . . . People like ourselves, beginning life again" (p. 121). Woolf herself showed such sympathy when she sold her *Three Guineas* manuscript to help refugees, but she cannot tolerate the Jew's presence in her fiction of English history.

At the very moment when history was taking a radical turn, Woolf's representation of the Jew is justified by her views of historical process. The title, *Between the Acts*, evokes the two world wars, suggesting that history is both successive and regressive, and that intervals dramatize the conflicts in personal and social relations that make war continuous. Historical time marks continuous sequences of conflict that repeat themselves, because the belief in change is more expedient than recognizing the return of repressed violence. As Rachel Bowlby shows, *Between the Acts* undoes "any stable conception of time on which to peg a conception of history or historical change" because it challenges "the distinction between serial time and repetitive time."[24] Because serial time is a masculine construct that denies the repetition of man-made violence, it takes the woman writer, as Judith Johnston asserts, to end such repetition, to create the possibility for historical change "even with only the end of an old inky pen" (p. 274).

As Woolf's historical critiques show, change from violence to peace is possible only if authoritarian impulses are recognized as destructive. Reading Freud in 1939 confirmed her belief in "subconscious Hitlerism" but also prompted her revisionary idea that "though many instincts are held more or less in common by both sexes, to fight has always been the man's habit, not the woman's" (*Three Guineas*, p. 6). Woolf committed her writing to the political act of exposing the more insidious aggression sanctioned by social structures. But as Freud also argued, unresolved ambivalence only activates aggression, and this is a dynamic embedded in images of those oppressed people Woolf would save from such hostility. Woolf's construction of gender and unconscious aggression are connected by one of *Three Guineas'* correspondents, Vita Sackville-West: "Is it not true that many women are extremely bellicose and urge their men to fight? . . . I am entirely in agreement with you that they ought not to be like that, but the fact remains that they frequently are."[25]

Woolf's failure to recognize her ambivalence toward her fellow outsiders is made possible by her visionary historical "farsightedness that thought in centuries rather than in decades" (Johnston, p. 260) and across culture and nations.[26] Just as she sees World War II growing out of the chaos of World War I and their "similarities" greater than their differences (Zwerdling, p. 288), so she identifies fascism in English patriarchy as indistinct from German and Italian. That Woolf viewed the Second World War as both coterminous with the last and yet apocalyptic in its own right destroyed her belief in a struggle for change. With boundaries between past and present and war and peace dissolving, there can be no action, including writing, that will turn civilization away from its death instinct. Her conclusion agreed with Freud, as she recorded in her diary on December 9, 1939: "If we're all instinct, the unconscious, whats all this about civilisation, the whole man, freedom &c?" (vol. 5, p. 250).[27] This transhistorical, pancultural view collapses distinct events into an epic battle with the barbarians within and at the gates, and disrupts belief in "individuality and the words and names used to protect this identity."[28]

Woolf's historic vision is challenged by her own creative process. In the second draft of "The Duchess and the Jeweller," the jeweller's name, Isidore Oliver, marks him as Jewish. Like his compatriot, Ralph Manresa, he disappears but is then resurrected as other outsiders: he becomes Oliver Bacon, oppressed by a narrator in league with social prejudice, and supported only when he becomes a gentile woman — Isa Oliver — whose oppression can now be blamed on patriarchal fascism. If Woolf does not distinguish between English patriarchy and the fascism of Hitler and Mussolini, neither does she distinguish her own rhetoric of sympathy for the Jews from her stereotypical portraits and omissions. Woolf's recognition of the political consequences of unconscious aggression is the reality test by which we can view her ambivalent images of Jews and their disturbing presence in her construction of a mythic history and pessimism about change.

In the same years Woolf was writing *Three Guineas*, other British women writers were self-consciously confronting British antisemitism as a phenomenon deeply entrenched in British culture but distinguished from other political injustices for its particular dangers in the 1930s. One writer who serves as a respondent to Woolf is the poet Stevie Smith, who wrote *Novel on Yellow Paper* in 1936 and *Over the Frontier* in 1938. Smith's experimental forms and narrative voice construct an inquiry into war and oppression that questions the political implications of Woolf's vision of history. Smith's narrator confronts both herself and her readers with an ambivalence toward Jews that impugns the viability of a "Society of Outsiders" at a time when a form of fascism had emerged under a particular "tyrant/dictator" whose racial politics were unique in their enforcement. Read together, Woolf's polemics and images of Jews and Smith's novels provide a critique of women's construction of their own roles in a total war on the outsider.

In two volumes of unmediated, monologic discourse, Smith's female hero, Pompey Casmilus, conducts an inquiry into the role of individual and collective consciousness in the history of war and aggression. With great glee, she indicts Britain's imperial past, as the perpetrator of violence in both its acts and rhetoric, but confronts personal political consciousness as having a formative role in the collective.[29] Historical event is represented in personal reflection which, because it is driven by unresolved ambivalence, emerges as hostile speech that colludes with a masculinist war machine. In 1938, the year *Over the Frontier* is published, the aggressive impulses that were seething in the first volume materialize in a midnight ride over the frontier of reality and fantasy, enacting a "racial hatred that is running in me in a sudden swift current, in a swift tide of hatred" (p. 159). But Pompey does not ride alone, for although her lover, Major Tom Satterthwaite, is too sick to accompany her, she makes sure that we do, for in her direct discourse she not only shares her words with us, she implicates us in them. Unlike Woolf's construction of harmonious correspondents, Smith challenges her readers to react against her and thus discover their own politics.

Like Virginia Woolf, Smith preferred writing as her act of political protest, and also experimented with forms that would question intersections of realism and representation. Instead of reifying mythological structures to envision historical process, however, Smith deploys them to expose their dangers to political discourse. Thus even Pompey Casmilus's name ironizes her political consciousness. The men for whom she is named signify a historical continuum of aggression that infuses her identity and consciousness by inscribing her into the myths that justify violence and war. The war god and the general whose patronymics she bears and whose violence she inherits are the icons of myths that give us power over the "dreams that come to us in the night that are full of cruelty" (p. 56). As Pompey's name and the novel imply, art and myth are implicated in both power and cruelty, because their persuasive force often serves ambiguous representations of power and cruelty. The only plot these novels can claim is the unraveling of Pompey's ambivalences as a critical exegesis of art's collusion with myths of power. Her zany, whirlwind associations, readings of history, painting, and myth, decenter the power of coherent explanation by revealing how it occludes distinctions between self-determination and the oppression of others. The result, she shows, is how easily art and myth are appropriated to justify violence and war. Pompey's "januslike-double-faced" feelings toward "Jewfriends" represent that occlusion in order to show how oppression of the other inheres dangerously in self-determination (*Yellow Paper*, p. 13).

Over the Frontier begins with Pompey's ironic self-reflections on Georg Grosz's painting of a horse and rider, "Haute Ecole." She analyzes not only her reactions to the painting but her associations with its historical and political contexts. It thus becomes impossible for her to appreciate the "passion and integrity" of the "ferocious and captive animal" without considering the artist's and viewer's complicity in the enigmatic quality of "his degenerate rider" (pp. 16, 11, 15). As Pompey veers through Grosz's career and life, her reading of "Haute Ecole" is clarified by its relation to his "cynical and malicious" satires, his portfolio of "war suffering," her associations with "the tearing seering suffering of Germany after the war," Grosz's "escape to America," and her own escape into art from "the shame and dishonor the power of the cruelty" that stretches "to the very last outposts of the black heart of despair" (pp. 12, 14, 15, 16). The allusion to Conrad's *Heart of Darkness* invokes not a male bastion of brutality, but Pompey's questioning "of the heart feminine," which, because it is just as "numb and ripe for death," can mobilize the cruel messages of art and myth as her ride over the frontier testifies (pp. 17, 18).

Pompey's ride into war's theater of cruelty begins in *Novel on Yellow Paper*, when she confronts her "mixed feelings towards the Jews" (Spalding, p. 18). Indulging her self-pity at being "the only goy" at a party hosted by Jewish friends, she discovers a miracle cure by identifying with the aggression of her namesakes (*Yellow Paper*, p. 11). She can be "shot right up" by deciding that "a clever goy is cleverer than a clever Jew" (p. 11). This is the power that she would later realize is part of the "cruelty [that] is very much in the air now, it is very dangerous, it is a powerful drug that deadens as it stimulates" (*Frontier*, p. 56). In 1936 and 1938 Stevie Smith interrogates myths of Anglo-Saxon moral hegemony by implicating a woman's voice in the rhetoric of the enemy's racial politics. Oppressed as much by the self-containment of her Jewish friends as she is by identifying with their oppression, she assumes an ambiguous position of addressing and expressing the social and political constructions of antisemitism:

Do all goys among Jews get that way? Yes, perhaps. And the feeling you must pipe down and apologize for being so superior and clever: I can't help it really my dear chap, you see I'm a goy. It just comes with the birth. It's a world of unequal chances, not the way B. Franklin saw things. But perhaps he was piping down in public, and apologizing he was a goy. And there were Jews then too. So he put equality on paper and hoped it would do, and hoped nobody would take it seriously. And nobody did. (*Yellow Paper*, p. 11)

Given Pompey's self-parodying voice, we could easily add: and neither does she, were it not for the fact that this passage represents the start of her journey to "the other side of the dividing line of pain in art" and between "the awful aloofness of the artist" and her cooptation into feeling morally superior (*Frontier*, pp. 67, 61). Never letting either us or herself off the hook, Pompey warns: "For you see I will not let you escape the issue, nor myself either" (p. 67).[30]

Pompey's journey takes her through a history of personal vulnerability that is transmuted into imperial aggression. The change occurs when she denies that her insecurity leads to defensiveness that in turn must find a scapegoat to feel safe. That Stevie Smith should choose the figure of the Jew and antisemitism as her test case in 1936 and 1938 testifies to her recognition of "the full danger in [Pompey's] pride at being a goy, for it is 'as if that thought alone might swell the mass of cruelty working up against them [the Jews]'" (Spalding, p. 120). So vulnerable herself, Pompey situates her ambivalence toward the Jew in social and historical contexts that expose the precariousness of both representing and identifying with the Jew. Unlike Woolf's Jewish jeweller, who despite revision is nonetheless indelibly branded with the dirt of his search for gold, Smith's Jewish entrepreneur is saved by Pompey's uncensored "play" with "Mr. Freud['s]" idea that "Gold is Dirt," allowing her to see that

hostility burns from empire blue eyes to the dark eyes of Israel, lord of the hidden river. And in each separate mind the significance of gold is a separate thing . . . in the mind of Empire-Blue-eyes, the significance of gold is fury and pride and a great beacon of light and power. Blue-eyes looks like he would lay a trail of bullets around the Board Room table. . . . And in the eyes of Israel what is the significance of Gold? Unity, flexibility, secrecy, control. Israel has lapped round that course already so many times, so many, many times, and his eyelids are a little weary. O.K. Israel, keep it under your hat. (*Frontier*, pp. 84–85)

Pompey has no access to the power of "Board Room tables," but her position as narrator privileges the voice of the vulnerable woman as sharing and shaping the forces of oppression, which in turn shape the representation of the Jew. Her position as participant-observer in the history of British imperialism is thus one of both power and powerlessness, but never one of absence or passivity, a status that is particularly important because all other voices in the novels are filtered through Pompey's. It is by dint of her position as audience that we can assess Pompey's relation to her "Jew-friend," Igor Torfeldt, whose "so-racial bonework of the face, and the blond blond hair and blue-grey eyes" make Pompey think Jews "look so patient, so souffrant, so sicklied o'er, bleached, albinoed and depigmented, by What of the Sorrows of Werther by the Dark Tarn of Auber, With-Psyche-his-soul-and-nobody-to-hold-his-paddy-paw" (*Frontier*, p. 72). The Jew "bleached" of his otherness is no better off, however, than Pompey's other Jew-friend, "very essentially civilized, urbane and international . . . old Jew Aaronsen," who also performs for her, not only on the piano but on the international stock market (*Frontier*, p. 197). As consumer of the Jews' gifts, Pompey is no innocent bystander, but implicates herself in myths that construct the Jew's character as originating not only in that of *"Our Lord,"* but in that of crucifier, both victim and villain, always responsible for his own vilification (p. 73).

The myths that construct the Jew as timeless Other are historicized by Pompey's representation of Igor's audience. She mimics those onlookers who praise the blond Igor as the Aryan "saviour . . . among the best type of young Jew, the aristocracy of Israel" (p. 73). Her next move, however, reveals the danger embedded in this praise, for she connects this revision of the Other to her nation writ large—Britain, the colonizing empire, and Britain's historic similarity to Germany, the supremacist, colonizing enemy (p. 73). In the face of the coming war, Pompey reviews the propaganda and jingoism that have historically justified Britain's imperial infamies through its rhetoric of pragmatism and restraint.[31] But it takes her reading of a German military memoir to provide the perspective from which Pompey can be critical of her own complicity with her nation's rhetoric and its construction of the Other. Pompey's reading is infused with satiric glosses that debunk myths of "our so darling pet Lion of these British Isles" by mocking Germany's admiration for Britain's "ethical imperialism" (pp. 104, 101). The joke is on both nations, for Britain's succès d'estime is based on convincing itself and her admiring enemy of an untroubled correspondence between its rhetoric of "justice and freedom" and its colonizing much of "the earth under its sway" (p. 102). But just as Pompey must join the ranks of the genteel antisemites in order to authenticate her mockery of them, so she must become a warrior in order to gain the authority of her anti-imperialist gloss.

Pompey's journey into "a heart of darkness" takes her through England's ignoble past and Germany's threatening future to argue on the basis of their similarities that her vision of history will locate their differences in her responses to war and the Jews (p. 48). War breaks out for Pompey at British headquarters in a German schloss, where her holiday becomes a nightmare flight into espionage, death, and imprisonment. Embedding a British spy maneuver into the German landscape erases and yet imprints boundaries between offensive and defensive, allies and foes, male militarism and female pacifism. In uniform and on horseback, Pompey is transformed into Georg Grosz's military icon, and once she discovers her "secret heart of pride and ambition, of tears and anger," she assumes the character of crucifier, of Grosz's "degenerate rider" (pp. 221, 11). Calling herself "Pompey *der* Grosse," she defends herself by shooting the "rat face" monster who reflects the "cruelty" she has seen on faces in all the places she values as civilized, including her own (pp. 228–29, 252). Cruelty, she discovers, is a function of civilization itself, whether defined as the British lion or as one's friends, because by nature of its collective self-interest, civilization is exclusionary and constructs the outsider as antipathetic.

When Pompey is finally challenged by another voice, it is to clarify the origins and impact of her "sensitive conscience," whether it has been constructed by her own narrative or as the object of patriarchal military history (p. 158). Both her lover and her military commander ask her, "On whose side are you?" and then press her even further when she chooses her friends: "And the Jews?" (pp. 158–59). Still choosing friends, she sacrifices the antipathetic Other to the very history in which she colludes as writer and as actor. As a result, she confirms art's conspiracy with myths of power; and until she realizes that her uniform is no outer garment, but rather an expression of "the racial hatred that is running in me," she remains a prisoner of war (p. 159). The running narratives of Pompey's personal and political monologue reach their final destination at the intersection of her perspective and ours. She sees herself reflected in the German Prince Von's celebration of British imperial history, but we can see her two volumes as a process of self-questioning that is very different from the prince's mythic construction of her homeland.

Out of that interrogation emerges a vision of history that is concurrent with modernism and with fascism but that identifies the historic moment as riven with a unique fascistic danger.[32] Going over the frontier for Stevie Smith explodes boundaries between offensive and defensive cruelty and universalizes guilt for war's violence, but it also constructs differences that become Pompey's saving grace. Whatever surreality Pompey's fantasy of war assumes, through her meditations and reflections, war's events are transformed from mythic representation to an analysis of culture. This analysis takes English history out of Prince Von's hands and subjects it to a kind of scrutiny that celebrates a different kind of Englishness. As one myth after another is demolished by Pompey's fantasied experience, it is replaced by the developing sense that:

In England there is no national ideology . . . to be carried through, to be expressed in a word and impressed upon a people, as in Germany it is expressed and impressed, with what of an original pure intention we cannot know, with what of a calamity in event we know too well. (pp. 258–59)

Smith's prophecy of that calamitous event, a second world war, disrupts pancultural views of fascism, distinguishes past from present, and her voice from that of Woolf's. She imagines historic process as a debate which is knowledge-bearing in its confrontation not only with herself and her correspondents but with the consequences of discovering differences between a self-questioning rhetoric and that which is already persuaded of its truth. Through her relentless questioning, Pompey Casmilus represents the possibility for historical change and for freeing the representation of the Jew from the historical dangers of ambivalence.

CHAPTER TEN

The Protection of Masculinity: Jews as Projective Pawns in the Texts of William Gerhardi and George Orwell

ANDREA FREUD LOEWENSTEIN

In *Difference and Pathology* Sander Gilman names the need for control or power as perhaps the most important motivation behind the formation of the stereotypical systems which arise around the idea of difference.[1] In the society in which George Orwell and William Gerhardi lived and wrote, power was located, as indeed it is today, in the middle- and upper-class construct of masculinity. Especially for middle- and upper-class boys, this construct was associated with the institution of the public school, where it had long been encoded as "Muscular Christianity." Its embodiment was a strong, healthy, and courageous public-school boy, an athlete who, though no fool, preferred games to books; a patriot whose lack of guile and inability to express himself in words concealed an overweening loyalty for his country, his school and "house," and his male chums. During boyhood the muscular Christian remained healthily asexual, but his identity was strictly heterosexual, and upon coming of age he married and produced sons. These qualities, which appear over and over again in schoolboy literature of the time, stood in direct opposition to those qualities generally encoded in this society as feminine, and in equal opposition to those ascribed to male Jews.[2]

It is not surprising that many bookish boys, including Orwell and Gerhardi, found this ideal a difficult one to live up to. As George Orwell put it in his powerful condemnation of the public school system, "Such, Such Were the Joys":

By the social standards that prevailed about me, I was no good, and could not be any good. But all the different kinds of virtues seemed to be mysteriously interconnected and to belong to much the same people. It was not only money that mattered: there were also strength, beauty, charm, athleticism, and something called "guts" or "Character" which really meant the power to impose your will on others.[3]

This perceived failure haunted Orwell's life and permanently damaged his sense of self-respect, just as it haunted the lives of Gerhardi and countless other middle- and upper-class British men.

It also permanently marred their ability to relate to women. In her psychoanalytic classic of 1932, "The Dread of Women," Karen Horney describes the process in which the young boy's longing to be a woman, originating in his primary identification with the mother, is challenged in a way that creates a terrible "menace to his self respect" and traumatizes him in all future relations with women.[4] His primary task at puberty is, accordingly, "not merely to free himself from his incestuous attachment to his mother, but more generally, to master his dread of the whole female sex" (p. 355). Nancy Chodorow, citing Margaret Mead, comments that in societies in which females are the primary caretakers for the young, and in which gender roles are fiercely enforced for boys, the practice of harsh male initiation ceremonies, whose purpose is to exorcise the female role or to "brainwash the primary feminine identity and to establish firmly the secondary male identity," are common.[5] The punishment for transgressing these roles is severe, and boys are often left with fear and hostility toward women.

The combination of longing for and dread of the powerful female recurs in the literature by public-school men and would-be public-school men of this time.[6] It is expressed in images of large women who threaten to physically or symbolically squash or obliterate smaller, weaker men; in the image of men who are actually transformed into females; in a loathing of and need to punish the "female" or weaker, more vulnerable self, and in a compulsive longing for women, both as nurturers and as objects upon whom to act out masochistic or sadistic sexual fantasies.

The Jewish character, in particular the male Jew, offered the male gentile author a less complicated and less conflictual web of signs and referents upon which to inscribe his fear and loathing of the female. Historical and cultural circumstances placed the Jew in an ideal situation for this purpose. As a symbolic entity he was, and still is, ingrained in the consciousness of most even semiliterate English people by his continuing representation in everyday texts, from pre-Chaucerian ballads to present-day radio jokes.[7] As a relatively small but visible presence in England between the two wars, and one whose differences could generally be called upon in humorous or disapproving common references, he was reassuring and ever available.[8]

In her important book on George Orwell, Daphne Patai refers to Allen Greenberger's study of the image of Indians in British literature. Greenberger describes "a whole series of characteristics . . . attributed to Indians, all of which stress their similarity to children and women as traditionally perceived: lacking in self-discipline, governed by emotion rather than reason, untrustworthy, senselessly cruel, tending toward hysteria." Patai concludes that "British servants of the empire did not need to acquire a new ethical code in order to step into the role of domination; such an ethic was already available to them in their ideas about masculinity. They merely extended it to a different object, a new kind of 'woman'" (p. 925).

In a direct parallel, the Jewish character's long-established characteristics are in many aspects identical to those of the Indian — and the female. In addition to cruelty, childishness, and hysteria these characteristics include cowardice; miserliness and avariciousness; a bestial sexual voraciousness or its converse, sexual impotence; uncleanliness; secrecy and guile; hypocrisy and dishonesty; vulgarity; a sharp cleverness that differs from true intelligence; and a fawning masochism.[9]

For the middle-class gentile men who attended British public schools in the 1930s and 1940s, Jews were men like themselves and yet unlike. On the border of femininity, objects both of physical distaste and fascination, Jewish characters provided (and, I believe, still provide) a slate on which these authors were able to inscribe their gender anxiety, as well as the sado-masochistic patterns which they used to express their conflicted feelings for women.

In *Autonomy and Rigid Character* the clinician David Shapiro describes rigid individuals, usually male, who are able to visualize or experience only relationships "between superior and inferior — the degradation or humiliation of one by another, the imposing of will by one, the surrender of the other."[10] Shapiro reasons that for such a man, the erotic is located not in his own feelings (these are inaccessible) nor in mutual engagement, but rather in the degradation of the other: "Such persons — who, for certain rigid men, may include women in general, and even more, 'effeminate' men — embody what the rigid individual is ashamed of, defensively repudiates, and therefore hates. [His] contemptuous punishment of weakness or inferiority . . . is what we call Sadism."[11]

William Gerhardi and George Orwell (as well as Wyndham Lewis, Graham Greene, Charles Williams, and other male authors of this period) encoded their textual sado-masochism through a number of textual stratagems. The male self could be inscribed in the role of a helpless victim in the grasp of the all-powerful woman or Jew, a role reversal that corresponded to the man's own interior experience, and that textually justified subsequent sadism against the woman or Jew. Alternatively, the male self was overtly textualized as the more dominating and powerful, and the woman or Jew as the victim, while a subtext portrayed the female or Jew as a potentially dangerous, even lethal force, biding his or her time to attack. Such a scenario, as well as encompassing both the overt and the inner reality, allowed the male to protect himself by (to use the highly appropriate language of modern male warfare) engaging in a preemptive strike.

Sadism is most commonly associated with the male role, while masochism is traditionally attributed to both women and Jews. This encoding, too, is a convenient one: it is arguably more justifiable to oppress or victimize those who "ask for it." When such desire is not verbalized, it can easily be produced through the process of projection. Robert Stoller, describing the views of a relatively liberated man of his time, Sigmund Freud, concluded that Freud held women to be innately masochistic.[12]

For both George Orwell and William Gerhardi, a kind of sexual sadomasochistic play in which the roles of victim and victimizer were often reversed or obfuscated served as an important textual device in each man's struggle to protect his threatened masculinity.

William Gerhardi: The Masochist Strikes Back

William Gerhardi may be best known today for his virulent reaction against Virginia Woolf, whom he decried as a "bloodless, fuckless anaemic . . . oh, the bitch!"[13] Gerhardi, who was desperately poor for most of his life, attempted, with the assistance of the noted antisemitic newspaper magnate Lord Beaverbrook, to promote himself as a misogynist and compulsive womanizer. His autobiography, *Memoirs of a Polyglot,* written in 1931 when Gerhardi was thirty-six years old, is in part an attempt to promote this image.[14] Gerhardi's sympathetic biographer, Dido Davies, notes the parodic elements of this text but concludes that Gerhardi's flaunted misogyny is more than a pose: "His published views on women . . . are the result of a complicated personal prejudice: his utterances clearly waver between affectation and phobia" (Davies, p. 207).

William Gerhardi was not a particularly successful little boy as measured by the standards of muscular Christianity. The child of manufacturers who retained a kind of frozen upper-middle-class English identity despite having lived in Russia for two generations, young William grew up with an idealized vision of the British public school and a feeling of belonging nowhere. His father, an unpredictable and meticulous man, possessed "an almost insane irritability" (*Memoirs*, p. 47) which he often turned upon the delicate, dreamy second son in whom he saw only "effeminate ineptitude" (Davies, p. 13). Gerhardi later blamed "a certain nervousness of disposition" on his early fear of the harsh father who despised him and called him womanish (*Memoirs*, p. 72). He recalled stifling sobs in his pillow when his older brother informed him that both parents regarded him as "the fool of the family," a title he would use again and again in his writing.

In his memoirs, Gerhardi describes his dependence on his much-loved governess, Liebe, and recalls an unsettling occasion in which Liebe was out and a maid came to kiss him goodnight instead, and he held up a piece of glass between his lips and hers, eager for the kiss but anxious about infection. The fear of infection by despised women, coupled with a compulsive need for their attentions, would attend Gerhardi throughout his life and would emerge as a major theme in his fiction.

Gerhardi's father preferred his elder brother, offering him the opportunity William yearned for — to attend an English public school. Later, his father similarly thwarted his younger son's desire to attend Oxford, pointedly sending him to a largely female secretarial college instead. When "the call to manhood became more urgent, the secretarial college more dreary," Gerhardi enlisted in the English army in 1915 (*Memoirs*, p. 84). He served his time safely in the north of England, but as Davies points out, "to one by now obsessively hygienic, the infrequent bathing, stinking urinals, filthy and exhausting fatigue duties, and the constant proximity of sweating bodies were a source of torment" (Davies, p. 48). Years later, Gerhardi's fellow officers remembered both his obsessive need to conquer women and his strange preoccupation with hygiene. After the army, Gerhardi did attend Oxford, but it was too late — he was crushed to find himself regarded as a strange outsider with a foreign accent.

Gerhardi's most sustaining relationship was with his mother, Clara, whom he describes in the autobiography in a particularly narcissistic manner: "Her eyes like glass reflected(ed) my own image" (Davies, p. 173). He shared every thought and hope with her and wrote to her that he hoped to die at the same moment she did. Clara Gerhardi died when her son was fifty-three, and he lapsed into a state of despair, never fully entering society again. Women other than his mother, with the exception of certain devoted servants, inevitably demanded too much. As if rebutting his father's mocking voice, he repeatedly argues in his texts that male impotence is the woman's fault, not a proof of the man's lack of masculinity: "For physiological reasons, a man's impotence to satisfy the passion of a woman who loves him, but whose body does not excite him is not . . . a proof of his emasculation. . . . she reproaches him with a temporary disability due only to herself" (*Memoirs*, p. 303).

Like Wyndham Lewis, who boasted of his venereal infections, Gerhardi frantically reported his visits to prostitutes, conquests of women he had "overtaken" in the street, and affairs with his servants, secretaries, and other people's wives.[15] His need for sex was far "beyond the capacity of a single woman to satisfy" (*Memoirs*, p. 355), and he regarded women as a commodity whose obligation was to "help the few of us afflicted with genius to bear our cross with good grace . . . through sympathy, understanding and the stanching of male hunger" (p. 330). Like Wyndham Lewis, he believed in the segregation of women, and he suggested that in wartime they should be kept "in a sort of recreation and refreshment ground for the soldiery" (p. 153).

Although Gerhardi often appeared masochistically to relish his own experience of himself as a helpless victim of powerful and sexually aggressive women, he repeatedly inveighed against such women, repeating "no more is demanded (than) that she submit herself passively to a will not her own" (p. 330). He protests: "I don't know what women want. All I want is not to give them any money. Not to take them out. Not to buy them anything. To have them at my beck and call and not to bother me when I do not require them." [16]

In his metaphors, women are fierce animals savaging soft and innocent males: "When from time to time, I take up my pen to suggest in the Press that women have no position to speak of in literature, female writers spring out at me like hyenas and tear me with their claws" (*Memoirs*, p. 346).

In later life, increasingly obsessed with infection, Gerhardi became a recluse, remaining in his flat. His sister noticed that "he grew agitated at the thought that she might have wiped her hands on his towel" (Davies, p. 199). He became especially upset at the thought that anyone might use his lavatory, and sent for a specially designed set of discardable lavatory covers. Gerhardi was also notorious for beating women with dog whips, a predilection in which he resembled Charles Williams, who desperately needed women, while at the same time finding them to be teeming with evil and repulsive female carnality. Through an elaborate system of quasi-religious ritual, including ceremonies in which he "punished" women by beating them, Williams, like Gerhardi, managed to control his panic. Gerhardi was especially drawn to Jewish women, who figure prominently in the memoir and in his fiction, and whom he identifies as particularly dirty and infectious, labeling them as prostitutes, and male Jews as pimps. He also regarded male Jews as particularly responsible for his lack of financial success: it was the Jews who had taken what was rightfully his.

When Wyndham Lewis's beloved mother died, he married a young, working-class woman whom he despised and kept in virtual purdah, and who treated him as her child and looked after all his physical needs. Gerhardi, who never married, was lucky enough to find two women, a secretary and a maid, who similarly serviced him. Patsy Rosenstehl, his secretary, soothed and admired him, addressed him as a "genius," and typed his work and took dictation. Francis Campion, the maid, took care of meals and housekeeping. It was only when Patsy left him for better employment during the war and Francis became terminally ill that Gerhardi himself completely withdrew into invalidity and ceased writing.

*

William Gerhardi's fiction, like that of Wyndham Lewis and Charles Williams, contains no characters who assume any sort of verisimilitude.[17] In Gerhardi's fiction, as in his memoir, the prevailing tone is a wry, at times cloying self-consciousness, as if the writer, half proud, half ashamed, is inviting us as readers to admire his cleverness.

Two stories in the collection *Pretty Creatures*, published in 1927 when Gerhardi was thirty-two, are typical in their preoccupation with and treatment of both women and Jews. "In the Wood" features Lieutenant Barahmeiev, an impecunious no-good who is deeply in debt to his landlord, Finkelstein, a handsome, self-assured broker, "inordinately proud of being a Jew and always selling foreign currencies to his guests at table."[18] Although Barahmeiev flirts openly with his landlord's wife, Vera Solomonovna, a "Jewish lady of thirty," Finkelstein refuses to take him seriously and goes off to bet on cards, leaving the two alone. The lieutenant begins his seduction by telling Vera the story of another occasion in which a woman offered herself to him. As she listens to the story of the other woman who, stripping off her clothes to persuade her unwilling lover, begins to "breathe in a queer panting way," Vera herself grows "fidgety with excitement" (p. 147). Suddenly, just as the story seems about to reach its climax, the lieutenant breaks it off, seemingly losing interest in the whole affair. Humiliated and frustrated, Vera leaves the room, and the story ends with the landlord and the lieutenant debating as to whose bedroom she has withdrawn to.

The lieutenant, on the surface a penniless gambler and fool, has a surefire method for dealing with women: in both the outer story and the inner story he systematically excites them, forces them to beg, then frustrates their desires. The Jewish landlord and businessman is revealed as a greedy pimp and a cuckold, while the Jewish woman is a shamefully sexual creature left panting with sexual frustration. Originally introduced as a "fool of the family," the Gerhardi persona here gets his revenge on everyone—even on the reader, whom he mocks by his refusal to reveal the ending. Gerhardi, obsessively worried about his potency, enslaved by his dependence on bestial women, in debt to greedy Jews, and unappreciated by vulgar readers who do not buy his books, here achieves a small but fitting textual revenge.

In another story in this collection, "Tristan and Isolde," the Gerhardi persona is a young American studying in Vienna who was having an affair with a young woman called Isolde, in keeping with her self-presentation as an unconventional romantic. "Tristan" soon discovers that she is instead a mercenary and conventional Jewess, who already has a fiancé, a doctor who works (fittingly) in a venereal-disease hospital. Despite this knowledge, Tristan's sexual enslavement forces him to propose marriage. Immediately after the proposal, however, he torments himself with regrets: "She won't let me drink my coffee as I like. She won't let me do anything as I like. I'm a lost man."[19] He is especially haunted by a gloomy vision of his "dark bride's" relatives and the infection they will bring: "They'll want to . . . see the ring, touch it maybe — all the dark Jewish brood, dentists, skin-disease doctors, stock-exchange frequenters. A nosing father . . . offering a wedding ring 'cheap' in advance. . . . It was unbearable" (p. 191).

As his regret escalates, he pictures his fiancée: "A grey-haired gouty old woman, with a deep black mustache and a beard, lying in bed with one complaint or another . . . her teeth in the glass at her side . . . their children, little hairy black Jews creeping about everywhere" (p. 193).

This hysterical vision inscribes Gerhardi's fear and loathing of both women and Jews, as well as his terror, shared by Lewis and Williams, of the loss of sexual boundaries and the possible transformation from male to female or female to male. As in Charles Williams's *All Hallows Eve*, the Jew appears here as a loathsome black beetle, especially terrifying because of her hermaphroditic characteristics. "Isolde," whether because she senses her lover's disgust or because she has other plans, turns down the marriage proposal, a mollifying measure which provides a note of self-mockery, and is perhaps what leads Davies to call this one the finest of Gerhardi's stories.

The 1939 novel *My Wife's the Least of It* is even more directly autobiographical. It concerns the efforts of a forgotten writer, Charles Baldridge, to sell a screen synopsis to Hollywood; an unsuccessful attempt Gerhardi himself made. Mr. Baldridge, like Gerhardi at that time, lives a financially precarious life in a boardinghouse, waited on by his comic Cockney char, Marigold, modeled on Gerhardi's maid, Francis Campion. Although Gerhardi was only forty-four in 1939 at the time of publication, he had already withdrawn into invalidity and pictures himself here as a frail old man. In the course of his efforts, Baldridge suffers an endless series of misadventures at the hands of women and Jews, "comic" indignities which quickly escalate to the pathetic and humiliating. The Gerhardi figure here revels once more in his victimized stance — a position which gives him license to indulge in the vicious textual misogyny and antisemitism in the book. It is as if Gerhardi is reminding the reader, with a childish smirk, that he is just a helpless, victimized old man, who cannot be held to account.

The beleaguered Baldridge is sustained only by his relationship with Marigold, who treats him as an adorable but troublesome child. However, while Baldridge's helplessness at the hands of the women and Jews who have power over him is humiliating and unmanning, he remains Marigold's indubitable master, while she remains firmly stuck in the role of uneducated and naive maidservant. Within this structure, being dominated ceases to be emasculating and becomes instead an enjoyable and carefully structured interaction in which it is always clear who has the real power. The cozy mother-son scenario is sometimes alternated with another one, involving a governess and pupil:

"You're not my governor, Marigold!"
"I govern your life, don't I? I look after you. I'm your governess, aren't I?"
"Of course."[20]

Most of the book consists of a series of scenes in which Baldridge, himself in the role of frustrated victim he had assigned to the Jewish woman of "In the Wood," waits abjectly for news that never comes. When he cannot pay his bills, first his flat, then all his furniture is seized by his sadistic and powerful landlady. His efforts to sell the screen synopsis land him in a virtual cesspool of rich Jews, all of whom have succeeded in the industry through their vulgarity and mediocrity. The most repulsive of these is Gus Oppenheimer, formerly a doorman in Graz, now "the genius of celluloid," who produces "imbecile conceptions most likely to sustain the attention of the lowest common denominators" (p. 163). Oppenheimer is an obese, pushing Jew, eager to penetrate British nobility. On his first appearance he does not speak but "merely squealed and grunted a little in a language which need not have been English or German" (p. 175). He has a "square porcine head with the blond bristles on top and the tiny pink eyes" (p. 178). Later, he is seen coming out of the lavatory (we must remember Gerhardi's feeling about lavatories): "The hog's head of Gus Oppenheimer, son of sow, emerged and sniffed by, supporting his weight as best as he could on his trotters" (p. 436).

All Baldridge's efforts to rework an old novel for the screen are in vain, as "the English have bowed down to the ghettos of Europe" (p. 255). In fact, his English honesty and lack of guile actually work against him: "You're just the sort of blunt honest-to-God Baldridge they don't want in the British films" (p. 270). Baldridge himself notes that "Elstree," the British film studio, has become "nothing but a Berlin ghetto" and realizes that Jews are "at the back of it all" (p. 358).

While Jews steal this Briton's birthright, women are busy emasculating him in other ways. In the boarding house, Dorothy, a bald woman with a stutter and the insatiable forwardness of all Gerhardi's female characters who are not servants, thrusts herself upon him. This large, aggressive young woman looms above the frail man in the chair below her and proclaims, "I'm made for strain, for intense service! I want passionately . . . to give myself to be used" (p. 97). Repulsed and ashamed at his inability to perform, Baldridge fends her off, protesting frantically to the reader that the problem lies in her ugliness and aggressiveness, not his inability.

Baldridge is also humiliated by another large and aggressive woman, his friend's wife, Mrs. Bess Devonshire. In a scene at a coronation party which has the quality of a nursery nightmare, Bess brings in plate after plate of mouth-watering food, which she gives to others, leaving Baldridge to stare at his empty plate. Then she sadistically places food on his plate but whisks it off before he can eat it, accusing him at the time of greed. Here, the hungry old man is treated as a helpless infant who is deprived of food by the cruel mother/nanny. As in a similar scene in Wyndham Lewis's *The Apes of God*, in which a young man is tormented, stripped, and forced to put on women's clothes in an obscene nursery, "Mrs. Bosun's Closet," the nursery here is the scene of humiliation and emasculation, a torture chamber in which large, powerful women torment a helpless male child.[21] After his humiliation at Bess's hands, Baldridge has a dream in which, significantly, he is soothed and comforted by another, more powerful mother/nanny figure, the queen.

Meanwhile, as Baldridge waits for the final decision on his script, the invective grows more heated. Gerhardi, like Lewis and like Charles Williams, pictures "the masses" as a dirty, vulgar mob easily seduced by the feminine wiles of the Jew. Gerhardi and Lewis agree that it is the male British artist-genius, by nature incapable of guile or feminine stealth, who is the victim of this collusion:[22] "While the Englishman was capable of writing like Shakespeare, like Milton, Wordsworth, Shelley, and Keats . . . the Jew was capable of what the Englishman was incapable, of glossing the fine mane of life with the fake lustre of cheap brilliantine" (p. 256).

Gerhardi's preoccupation with infection by foreign elements and substances increasingly comes to the fore as the book progresses and begins to bear an uncanny resemblance to Nazi rhetoric: "Those anonymous millions . . . wanted blood and were not too fastidious if what they got was the excrescence of Jewish hide — oil" (p. 256). Eventually, in a bizarre reversal of the Shylock/blood-libel myth, Job Devonshire suggests that in order to succeed, Baldridge must drain out his own blood and have Jewish blood transfused into him, as a way of showing philosemitic feelings: "Religion doesn't matter a hang. It's a question of race," Devonshire assures him (p. 269). This scheme, however, is rejected as unlikely to succeed, since the Jews will certainly be too selfish to donate any blood.

In the last fifty pages of the book, all is quite suddenly reversed. In despair, Baldridge steals Gus Oppenheimer's wallet and is put in jail. Upon his release, he begins to make a living as a quack faith-healer, and in this occupation meets a rich and ugly old woman, Miss Crossland. He marries her, but despite her begging, cannot bring himself to consummate the marriage, insisting on maintaining it "on a higher spiritual level" (p. 485). Her demands madden him, and when she attempts to interfere with his relationship with Marigold, it is the last straw. Having learned that there is a history of insanity in her family, he convinces her that she is insane, condemns her to a lunatic asylum, and inherits all her riches.

Although Baldridge never sells his script, he does end up rich and satisfied. For the moment, the Jewish conspiracy takes a backseat to the female one, and his sadistic punishments are confined to Dorothy, Bess, and his wife, whom he confines in smaller and smaller spaces. Women who humiliate men by demands for sex are a constant in Gerhardi's work, just as they are in the work of Greene, Lewis, Williams, and Orwell. In the novels of the other authors, such women usually meet a fitting death, and, because of its ending, *My Wife's the Least of It* could as easily be called *The Masochist Strikes Back*. It is not, however, the abbreviated and seemingly tacked-on "happy" ending that remains with the reader here. *My Wife's the Least of It* is primarily a text about masculine humiliation at the hands of women and Jews, and it is the authorial masochistic delight in this humiliation that gives this book its peculiar and bizarre flavor.

Big George Orwell and Little Eric Blair

As we have seen, William Gerhardi carefully manufactured an image with which to appeal to a neglectful public: the mischievous "bad boy" whose hatefulness could not be held against him; the charming but powerless child more sinned against than sinning. George Orwell's chosen authorial persona, in contrast, was that of the lone defender of the weak. Unlike Gerhardi, Orwell took significant moral stands against oppression and injustice. And yet, Orwell's public persona, "the wintry conscience of a nation," hid a tormented, self-hating, and conflicted man whose desperate effort to retain his masculinity was perhaps the prime task of his life and was a hidden agenda in each of his texts.[23] It was a task which determined his textual animosity toward women and his almost phobic hatred of homosexuals, and what I will chiefly focus upon here, his ambivalent and changing stance toward Jews.

As a small child, Eric Blair was chubby and unathletic, remembered by one of his disgusted contemporaries as "stinking little Eric . . . full of 'nobody loves me' and torrents of tears."[24] Like most British men of his time and class, he spent his early childhood in a largely female society. Eric

Blair's father, whom he remembers only as "a gruff-voiced elderly man forever saying 'Don't,' was away in India until Eric was eight, pursuing the
empire's opium trade ("Such," p. 360). In an unpublished notebook, Orwell remembered his sheltered childhood among women, marred only by
his impression "that women did not like men, that they looked upon them
as a sort of large, ugly, smelly and ridiculous animal who maltreated women
in every way, above all by forcing their attentions upon them."[25] His father's return when Eric was eight marked the son's removal to the hell of
St. Cyprian's prep school. In "Such, Such Were the Joys," first published
posthumously in 1954 and probably written around May 1947, Orwell documents the traumatic effect of this sudden severance from home, a trauma
for which he held his mother responsible and for which he would never
fully forgive her:

Your home might be far from perfect . . . but at least it was a place ruled by love
rather than by fear, where you did not have to be perpetually on your guard against
the people surrounding you. At eight years old you were suddenly taken out of this
. . . and flung into a world of force and fraud and secrecy. ("Such," p. 349)

At prep school, Eric Blair learned "a deep grief which is peculiar to childhood . . . a sense of desolate loneliness and helplessness, of being locked
up . . . in a world where the rules were such that it was actually not possible
for me to keep them" ("Such," p. 334). Significantly, this new world was
also dominated by a woman, the capricious and sadistic Mrs. Wilkes, or
"Flip," who was especially cruel to the unhappy and unathletic scholarship
boy. Flip attributed his cough, due to the weak lungs that would eventually
kill him at forty-four, to greed. When the homesick eight-year-old wet the
bed, he was humiliated by Flip and a female friend in a sadistic ceremony:

To this day I can feel myself almost swooning with shame as I stood, a very small
round-faced boy in short corduroy knickers, before the two women. . . . I felt that I
should die if "Mrs. Form" was to beat me. But my dominant feeling was not fear or
resentment: it was simply shame because one more person, and that a woman, had
been told of my disgusting offence. ("Such," pp. 331–32)

Long after leaving school, he continued to believe that he smelled and
was "preternaturally ugly" (p. 361). The self-hatred and despair Orwell
learned at prep school were in fact so profound as to make him doubt his
very right to survive, let alone his ability to take his place in the world as a
man among men. He also learned the rules of this world: "Virtue consisted
in winning . . . in being bigger, stronger, handsomer, richer. . . . Life was
hierarchical and whatever happened was right. There was the strong, who
deserved to win and always did win, and there were the weak, who deserved to lose and always did lose, everlastingly" ("Such," p. 359).

Orwell's character George Bowling, in his 1939 novel, *Coming Up for Air*, says of survivors of the public school experience, "Either it flattens them out into half wits or they spend the rest of their lives kicking out against it."[26] Orwell was proud of his kicking out, and of the "incorruptible inner self" he managed to retain at St. Cyprian's, at Eton, and later during his five years of service in the Burmese Civil Police. In a world that was split into the oppressed and the oppressors, he steadfastly refused to join or identify with the oppressors, growing uncomfortable and even sometimes changing sides when his support for an oppressed minority was adopted by a larger group. Nevertheless, the role of the victim was far too close for comfort. Throughout his life, Orwell desperately needed to disassociate himself from Eric Blair, the cringing, victimized child who lived on inside the austere, hyper-virile man. While on one level rejecting the hierarchical system of his prep school, he unconsciously accepted its equally hierarchical code of muscular Christianity, which denigrated the "feminine" and privileged the "masculine." These two strong, but often opposing, needs left Orwell conflicted and agonized, and determined his stance toward different groups at different times and in different contexts.[27]

One unwavering hatred was toward male homosexuals. Like Gerhardi and the other authors I have studied, Orwell found any weakening of boundaries between the genders especially threatening, and his own attraction to working-class men made men who actually acted out such attractions especially terrifying to him.[28] He was far more ambivalent in his stance toward women, whom he, like Williams, Lewis, Greene, and Gerhardi, desperately depended on while simultaneously despising and fearing them.

Orwell's own relationships to women and his textual treatment of them reflect his dependence and his need to render them powerless and submissive. Until her death, his wife, Eileen, like Gerhardi's maid, seems to have devoted herself entirely to his needs, abasing her own needs and self. Although she was aware of growths in her uterus, she did not seek a medical opinion or medical care, in case a diagnosis of cancer might hurt her husband's chances of obtaining the son he was determined to adopt, despite his own worsening lung condition. After the adoption, she cared for their son, Richard, and as she contemplated the operation that would kill her, her concern was only for him and for her husband. As for her own concerns about the operation, as she wrote to him, "What worries me is that I really don't think I'm worth the money."[29]

After Eileen's death, Orwell, whose own condition had worsened, offered marriage in quick succession to one woman after another. In each of these pathetic proposals, the famous writer George Orwell is all but forgotten. Instead, he presented himself as an unattractive invalid in desperate need of a mother for his child and "someone to be fond of me." Sonya Brownell, who did not love him but was apparently interested in the inheritance he offered her, including the role of a famous writer's widow, accepted his second proposal four months before his death, when he was already permanently hospitalized. At the end of his short life, Eric Blair had returned to a relationship that recapitulated his childhood trauma — life as a small and helpless boy, stuck in an institution he could not escape, and at the mercy of an erratic and all-powerful school mistress.[30]

*

In *The Orwell Mystique*, Daphne Patai illustrates how Orwell's "adherence to a traditional and damaging notion of manhood" seriously flawed all his work, and demonstrates that all of Orwell's novels are in some sense "narratives of a process of masculine self-affirmation" (pp. 19, 54). Instead of recapitulating Patai's findings on Orwell's textual treatment of gay and female characters, I will concentrate here on his interrelated treatment of Jews.[31]

One of Orwell's first published articles, "Hop Picking," the result of the same research that produced *Down and Out in Paris and London*, contains a portrait of a filthy, louse-ridden Liverpool Jew of eighteen, a boy who, Orwell declares, disgusts him more than anyone he has ever seen: "He was as greedy as a pig about food . . . and he had a face that recalled some low-down carrion-eating beast. His manner of talking about women and the expression on his face when he did so, were so loathsomely obscene as to make me feel almost sick."[32]

In the shadow of this portrait it is not hard to discern the child who was taunted by Wilkes for his greediness, and told so convincingly that he smelled that he would believe it for the rest of his life. The young Jew, an accurate embodiment of Orwell's own self-loathing, is also "filthy and obscene" in his manner toward women; in Orwell's projection, this alter-ego is allowed to express the rage against women which is so evident in all his texts but which his conscious persona did not and could not allow.

This Liverpool Jew, a kind of hateful shadow-self, reappears in *A Clergyman's Daughter* as "The Kike" or "Kikey." In this book, in which Orwell inflicts an attack of amnesia on Dorothy, his already strangely vacant and passive female main character, there is another Jewish presence, a vicious, bullying shopkeeper who, taking advantage of Dorothy's destitution, attempts to turn her into a prostitute: "The thought [of her prostitution] made his mouth water. When he saw her coming he would post himself at the corner . . . one black lecherous eye turned inquiringly upon her."[33]

A Clergyman's Daughter, which seems to lack any thematic center, has bewildered most critics; only when it is read as a sadistic fantasy against women do the fragments cohere. Orwell's overt authorial stance toward his main character, however, is one of removed "objective" sympathy. To verbalize overt sadistic lechery, a Jewish merchant is required.

Down and Out in Paris and London contains several other portraits of greedy, lecherous, and avaricious Jews, including one who is seen "in a corner by himself . . . muzzle down in the plate . . . guiltily wolfing bacon."[34] Orwell continually projected his own shame and guilt onto Jews, and Jews who confounded this projection were special targets. Even in the overtly philosemitic article of 1947, "Antisemitism in Britain," he recounts the amazement he felt when he encountered a boy who introduced himself openly as Jew. In *Down and Out*, Orwell's Russian friend, Boris, who is portrayed as a dashing, virile character, tells Orwell about his roommate, "A Jew mon ami, a veritable Jew! And he hasn't even the decency to be ashamed of it" (p. 33).

Jews also provide further opportunities for projected sexual sadism in *Down and Out*. Boris tells Orwell the story of "a horrible old Jew, with a red beard like Judas Iscariot," who attempts to set up his own daughter as a prostitute — "That is the Jewish national character for you" (p. 33). In the same sequence, a youth called Charlie also tells a story about the happiest day in his life, when he raped a peasant girl whose parents have sold her into slavery: "Ha, *messieurs* need I describe to you —*forcement*, you know it yourselves — the shiver, half of terror and half of joy, that goes through one at those moments?" (p. 12).

The attribution of his own feelings to another character, a technique Orwell often uses, allows him to take the role of the detached narrator, shaking his head in scientific interest. Indeed, Orwell condemns Charlie as "somehow, profoundly disgusting" (p. 14) and, lest we attribute Charlie's sadistic frisson to him, assures us that he has told the story of this "curious specimen" "just to show what diverse characters could be found flourishing in the Coq d'Or quarter" (p. 14). The phrase "you know it yourself" is another of Orwell's frequent techniques, in which he quietly invites the (male) reader into a universe of shared assumptions, in this case assumptions of shared sadistic pleasure. In *Down and Out in Paris and London* the sniveling little boy terrorized by the masculine woman with a hunting crop has become that most powerful and desirable of objects to Orwell, a man among working-class men. It is the sadistic abasement of women and of Jews that makes this possible.

Once the Holocaust became public knowledge in England, Orwell's "defender" button was pressed, and he was often, although not always, able to move Jews into the category of the worthy oppressed, a reversal he was never able to make in the case of either women or homosexuals.[35] In his journalistic essays during and after the war years, Orwell wavers

between defending Jews, when he sees them as deserving ·victims of oppression, and a kind of querulous irritation, when they appear to him to be
insufficiently grateful for his patronage, or when his own role of lone
defender is threatened by too much patronage on the part of the larger
public.

In August 1940, for example, after several articles and letters in which he
challenged British antisemitism, he suddenly complains that he has "heard
enough" about concentration camps and the persecution of the Jews, and
would welcome something that "told what it was like to be a Nazi."[36] The
humble, hard-working, and uncomplaining Jews in the 1939 essay "Marrakech," on the other hand, present a sharp contrast to the equally filthy
ones in *Down and Out*. The Jews of Marrakech are dirty because of oppression instead of inner filth, and instead of criminals and pimps they are re-
spectable laborers who "work no less than twelve hours a day."[37] In a passage unusually sympathetic to women, Orwell even compares them to
"poor old women (who) used to be burned for witchcraft when they could
not even work enough magic to get themselves a square meal" (p. 390).

A review of *Mein Kampf* is more ambivalent. Orwell, clearly resenting
his majority position, writes that although he would like to kill Hitler on
sight, he has "never been able to dislike him."[38] By 1943, Orwell, who in
other circumstances decried nationalism,[39] has begun to identify with
Britain, which he pictures as helpless male, victimized by a demanding un-
grateful female, the Jewish refugees.[40] In "A Wartime Journal" of 1943, he
offers a kind of stream of consciousness on the subject of these Jewish
refugees. Having determined, without evidence, that the underground
shelters are used by an abnormally high number of Jews, he describes

a fearful Jewish woman, a regular comic-paper cartoon of a Jewess [who] fought
her way off the train at Oxford Circus, landing blows on anyone who stood in her
way. . . . Surprised to find that D, who is distinctly Left in his views . . . says that
Jews in business circles are turning pro-Hitler . . . according to D they will always
admire anyone who kicks them. What I do feel is that any Jew . . . would prefer
Hitler's system to ours if it were not that he happens to persecute them. . . . They
make use of England as a sanctuary, but they cannot help feeling the profoundest
contempt for it. You can see it in their eyes, even when they don't say it outright.[41]

The level of paranoid projection is quite startling here. In his usual tactic, Orwell disowns the most extreme statement, attributing it to "D,"
who, as he is a leftist, certainly would not make such statements unless they
were true. The Jew here is at first a fearsome and aggressive woman, then a
masochist who "love[s] being kicked" (and so must have brought Hitler's
persecution on herself), and whose unspoken but powerful contempt and
intention to "make use of" her poor host country are clearly visible, if only
"you" look into her eyes.

Orwell's angry defense of other writers accused of antisemitism makes it clear how defensive he himself felt on the subject as the war progressed.[42] Nevertheless, in two essays of 1946, "Antisemitism in Britain" and "Notes on Nationalism," he makes a conscious effort to confront his own antisemitism. In this, he differs from any of the writers I have studied, including Graham Greene, who quietly changed the antisemitic references in the post-Holocaust versions of his books but made no statement about his reason for making the change. While Orwell does not actually acknowledge his own previous textual antisemitism in these essays, he does recommend looking inward and examining oneself before pointing the finger at anyone else.

The starting point for any investigation of antisemitism should not be "Why does this obviously irrational belief appeal to other people?" but "Why does antisemitism appeal to *me*? What is there about it that I feel to be true?" If one asks this question one at least discovers one's rationalizations, and it may be possible to find out what lies beneath them.[43]

In this essay and in "Notes on Nationalism," Orwell had come, as Walton puts it, "as near as he could to acknowledging publicly his own antisemitic tendency" (p. 30). Orwell's feelings about Jews were not firmly fixed but were instead bound up with his feelings about women, and ultimately with his contempt for and need to protect young Eric Blair, his vulnerable childhood self. Without the ability to explore this larger web of associations, his analysis necessarily stopped short. After his call for self-examination in February 1945, he continued to waver in his public and textual attitude toward Jews. Thus, while he became one of the few writers to publicly challenge Britain's closed-door policy for Jewish immigration, he experienced the founding of the state of Israel as a personal affront.[44]

Sexual Politics in 'Nineteen Eighty-Four'

The enormous success of *Nineteen Eighty-Four* must be attributed in part to Orwell's achievement of a highly believable and human character, Winston Smith, through the successful integration of George Orwell and Eric Blair. In addition, in *Nineteen Eighty-Four* Orwell demonstrates a new awareness of the interconnectedness of symbolic systems of power and control; that is, he begins tentatively to connect oppressions.

There are no identified Jewish characters in the society of *Nineteen Eighty-Four*, just as the population, as far as we know, appears to be only Caucasian.[45] Nevertheless, many of the mechanisms Orwell uses so well to recreate the horror of the totalitarian state are based not only on Stalinism but on the Nazi state and its use of scapegoating.[46] Most importantly,

Emmanuel Goldstein, the "Enemy of the People," is a Jew, whose "vast shadowy army, an underground network of conspirators dedicated to the overthrow of the state" is a direct echo of the Jewish conspiracy myth and whose book, "a compendium of all the heresies," is a direct reference to the influential and famous forgery, *The Protocols of the Elders of Zion*.[47] Through showing how the dictatorship employs the myth of the demonic Jew to gain control over the people, Orwell demonstrates his understanding of the projective uses of systems of stereotype. In this, he parts company with most of his contemporaries, including the other authors I have studied, who accept and utilize this literary stereotype as they find it, rather than holding it up for examination.[48]

Besides Goldstein, the only other Jewish character in *Nineteen Eighty-Four* is a woman in a boat, holding a little boy, whom Winston sees in one of the war films and writes about in his diary. As in the case of Orwell's labeling of the aggressive woman in the underground as a "Jewess" in his own wartime diaries, Winston determines that she is a Jew without any evidence, solely on the basis of his projective associations. However, in this case the labeling is tentative, and the projection very different. Winston sees

a middle aged woman who might have been a jewess sitting up in the bow with a little boy about three years old in her arms. Little boy screaming with fright and hiding his head between her breasts as if he was trying to burrow right into her and the woman putting her arms around him and comforting him although she was blue with fright herself. (p. 11)

This mother cannot protect her son, who is blown to bits in the next shot, but she risks herself to make the attempt. The tone of open loss and longing for lost female protection is new here—and the grouping of mother/Jew/little boy as common victims is a contrast to Orwell's usual grouping in which the Jew and/or female victimizer is grouped in opposition to the male child. In Winston's next image of the Jewish woman, after he has been humanized enough by his relationship with Julia to wake up from a dream with his eyes full of tears, he connects her with his own mother, whom he is for the first time able to remember with grief and loss rather than with the guilt and anger he felt earlier. "The dream had . . . consisted in—a gesture of the arm made by his mother and made again thirty years later by the Jewish woman he had seen on the news film, trying to shelter the small boy from the bullets, before the helicopters blew them both to bits" (p. 132). The "jewess's" gesture of protection (one that Orwell must have seen actual Jewish mothers making in war photographs and footage) is one of the few selfless gestures left in the world of *Nineteen Eighty-Four*, and one that neither Winston nor Julia can finally claim for themselves.

In *Nineteen Eighty-Four*, Orwell also appears aware for the first time of the connections between sexual oppression and other oppressions. Though neither he nor his characters seem to realize that sexual oppression operates differently upon men and women, they do realize that sexuality is a key to control. As Julia explains to Winston:

It was not merely that the sex instinct created a world of its own that was outside the Party's control and which therefore had to be destroyed if possible. What was more important was that sexual privation induced hysteria, which was desirable because it could be transformed into war fever and leader worship. (p. 110)

Winston realizes that the party works by "bottling down some powerful instinct and using it as a driving force" (p. 111). During the three-minute hate, he experiences this force himself as, unable to avoid the electric current of hatred that flows through him, he obediently directs it at the mythic Jew, Emmanuel Goldstein. With a tremendous effort, he succeeds in transferring it—from the Jew to the dark-haired girl behind him: "Vivid, beautiful hallucinations flashed through his mind. He would flog her to death with a rubber truncheon. He would tie her naked to a stake shoot her full of arrows like Saint Sebastian. He would ravish her and cut her throat at the moment of climax" (p. 16).

Through Winston, Orwell demonstrates how a dictatorship can manipulate people to project the hatred and misery they feel about their own lives toward an entity they are taught to name "Jew." And yet, when Winston redirects that same hatred toward an unknown female, Orwell explains this phenomenon not as another example of the same manipulation, but rather as the result of Winston's deprivation of an object which should by right be his—the body of the woman. The sadistic fantasy about Julia sets off a chain of associations in Winston's mind: a disgusting sexual encounter with a repulsive, toothless, "prole" prostitute, who cheated him by concealing her age, and his frigid, sexually withholding wife, a woman who had "without exception the most stupid, vulgar, empty mind that he had ever encountered" and whom he had also contemplated killing. "Why could he not have a woman of his own?" Winston whines to himself, as he remembers the past (p. 59).

Once Winston gets over his fear of Julia's largeness and good looks, and once he manages to "pull her down on to the ground" and find that "she was utterly unresisting, he could do what he liked with her," he gives up his murderous fantasies about Julia, although he continues to produce them when he meets other women (p. 100). Later, a Winston humanized and healed by regular sexual contact feels "she had become a physical necessity, something that he not only wanted but felt that he had a right to" (p. 115). In a truly just world, Orwell reasons, each man has a right to a woman all his own.

To readers with a feminist awareness, it is clear that the sadistic control O'Brien and the other party officials exert over Winston is merely another version of the sadistic fantasies Winston entertains about every woman he encounters. Just as the party needs its people prone and vacant in order to control them, so Winston can only penetrate Julia when she is limp and "utterly unresisting." And just as the people of *Nineteen Eighty-Four* will not ultimately be able to revolt as long as the proles are divided from the intelligentsia, so Winston Smith cannot become fully human as long as he regards an oppressed old woman as a yawning hole of corruption designed to entrap him.

Like the antisemitism of his enemy and political antithesis, William Gerhardi, Orwell's own antisemitism, with its sado-masochistic elements and its reversals of the roles of victim and victimizer, was deeply bound up with his fear and loathing of women and his desperate need to prove and retain his threatened masculinity. Orwell, unlike Gerhardi, struggled hard against his own antisemitism. But like Winston Smith, who is finally unable to make the connections that will lead to true liberation, George Orwell was unable to fully eradicate his antisemitism because he failed to recognize it as part of a larger symbolic web.

CHAPTER ELEVEN

Some Uses for Jewish Ambivalence: Abraham Cahan and Michael Gold

ERIC HOMBERGER

Ambivalence is an undignified attitude, betraying indecision and regret in equal proportions. It is what one feels about ideas, institutions, and also people, one knows all too well. Unqualified admiration is long gone, yet these things, these people, are too close, too much a part of our inner landscape, to jettison without misgivings. "Fondness" is too distant; "loyalty" too unthinking; and "loathing" altogether too crude and oversimplified. I will be arguing, through a divagation upon a contemporary novelist who has boldly used antisemitism, that ambivalence is not self-hatred; that in fact ambivalence has been a significant though often silenced current within Jewish culture, one which has played a part in the emergence of Jewish writers in the United States. The politics of ambivalence has shaped the sometimes uncomfortable dealings of the American left with the Jewish immigrant community.

Jonathan Kellerman's *The Butcher's Theatre* (1988) is a long (620-page), efficient example of the contemporary police procedural. The plot, which resembles Thomas Harris's *Silence of the Lambs*, turns on an American sociopathic serial killer who has come to Jerusalem under the false identity of an administrator of a UN hospital. *Pakad* — that is, chief inspector — Daniel Sharavi, an observant Yemenite Jew, leads a team of National Police detectives in the hunt for the killer, who, we learn, is the child of a supremely dysfunctional mixed marriage (his father, a Jew, was a surgeon). Having absorbed from the ugly antisemitic taunting of his gentile mother an ex-treme version of Nazi racial doctrine, the killer hopes by the ritual murders of young Arab women to exacerbate the already fierce hostilities between Israelis and Palestinians. As the investigation widens, detectives find post-ers in Jerusalem denouncing an American Hasid named Malkovsky as a child molester. In an interview at a luxury penthouse west of the Old City, Sharavi finds Malkovsky to be an overweight, unpleasant figure, with "per-spiration stains browning the armpits of a tentlike V-neck undershirt." When Sharavi shows the denouncing poster to Malkovsky, he is sickened by the willingness of the Hasid to blame everything on an evil spell. "The sight of the man, with his beard and *peyot* and religious garments, dredged up feelings of revulsion that were almost overwhelming." [1]

Pakad Sharavi's visceral reaction carries with it layers of cultural, reli-gious, and political nuance: there is a professional relation of policeman and suspect, but between the two men there is also the detestation of the Yemeni-born for the American; the sharp-eyed scorn of the observant but secular-minded Jew for the professionally orthodox whose cultivation of piety reeked of corruption and dishonesty. None of which quite explains Sharavi's feeling of sheer physical revulsion. In another context, Malkovsky would be little more than an ugly stereotype of the physically gross and morally corrupt Jew which has been so prominent in antisemitic tracts. Perhaps Sharavi is upset because Malkovsky *confirms* the ugliest of stereo-types. Jews should be flat-bellied, sun-tanned, powerful people of the mod-ern technological age, not a disgusting, overweight, pale figure like the man before him, who looked as though he had just crawled out of the sour herring-smelling world of the shtetl. Jews had no business looking like that. It made the work of enemies too easy.

Elsewhere in the novel there are pages of antisemitic diatribe between the killer's mother and father. It was a poison planted early, and which had done its vile work of producing a murderer. Kellerman understands the mechanism, and in his other books has clearly shown the processes of psy-chological deformation and its violent consequences. Antisemitism is an explosive ingredient in fiction. A "nervous little chap" in the first chapter of John Buchan's *The Thirty-Nine Steps* (1915) advises Richard Hannay that "the Jew is everywhere, but you have to go far down the backstairs to find him. . . . If you're on the biggest kind of job and are bound to get to the real boss, ten to one you are brought up against a little white-faced Jew in a bath-chair with an eye like a rattlesnake. Yes, sir, he is the man who is rul-ing the world just now." Writers of popular fiction in America have, in the past three or four decades, and for understandable reasons, generally shied away from more than glancing use of antisemitism. (Was it the first of the great "incorrect" bigotries and biases to drop from polite use?) Where antisemitism has a role to play in the construction of a character, it is more likely to be alluded to, hinted at, than given full expression. *The Butcher's Theatre* boldly uses antisemitism, and the boldness is all the more striking in a novel written by a Jew, with a *shabbat*-observing Jewish detective-hero. We are shown that the major exponent of antisemitism in the novel is a sadistic perverted sociopath. No mistaking authorial intent here in the course of a narrative that registers an extraordinary range of hatreds toward Jews and Jewishness.

Jewish writers who deal with the subject of antisemitism run great professional risks of being charged with "self-hatred," an accusation difficult to deny (both because "self-hatred" is itself the denial of the "essential Jew within" and because it reflects an unconscious process of the internalization of an antisemitic myth whose core mechanism is an "identification with the aggressor").[2] Sander Gilman's thesis on the nature of Jewish self-hatred focuses on the *process* of identification with gentile attitudes, inevitably assumed to be hostile, and which functions through the internalization of the notion that Jews collectively possess a hidden language.

The expression by Jews of what are described as negative emotions about Jews and Jewishness brings the inevitable accusation of self-hatred. In journalistic practice, it has been effectively used to discredit and intimidate critics from "within." The likelihood of being sneeringly accused of self-hatred can certainly have a chilling effect on so-called internal Jewish criticism, or even on the willingness to discuss certain questions. The accusation that a critic is consumed by Jewish self-hatred is an effective silencer; it is literally unanswerable. Of course the category of self-hatred has been used politically, and in part should be understood as such. But I do not find the concept as formulated by Gilman to be helpful, because, for all the formidable intellectual apparatus and scholarship at his disposal, it rests upon a comprehensive obliteration of nuance through the process of reification—of "the Jew," of "the Other," of antisemitism itself—and because Gilman does not appear to grasp the need for space between the self-hating Jew's absorption of a self-image of the Jew based upon antisemitic stereotypes and a self-image, a space, within which the writer lays claim to objectivity, independence, and critical distance—distance from Jewishness, perhaps—upon which secular intellectual integrity depends. Consider a comment by Lionel Trilling on Jewishness, made in in 1944: "As the Jewish community now exists, it can give no sustenance to the American artist or intellectual who is born a Jew. And so far as I am aware, it has not done so in the past. . . . I know of no writer in English who has added a micromillimeter to his stature by 'realizing his Jewishness,' although I know of some who have curtailed their promise by trying to heighten their Jewish consciousness."[3] It is precisely Trilling's brave and indeed reckless words which open up a terrain for analysis: not of Jewish "self-hatred," but Jewish ambivalence, the burden of being of two minds about Jewishness itself.

Jewish writers who, however guardedly, give to their characters anti-semitic sentiments are vulnerable to the accusation that morality and de-cency are ill-served by giving Satan at least a minimum of coherence and persuasiveness. But between antisemitism, "self-hatred," and social criti-cism, there is a minefield upon which Jewish writers have only occasionally chosen to pitch their tent. Kellerman, in other words, is an unusual exam-ple of a Jewish writer self-consciously prepared to engage with and *use* the explosive emotions of antisemitism. How he does so, the fictional context, obviously shapes the meaning of the attitudes toward Jews which appear in the pages of *The Butcher's Theatre*. The impact of disturbing material like this on many kinds of readerships is so explosive that there remains a fierce contestation between those who would censor any expression of these sen-timents and those who defend artistic freedom and reject the idea that *any* subject need be forbidden. It is not surprising that "commercial" genre fiction has had little sense of what to do with and about such content.

In the hands of Jonathan Kellerman, and many other Jewish writers (not least his wife, the novelist Faye Kellerman),[4] we can find a panoply of atti-tudes toward Jews and Jewishness. For every novelist who has piously sought to present favorable "role models" of Jewishness, from Leon Uris to Chaim Potok, there are uncomfortable writers, veritable "trouble-makers" like the early Philip Roth, who have been prepared to confront the ambiva-lences and worse that many people have felt about their own and other people's religions. Since many of the leading figures in our culture, politics, and intellectual life have had, and perhaps continue to have, as they say, "problems" with Jews, it might also be worth reminding ourselves that Jews—let us say, *some* Jews—have had their own problems with Muslims, gentiles, mixed marriages, and African Americans.[5] There is a character based on Rabbi Meir Kahane in *The Butcher's Theatre*, reminding us that within the Jewish community there has been an outspoken and violent, though decisively minority, vein of fundamentalist racism and bigotry. In other words, on the subject of antisemitism there is not a *them* and *us*: when Jews are bigoted, we should candidly and publicly affirm that there can be no special exemption offered on their behalf.

It is not always easy to say what Jewish writers think about their co-religionists. American Jewish literature has more than a few examples of the ways that Jewish writers have felt that Jewishness was not an unequivo-cal entity.[6] Jewish writers have been cautious about issuing their proclama-tion of *non serviam*, but James Joyce, and particularly *The Portrait of the Artist as a Young Man* (1916), retains an iconic significance. There is a need, in other words, to assert the value of a certain space, ideological as well as theological. This was what Henry Roth suggested, in an interview in 1973, when asked about the Jewish world of his early years: "All I had to do was just go a few blocks downtown, in New York's megalopolis, or a few blocks uptown, to leave my milieu, to obtain that kind of detachment in which everything, including your own folk, become elements for art, without a feeling of being profoundly committed — to them, to their exilic struggle."[7]

The characteristic note of secular Jewish imaginative writing in the United States is a sustained ambivalence about Jewishness and its "exilic struggle." At one point in his autobiography Abraham Cahan described a conflict within the Jewish immigrant community in New York in the 1880s. The young, better-educated Russian Jews, deeply influenced by the radical ideas of the European left, consciously rejected the Yiddish of the shtetl and spoke Russian among themselves. It was a badge of enlightenment and social liberation. Old-fashioned Jews were hostile to their left-wing politics and aggressive secular acculturation: "They considered us to be atheists and lunatics; we intellectuals thought of them as ignorant, primitive people."[8] The proponents of Yiddish-language propaganda, who were led by Cahan, and his German or Russian-speaking opponents, were not neutral before the somnolent mass of Jewish proletarians, who were so clearly in need of a rigorous ideological kick up the backside. The problem was to make use of the hostility they felt toward the backwardness, political underdevelopment, and petty-bourgeois inclinations of the workers around them. They too were struggling with ambivalence.

In his early years as a journalist in New York in the 1890s, Cahan willingly acted as guide to a small group of writers deeply curious about the mysterious "lower depths" of the Jewish immigrant ghetto in the lower East Side. He encouraged writers who were concerned with the problems of the slums, as well as those sympathetically curious about the Jews, to visit the street markets, cafés, booksellers, and theaters of the Russian-Jewish community. As editor, journalist, and novelist-historian of the Jews in New York, he argued the need to understand the world of Hester Street with the inner perspective of the participant.[9]

He was no less sure that the Jewish community needed to know more about the world in which they lived. Even things so fundamental as the political system of New York, social customs, social values, sport, and so on, were dark mysteries to the lower East Side. Addressing that need involved a lifetime of explaining, cajoling, translating. For Cahan, the immigrant generation of the 1880s and 1890s was trapped between a sentimental attachment to Jewish tradition and a facile yearning to redefine the self in the New World. The choice of an American identity for Jake in *Yekl* ("I am an *American feller*, a *Yankee*—that's what I am") and the intoxicating world of thought and literature to which the immigrant scholar Shaya was exposed in New York in *The Imported Bridegroom* (he felt a "fever of impatience to inhale the whole of Gentile language") was never, given Cahan's pervasive irony, quite liberating.[10] But where the individual craves freedom and self-expression, in Cahan's fiction it often takes the form of a hostile and bitter-sweet abandonment of what are perceived as restricting and indeed un-pleasant qualities designated as being "Jewish" and the adoption of the "unlovely" values of competitive, go-ahead America. Piety could not sur-vive in the New World, and assimilation was more like a defeat than tran-scendence. At the end of *Yekl*, Jake is a "defeated victor," a symbol of the price paid for radical surgery against tradition; David Levinsky is an even more comprehensively wounded figure, a failed human being despite his riches.

It is from Cahan that "Michael Gold" (1893–1967) learnt the particular flavor of ethnic irony with which he wrote his own family story in *Jews Without Money* (1930).[11] Cahan's first book concerned Yekl, the archetypal immigrant who had begun to make good in America and renamed himself Jake.[12] "Michael Gold" was born Itzok Granich, familiarly known as Isaac; to his schoolmates he was Irwin; and, from 1920, for political and legal rea-sons, he was remade as Michael Gold—universally referred to as Mike. When this protean master of nomenclature began his literary career as a contributor to Max Eastman's *Masses*, Cahan's reputation as a writer was at its peak. *The Rise of David Levinsky* appeared in 1917, and Gold, then Irwin Granich, reviewed it favorably for the *Liberator*.[13] He had grown up in a lower East Side tenement in the heyday of Cahan's *Forverts* and belonged to the first generation of Russian Jewish immigrant children born in Amer-ica. Although there was between the two writers a generational gap which, no less than their political differences, shaped their attitudes toward Jew-ishness, Granich beautifully invokes the shtetl world in Cahan's novel:

There is nothing more charming than those dreaming young old-world Jews who gave themselves up entirely to holy study, living as beggars that they might be wealthy in the knowledge of God. Cahan knew them well—was a *Yeshivah Bucher* himself, I suspect. And he writes of their life with a glow and affection that kindles the page. Levinsky is so young and tender and ardent, with the dim harmonics of heavenly wings ever rustling in his ears, with the earth and sky all significant to his adolescent vision; his transition to the successful American millionaire is . . . tragic.

Cahan, who had been born in Russia and was ever an ironic observer, gave to Levinsky a recollection of the shtetl world of simple devoutness and piety untainted by American materialism. What he had lost became a source of inner torment for Levinsky as he contemplated the compromises and corruptions which marked his rise upward in the commercial life of the New World.[14]

Granich, who carried no such memory of a world elsewhere, partici-pates in the Jewish collective memory secondhand. For his generation Jew-ishness is sharply dominated by a duality: the hearsay world of piety in the shtetl, on the one hand, as nourishment for his spirituality and emo-tional identification with "his" people; and the all-too-insistent, corrupting world of the urban slums in which he lives, and to which he unquestion-ably belongs. Even here, the sharp dichotomization is capable of misrep-resenting Granich's experience. Neither of his parents were proletarians, and his father's business in New York was a small workshop on Chrystie Street where, like a thousand "cockroach manufacturers," he produced small items for manufacturers scarcely larger than his own shop (cotton suspender ends for suspender makers). The exploitation they knew was self-exploitation, the reigning oppression of the self-employed. Although he grew up on Delancey Place, and attended nearby P.S. 20, Granich's ed-ucation, which included the reading of Herbert Spencer and Ruskin, was thoroughly engaged in the main currents of contemporary thought. At the University Settlement on Eldridge Street he played basketball and won a lead role in a production of Gilbert and Sullivan's *H.M.S. Pinafore*.[15]

It was the failure of his father's business, and his death soon after, which plunged the family into real financial hardship. Granich left school at fif-teen and worked for four years in a succession of unskilled jobs, from soda jerk to sales clerk and general laborer. In his first major article, "Towards Proletarian Art," Gold wrote of his impassioned identification—not with shtetl piety but with the world of the urban tenements:

All that I know of life I learned in the tenement. . . . The tenement is in my blood. When I think it is the tenement thinking. . . . Why should we artists born in tene-ments go beyond them for our expression? . . . Need we apologize or be ashamed if we express in art that manifestation of Life which is so exclusively ours, the life of the toilers? What is art? Art is the tenement pouring out its soul through us, its most sensitive and articulate sons and daughters.[16]

This difference defined the generational gap between Gold and the older religious men living in his tenement. When the pious Jews encountered whores in the streets of the lower East Side, "they shrugged their shoul-ders, and murmured: 'This is America.' They tried to live. They tried to shut their eyes. We children did not shut our eyes. We saw and knew" (p. 15). In Gold's eyes, the shtetl stoicism in *Jews Without Money* is simply social passivity and a failure to fully engage with America. Sitting and drink-ing endless cups of tea with other *altecockers*, Reb Samuel the umbrella-maker told stories about dybbuks; every day in the street the children watched strutting whores, drunks, gamblers, and gangsters. (In this con-junction one can see Gold's sense of the real subject matter for American

Jewish literature.) Such men showed the achievements of a thousand years of ghetto patience, the sigh and shrug as effective a form of self-defense as a raised arm to ward off a Cossack's whip. "He submitted to it as once he had submitted to the pogrom. He saw Jews working on the Sabbath, Jews eating pork, and practicing other abominations. He learned to shrug his shoulders and be silent" (p. 196). Gold's point was that however much pious Jews hated the immorality of the slums, they were impotent, had no choice in the matter; they were those who were acted upon. They would never accept the slums, but they could do little about them.

The home and the street are reality-instructors for a young Jewish boy. Cahan's autobiography recounts similar moments. When he made his first journey on the el in New York in the early 1880s, Cahan bought a ticket but didn't know what to do with it. The ticket collector gestured (correctly assuming that Cahan could speak no English) for him to deposit it in the box. But for Cahan the American's gesture had a different meaning than the same kind of gesture by bus conductors in Vilna, and he refused to part with the ticket. The collector had to pull it out of his hand before Cahan understood what he was being shown.[17] There were many such lessons to be learned on the streets (and in the schools) of the New World. Morris Raphael Cohen's schoolteacher once warned him: "Don't walk like a sheeny!" Samuel Chotzinoff was shocked when he was addressed by his teacher in the second grade by his surname. Arriving in Brooklyn in 1904, Joseph Freeman's mother refused to eat either tomatoes or bananas: "She had never heard of them." It was only when he persuaded his mother that tomatoes and bananas were kosher that they were admitted to the family kitchen. Walking through the Brooklyn Botanic Garden, Alfred Kazin's father remarked "Nice! but you should have seen the Czar's summer palace at Tsarskoye-Selo!"[18] To learn that you walked like a "sheeny"; to be addressed without the loving diminutives of Yiddish; to be confronted by strange foodstuffs; to live in one society but to carry the memory of another, more sharply recalled and more richly endowed with meaning: these were some of the burdens of immigration.

The street and the kitchen table offered different syllabi for an education, alternative ways of seeing the world. The real education of Mike Gold began when he started to contrast the lessons of the street with those imparted by his family. The old Jewish men either shut their eyes to the life around them or, like his father Herman, railed bitterly against the destruction of their dreams of success in America. Neither the old men nor his father could help him to acquire an education in life as it actually was. For Jacob Riis, like so many writers in the Progressive era, what was good about the lives he described in the New York slums came from family values; the ghetto itself exerted a malign influence.[19] But for Gold, the life of the ghetto nourished as well as brutalized. In the streets, the boys tormented cats: "It was a world of violence and stone, there were too many cats, there were too many children. . . . We tortured them, they tortured us. It was poverty" (pp. 63–64).

Of sex, there was much to be learned in the overcrowded tenements. In later years, when Gold moved among gentile radicals like Mabel Dodge, John Reed, and Max Eastman, he seemed worldly-wise, with a knowledge of things denied to his contemporaries. Life in the tenements was transparent. Sex was not hidden away in the lower East Side but brazenly on display on the streets. Along with his pal Nigger, Mikey watched a whore do her business with a customer. Everyone knew (and was powerless to do anything about) the fate of girls who were lured into the "camp" maintained by Kid Louie, former pugilist and king of the streets, and raped. Harry the Pimp, "mellow, conservative and fatherly" (p. 29), served as a role model for many of the boys. Predatory sexuality was a lesson all had to learn, particularly after an attempted sexual assault on Joey Cohen. Even young boys had to learn fear, Granich included. They taunted the prostitutes. Powerless to drive them out of the neighborhood, and too young to be customers, they hassled the girls. It seemed fun to drive them to tears. Rosie, one of the tearful hookers, took refuge in Momma's kitchen. Though she disapproved of the whores, Momma was too kind to deny them a sympathetic hearing and a cup of tea. Mikey was beaten for learning "those bad, nasty things" from the street: "Vain beating; the East Side street could not be banished with a leather strap. It was my world; it was my mother's world, too. We *had* to live in it and learn what it chose to teach us" (p. 19).

He learned about the corrupt system that tied police, prostitutes, landlords, and Tammany Hall together in the maintenance of vice and kickbacks. Zunzer, who owned the building where the Granich family lived, was a pillar of the synagogue though he let rooms to the whores. They paid more rent than poor people. That the almighty dollar corrupted was another lesson learned early, and often reinforced. He knew that pimps preyed on young girls and heard in his mother's kitchen the heart-breaking story of Susie, who later chose suicide because she could not escape from her life as a whore.

The streets themselves offered daily lessons in the way of the world. The structure of the streets on the lower East Side had been determined early in the nineteenth century by the imposition of a grid plan over the untidy pattern of colonial farms and landgrants. As the population density rose, the old private homes of merchants and artisans were turned into tenant-houses occupied by families on each floor. In turn these two- and three-story dwellings were replaced by larger tenements like Gotham Court on

Cherry Street, which could house as many as five hundred people. The Irish, who originally lived throughout the East Side, were supplanted by the arrival of large numbers of German immigrants, who transformed the streets east of the Bowery into *Kleindeutschland*. The Germans moved uptown and were in turn replaced in the 1880s by large numbers of immigrants from southern Italy and eastern Europe (including Abraham Cahan from Vilna and the Granich family, Herman from Romania, Mama Katie from Hungary). Growing up in such a world, with a score of nationalities to be found on every street, the young possessed an instinctive sense of the differences between streets, virtually between one tenement and another. Theirs is an urban geography as complex as any map of the Balkans, and as dangerous. Territorial battles between the Forsythe Street boys and the Chrystie Streeters, streets which were precisely one block apart just to the east of the Bowery, took place within the territory of the Eastmans, a gang named by the prince of thugs, Monk Eastman, who, during Itzok Granich's childhood, commanded more than twelve hundred warriors and ruled the territory between the East River and the Bowery below 14th Street with an iron fist. With its headquarters on Chrystie Street, near Herman Granich's workshop, the Eastmans waged deadly territorial warfare against the Five Pointers gang, who lorded over the territory between Broadway and the Bowery between City Hall Park and 14th Street.[20] The street battles in *Jews Without Money* reenact the fabled warfare between German and Irish gangs of an earlier generation in the same streets. Granich was attacked and driven away by Italian boys on Mulberry Street, dangerous territory to the west of the Bowery. It was their turf, and he knew it. Delancey Street, where the Granich family lived, was a borderline between Jews and Italians, and a traditional combat zone. A map prepared in 1920 for the Joint Legislative Committee Investigating Seditious Activity in New York State showed "racial colonies" of the city: Jews and Italians east of the Bowery and Fourth Avenue, Czechs and Hungarians on the East River below 14th Street, Irish at the foot of the Williamsburg Bridge, Chinese between the lower end of the Bowery and Centre Street.[21] At another level, the differences between *goy* and Jew, and the consequences of their conflicts, shaped perception and behavior.

Gold employs a pattern of "popular" racial stereotypes to define difference. Whenever an Irish family was mentioned, the Irish fondness for drunkenness and violence was soon remembered. The Golds lived near Chinatown, but few outsiders were successful in penetrating the inner life of the Chinese immigrants. It was just too easy to repeat the most banal of racial stereotypes:

They never seemed to sleep. All night long one heard a Chinese phonograph whining and banging horribly. The waiters held long explosive conversations all night.

They quarreled, playing cards, cooked queer dishes that filled the tenement with sweet, nauseating smells. An opium den, some of the neighbors said. A gambling house, said others. One morning there was a crash. Then the police came and found the house in wreckage. The young Chinese had disappeared. The nude body of a white girl lay on the floor. She had swallowed rat-poison. (pp. 177–78)

The Chinese add yet another element to the ethnic and racial mix of the lower East Side: "Negroes, Chinese, Gypsies, Turks, Germans, Irish, Jews — and there was even an American on our street" (p. 178).

Gold's attitude toward the Jews was drenched in ambivalence. There was much about ghetto life that he cherished, such as the Jewish passion for ethical idealism. Aunt Lena, who refused a brilliant marriage with Dr. Solow out of love for an imprisoned strike leader, exemplified a distinctively Jewish form of heroism. On the other hand, an account in *Jews Without Money* of a visit to the home of the Cohen family in Borough Park, Brooklyn, was fiercely ironic at the vulgarity of the Jewish nouveau riche. There was always in Gold's writings a sharp-edged scorn for the compromises and materialism of the bourgeoisie.

When he turned to religious life itself, he was equally sharp-eyed and unforgiving. Reb Moisha, "a walking, belching symbol of the decay of orthodox Judaism" (p. 65), ran the *chaider* Mikey attended. The *chaider*, remembered without fondness in scores of Jewish memoirs and novels, was calculated to return young boys to the streets as aggressive enemies of all religion. Elsewhere in Gold's book pious Jews like Reb Samuel and Mottke the vest-maker are studies in futility. Barney, an old Jew wearing a rag cloak, sits waiting for the Messiah. Reb Samuel has a nightmare that the old values are being undermined in America, but can only shrug his shoulders.

There must have been a middle ground among those he had known on Delancey Street, composed of garment-workers perhaps, finding unity in their epic struggles against the manufacturers.[22] But they occupy few pages in Gold's memoir. Between the old men, and the Cohens in Borough Park, Gold presents the extremes of Jewish response to New York: the unassimilable, and the *allrightniks* who find the prosperity of American life very much to their taste.

Gold uses stereotypes in *Jews Without Money* to construct the ethnically and religiously diverse world of the lower East Side, and draws upon the same system of cliché and stereotype to describe the Jews among whom he grew up. It is in his description of his parents, Herman and Katie, that he breaks away from stereotype and succeeds in fully representing the complexity of his feelings about Jews and their values. Born near Yassy (Iasi, near the river Prut on the present border with Moldova) in Romania, Herman was a superb story-teller. Mikey learned later that many of his father's best stories were stolen from the *Arabian Nights*. Herman's account of his childhood, and his promised betrothal, gave his son a glimpse into the remote and alien life of the shtetl. But his experiences in America suggest a more nuanced and politically pointed tale. A photograph sent to Romania, showing his cousin Sam Kravitz wearing a derby hat, deeply impressed everyone. Herman came to America in search of the magical success of cousin Sam. When times went well, Herman hauled the family to a photographer so that he, too, could send a photograph of his brilliant good fortune to Romania. But when Kravitz stole the suspender shop they had opened, the embittering of Herman Gold began in earnest. Forced to work for others as a painter, he suffered from lead poisoning and endlessly denounced Kravitz and bemoaned his bad luck: "Once I worked for myself and laughed and lived! But now I must die! It is all useless. A curse on Columbus! A curse on America, the thief! It is a land where the lice make fortunes, and the good men starve!" (p. 112).

Seeking to improve his luck by turning into a labor spy, Herman obtains the dismissal of the foreman, Abe Tuchman. With his improved prospects the Gold family buys a little house in Borough Park. An accident in which both of Herman's legs were broken ends his dream. Unable to work any longer as a painter, the house was soon lost. Sitting at home back in their little tenement apartment, denouncing unions as being un-American, he is a disappointed man, destroyed by ill fortune, whose final humiliation comes when he could find nothing to do but peddle bananas from a pushcart. The forlorn bananas were symbols of his utter defeat, the death of his hopes. Mikey saw his father as "a hunched frozen figure in an old overcoat" (p. 299).

Herman Gold's experience, typical in so many ways, becomes a different story in the hands of his son Mikey, that notorious baiter of the petty bourgeois among his fellow religionists. Cahan's treatment of Levinsky raises similar issues. He was a socialist of sorts, or at least had fairly recently been a paid-up member of the Socialist Party (which was not always the same thing). He had translated popularizations of Marx and Marxism in his early days and had argued socialist strategy with Daniel DeLeon, Marxist *capo regime* of the Socialist Labor Party.[23] Levinsky, on the other hand, was an *allrightnik*, a type familiar to the Jewish community. Cahan was alternately sympathetic and mocking toward his protagonist. The implied (and very public) values of the author gave to his account of Levinsky's career exploiting workers and breaking strikes a certain knowingness. Cahan had battled against such people for over thirty years before *The Rise of David Levinsky* appeared.

The same considerations apply to Gold. By the time of the publication of *Jews Without Money*, Gold had easily become one of the most visible and hard-hitting polemicists of the Communist Party. A man of the left from his first youthful publications in *The Masses*, Gold had been a regular contributor to *The Liberator* and was one of the founders of *The New Masses* in 1926, becoming its editor two years later. He also played a major role in the founding of the John Reed Clubs in 1929. He was the first writer on the left to have written in American periodicals about the artistic experiments of the Proletcult in the Soviet Union, and he led the campaign to create a proletarian literature in the United States. Though not a "socialist intellectual" of the stature of Cahan, and without much interest in Marxian dialectics, he was most definitely a mover and shaker on the American literary left in the 1920s and 1930s.[24]

If we look at Herman Gold from the vantage point of the Communist Party—especially in the late 1920s when Comintern doctrine was at the height of its Third Period, calling for maximum class conflict—it is quite clear that he stands for the most entrenched and recalcitrant of American labor types, the union-hating, individualistic, capitalist-sympathizing workman who viscerally rejected solidarity with others in the struggle for their mutual betterment. Herman Gold's wholesale absorption of the American dream was, in Marxist terms, a false consciousness. It is characteristic of Gold that he omits the jargon of Marxism, while reconstructing some of its most significant insights. His feelings toward his father were profoundly ambivalent.

Momma—Katie Gold—stands for everything which was the opposite of her husband. She was the supreme realist, Herman the romantic. When Herman betrayed his foreman, her response was to say "It is not right that after working ten years for a boss, a man should be fired, a sick man with a family" (p. 213). Katie was the keeper of the family conscience; her kosher kitchen gleamed. Having grown up amidst Hungarian peasantry, she tried to help her sons share what was so vivid to herself. Growing up in the streets of New York, the boys had no feeling for nature: "America, the thief, where children only see dry, dead mushrooms in grocery stores!" (p. 153).

She was generous with her time and labor, and also with her sympathy. Where Herman minded his own business, Katie was a "buttinsky," endlessly involving herself with others, cooking meals and cleaning the apartments of women who had fallen ill. She willingly stayed with a neighbor who feared she was losing her mind. When an unfortunate family was evicted, Katie went from door to door begging pennies for them. When young prostitutes sought her sympathy, it was not refused.

On the subject of the *goyim* she was regrettably closed-minded, retaining a European Jewish suspicion about gentiles: "Mother was opposed to the Italians, Irish, Germans, and every other variety of Christian with whom we were surrounded" (p. 163). When Herman read aloud a report of a train crash to Katie, her only concern was whether any Jews had been among the dead: "Christians did not seem like people to her" (p. 164). Her son absorbed these ancestral feelings, and was plagued by nightmares of Christian ogres screaming "Jew, Jew! Jew!" (p. 165). Despite these fears, he played with the children of his Irish neighbors, and in practice Katie made no discrimination among those who needed help. While working at a cafeteria, she was a tireless fighter for social justice and willingly confronted landlord and pawnbroker. An instinctive sense of shared humanity enabled Katie to rise above her ethnic and religious bigotry and help Irish families and Italians. Where Herman looked after his own interests, Katie the buttinsky defended everyone's. This "humble funny little East Side mother" (p. 158) "was made for universal sympathy, without thought of prejudice. Her hatred of Christians was really the outcry of a motherly soul against the boundless cruelty in life" (p. 166). If Herman represented the selfish worker and would have been an object of scathing left-wing satire and polemic, Katie was the embodiment of a wider proletarian solidarity of the poor. She was the "heroine" of the book, who lived to the end of her life in the same East Side tenement, and prayed in the same synagogue.[25] Her scorn for jewelry and her "dark proletarian distrust" of money-making (pp. 157, 214) enhanced Mikey's gut feelings of class solidarity and "morbid proletarian sense of responsibility" (p. 299). It was to her memory that he dedicated his later political development: "We could not worship her gods. But we loved our mother; and she loved us; and the life of this brave and beautiful proletarian woman is the best answer to the fascist liars I know; and it is in the bones of her three sons, and they will never betray their mother who was a worker and a Jew, nor their race and class, but will honor her dear memory, and fight the fascists in her defence until the bitter end."[26]

We are right to sense the politics of Michael Gold's presentation of Herman and Katie Gold, although contemporary reviewers complained of the absence of direct political material in *Jews Without Money*.[27] The book contains no strikes, no raised class-consciousness through political involvement. The conniving landlords and employers are mostly *schlemiels*; there is no political message save that which was exemplified by the contrasting portraits of Herman and Katie Gold, and by their son's career. It is ridiculous to describe *Jews Without Money* as "the first American proletarian novel"[28] — if the term *proletarian* has any specific meaning. Rather, Gold's book serves to remind us of the powerful contradictions of his relations to the American Jewish community and of some of the ways he represented his misgivings in terms of the dilemmas of the revolutionary movement.

When Gold drew up a list of the people who lived on their street ("Negroes, Chinese, Gypsies, Turks, Germans, Irish, Jews — and there was even an American"), he was expressing the left's fervent hopes about the ethnically and racially divided American working class. He dreamed that the persecuted and disadvantaged proletariat would forge a sense of community out of those things which united them. The tenement-dwellers shared a proud, hostile reaction toward charity investigators (pp. 292–94);[29] universal detestation was felt among the tenement young at the heavy hand of the police; they all hated the corruption represented by the whores who paraded night and day on the streets of the lower East Side and their pimp protectors: all these things were the rough-hewn materials out of which the solidarity of the poor was to be constructed. The instinctive generosity of the proletarians, as exemplified by Katie Gold, gave the book its basis for political hope.

It was a hope which flew in the face of "reality." Among the diverse anti-semitisms in America before the First World War, among the most virulent was precisely that of the immigrant working class, especially the Irish Catholics. Tauntings and assaults on Jews by the Irish were, as Gold recorded, an everyday occurrence on the lower East Side. These tensions were often resolved by the sound of (Irish) New York police batons cracking Jewish skulls.[30] The persistent fact of difference undermined the political hope of the left. By implication, Gold showed that Jewish hatred and fear of *goys* and gentile discrimination against Jews were mutually self-enforcing; the Irish regarded the Jews as Christ-killers; the Italians chased Jewish boys out of Mulberry Street; and old Jews shrugged their shoulders and cursed the *goyim*. To work with the Jews in the lower East Side, radicals like Gold would have to overcome their feelings of ambivalence, to leave behind the structure of bias.

Despite a heartfelt rejection of ethnic or religious chauvinism, radicalism in New York was an intensely ethnic and tribal phenomenon. Jews did not prosper in the Communist Party if they were too obviously "Jewish." Party names were invariably nondenominational. On all sides, the political alignments were laid over older fault-lines. We may take it as given that Catholic priests denounced the "Jew Reds"; that Jewish workers denounced the Jewish manufacturers in the rag trade (and voted for the Socialist Party candidate Meyer London for Congress); and that Communist Party cadres denounced both priests and rabbis and argued that Zionism was a form of collaboration with fascism. Immigrant radicalism had regularly contained a significant element of antireligious polemic. There was little inclination to pacify the religious Jews, and a bristling sense of hostility toward things Jewish. By the late 1920s, the Jewish Bureau of the Communist Party organized antireligious demonstrations on traditional Jewish holidays, and as a matter of principle the children's schools run by the International Workers Order excluded Jewish history or religion.[31] In his portraits of *chaider* Gold clearly did not distance himself from this Third Period leftism. But neither did he engage in its most aggressive forms of antireligious propaganda. He functions *within* the Third Period, but with inner reservations and qualifications. His is a kind of high-wire balancing act, ambivalent about so much of Jewish life yet unwilling to break with Jewishness. "Life for us," he wrote in "Towards Proletarian Art," "has been the tenement that bore and molded us through years of meaningful pain."

The paradox is that while envisioning a liberation from difference Gold used the racial and ethnic stereotypes which revealed the persistent traces of the bigotry which so divided the proletariat. Due to that mutual suspicion and fear the Jewish working class remained politically and culturally isolated from the Irish, Italians, and others who lived in the tenements of the lower East Side. The dream of Katie Gold that the oppressed would recognize their common identity in the fact of oppression, and act together to end it, remained unfulfilled. If there ever was a text which demonstrated, with some subtlety, the impotent frustration of the left in the slums of New York, it is *Jews Without Money*.

Gold's mixed feelings about Jewishness are present at the creation of an American Jewish literature. Indeed, I suspect that those ambivalences make a significant contribution toward the defining characteristics of American Jewish literature.

Notes

Notes

1. Cheyette

1. "Street Haunting: A London Adventure" (1927), in Leonard Woolf, ed., *Virginia Woolf: Collected Essays* (London: Hogarth Press, 1967), vol. 4, p. 157. See also Rachel Bowlby, "Walking, Women and Writing: Virginia Woolf as *Flâneuse*," in Isobel Armstrong, ed., *New Feminist Discourses* (London: Routledge, 1992).

2. For an extended version of this argument, see my *Constructions of "the Jew" in English Literature and Society: Racial Representations, 1875–1945* (Cambridge: Cambridge University Press, 1993).

3. Elleke Boehmer, "Stories of Women and Mothers: Gender and Nationalism in the Early Fiction of Flora Nwapa," in Susheila Nasta, ed., *Motherlands: Black Women's Writing from Africa, the Caribbean and South Asia* (London: The Women's Press, 1991), pp. 3–23.

4. On the relationship between Jewish women and messianic redemption, see also Nadia Valman, "Jews and Gender in Nineteenth-Century British Literature," Ph.D. thesis, University of London (1996), and Michael Ragussis, *Figures of Conversion: "The Jewish Question" and English National Identity* (Durham, N.C.: Duke University Press, 1995).

5. For the feminization of male Jews within racial discourse, see Sander Gilman, *Freud, Race, and Gender* (Princeton, N.J.: Princeton University Press, 1993). See also Daniel and Jonathan Boyarin, eds., *Jews and Other Differences: The New Jewish Cultural Studies* (Minneapolis: University of Minnesota Press, 1995).

6. Virginia Woolf to Violet Dickinson, 18 April 1935, to Ethel Smyth, 26 April 1935, and to Margaret Llewellyn Davies, 28 April 1935, in Nigel Nicolson, ed., *The Letters of Virginia Woolf, 1932–1935: The Sickle Side of the Moon* (London: Hogarth Press, 1979). My thanks to Tracy Hargreaves for these references.

7. For examples of this arbitrary Judaization see my *Constructions of "the Jew" in English Literature and Society*, p. 15 and pp. 190–91.

8. For an examination of draft versions of *The Years* in relation to the final published version, see Tracy Hargreaves, "Virginia Woolf and Twentieth Century Narratives of Androgyny," Ph.D. thesis, University of London (1994), pp. 229–38, and for the "slimy" conceptual Jew, see Zygmunt Bauman, *Modernity and the Holocaust* (Cambridge: Polity Press, 1989), ch. 2.

9. Cynthia Chase, "The Decomposition of the Elephants: Double-Reading *Daniel Deronda*," *PMLA*, vol. 93 (1978), pp. 219, 215–27.

10. Chase, p. 222, argues that in *Daniel Deronda* "Jewish identity" is "inherited, historical, and finally . . . genetic." For a more extensive critique of this argument, see my *Constructions of "the Jew" in English Literature and Society*, ch. 2.

11. For this, see Gilman, *Freud, Race, and Gender*, passim.

12. K. M. Newton, "*Daniel Deronda* and Circumcision," *Essays in Criticism* (1981), vol. 31, pp. 313–27, and Mary Wilson Carpenter, "'A Bit of Her Flesh': Circumcision and the Signification of the Phallus in *Daniel Deronda*," *Genders*, no. 1 (Spring 1988), pp. 1–23. Chase and Newton have been recently republished in K. M. Newton, ed., *George Eliot: Longman Critical Readers* (London: Longman, 1991).

13. For a detailed discussion of these issues, see Katherine Bailey Lineham, "Mixed Politics: The Critique of Imperialism in *Daniel Deronda*," *Texas Studies in Language and Literature*, vol. 34, no. 3 (Fall 1992), pp. 323–46, and also my "White Skin, Black Masks: Jews and Jewishness in the Writings of George Eliot and Frantz Fanon," in Keith Ansell-Pearson, Benita Parry, and Judith Squires, eds., *Cultural Identity and the Gravity of History: On the Work of Edward Said* (London: Lawrence & Wishart, 1996).

14. Gayatri Chakravorty Spivak, "Three Women's Texts and a Critique of Imperialism," in Henry Louis Gates, ed., *"Race," Writing, and Difference* (Chicago: University of Chicago Press, 1986), pp. 262–80.

15. See also Shelley Fisher-Fishkin, *Was Huck Black? Mark Twain and African-American Voices* (Oxford: Oxford University Press, 1993). For further examples of an arbitrary "blackness" in relation to Jewish literary representations, see my "Neither Black nor White: The Figure of 'the Jew' in Imperial British Literature," in Tamar Garb and Linda Nochlin, eds., *The Jew in the Text: Modernity and the Politics of Identity* (London: Thames and Hudson, 1995), and Sander Gilman, *Difference and Pathology: Stereotypes of Sexuality, Race, and Madness* (Ithaca, N.Y.: Cornell University Press, 1985).

16. E. M. Forster, *A Passage to India* (London: Edward Arnold, 1924). I will be referring to the Penguin edition throughout.

17. For a recent argument along similar lines, see Gillian Rose, *Judaism and Modernity* (Oxford: Basil Blackwell, 1993), ch. 1.

18. Dickens's rewriting of *Oliver Twist* (1837) to reduce the number of times the phrase "the Jew" is used in relation to Fagin has been documented by Harry Stone, "Dickens and the Jews," in *Victorian Studies* (1958–59), vol. 2, pp. 223–53. Graham Greene's rewriting of *Stamboul Train* (1932), *A Gun for Sale* (1936), and *Brighton Rock* (1938) after the war to rid them of their overt Jewish stereotypes has been recently documented by Andrea Freud Loewenstein, *Loathsome Jews and Engulfing Women: Metaphors of Projection in the Works of Wyndham Lewis, Charles Williams, and Graham Greene* (New York: New York University Press, 1993). For references to Woolf's rewriting of her earlier drafts to lessen the impact of her extravagant use of Jewish racial characteristics, see Hargreaves, pp. 229–38, and Lassner's discussion of the various drafts of Woolf's "The Duchess and the Jeweller" in this volume.

19. Zygmunt Bauman, "Allo-Semitism: Premodern, Modern, and Postmodern," in Bryan Cheyette and Laura Marcus, eds., *Modernity, Culture, and "the Jew"* (forthcoming). Bauman notes that the term *allo-semitism* originates in the work of the Polish Jewish literary historian Artur Sandauer, who foregrounded the Greek word for otherness, *allus*, when referring to the practice of representing "the Jews" as a radically different Other.

2. Galperin

1. *Semites and Anti-Semites: An Inquiry into Conflict and Prejudice* (New York: Norton, 1986), p. 102. For Jean-François Lyotard's postmodern reading of the Jews as *jews* — as an Other, who represent, in turn, a "deep unconscious," which is forgettable only insofar as it is represented or made conscious through the memory of, among other things, the murder of the "jews" at Auschwitz — see *Heidegger and "the jews"*, trans. Andreas Michel and Mark Roberts (Minneapolis: University of Minnesota Press, 1990).

2. *Rahel Varnhagen: The Life of a Jewish Woman*, trans. Richard and Clara Winston (New York: Harcourt, Brace, 1974), p. 38.

3. Although the "Jewishness" of modern romantic studies is too vast and various a subject to be entered here, I want to call attention to an early and possibly seminal instance of this phenomenon: Lionel Trilling's 1950 essay, "Wordsworth and the Iron Time," which was later and more appropriately titled "Wordsworth and the Rabbis" (reprinted in *Wordsworth: A Collection of Critical Essays*, ed. M. H. Abrams [Englewood Cliffs, N.J.: Prentice Hall, 1972], pp. 45–66). In this essay, Trilling stresses, in ways that might seem beside the point but presumably were of great urgency to the author himself, the link between the Rabbis in their stance to the Torah and Wordsworth in his stance toward Nature: "There existed for the Rabbis and for Wordsworth a great object, which is from God and might be said to represent Him as a sort of surrogate, a divine object to which one can be in an intimate passionate relationship, an active relationship . . . which one can, as it were, handle, and in a sense create, drawing from it inexhaustible meaning by desire, intuition, and attention" (p. 51).

4. *The Visionary Company: A Reading of English Romantic Poetry*, rev. 2nd ed. (Ithaca, N.Y.: Cornell University Press, 1971), p. xvii.

5. For a detailed account of the relationship between the Revolution and Jewish

emancipation, see Arthur Hertzberg, *The French Enlightenment and the Jews* (New York: Columbia University Press, 1968).

6. For Harold Bloom's reading of Shelley in conjunction with Buber's *I and Thou*, see *Shelley's Mythmaking* (New Haven: Yale University Press, 1959). The other (though perhaps not opposite) viewpoint is espoused, of course, by Viereck in *Meta-Politics: The Roots of the Nazi Mind* (New York: Capricorn, 1965), pp. 3–47, and, with particular relevance to my discussion of romantic narrativity, by Lacoue-Labarthe in *Heidegger, Art and Politics*, trans. Chris Turner (Oxford: Basil Blackwell, 1990).

7. Two relatively recent studies that stress the self-contestational aspect of English romantic writing are Anne K. Mellor, *English Romantic Irony* (Cambridge, Mass.: Harvard University Press, 1980), and Tilottama Rajan, *Dark Interpreter: The Discourse of Romanticism* (Ithaca, N.Y.: Cornell University Press, 1980).

8. Lines 33–48 from "A Jewish Family," in *William Wordsworth: The Poems*, 2 vols., ed. John O. Hayden (New Haven: Yale University Press, 1981), pp. 650–51.

9. Citations to this essay as well as to *The Romantic School* are to the translations of those works by Helen Mustard in *Heinrich Heine, The Romantic School and Other Essays*, ed. Jost Hermand and Robert Holub, The German Library, vol. 33 (New York: Continuum, 1985).

10. For Freud's analysis of jokes, which has frequent recourse to Heine, see *Jokes and Their Relation to the Unconscious*, ed. and trans. James Strachey (New York: W. W. Norton, 1960).

11. For an analysis of Heidegger's commitment to "the idea of a national revolution," or to "schema or historiality" with a sense of a German destiny, all of which ran counter to his philosophy of being in general, see, again, Lacoue-Labarthe, *Heidegger, Art and Politics*. According to Lacoue-Labarthe, Heidegger's affiliation with Nazism, especially as formulated in his infamous "Rectoral Address," represented a "national aestheticism," or an affiliation with narrative.

12. "The Rabbi of Bacherach," in *Heinrich Heine: Self Portrait and Other Writings*, ed. and trans. Frederic Ewen (Secaucus, N.J.: Citadel Press, 1948), pp. 259–91.

13. *Jewish Self-Hatred* (Baltimore: Johns Hopkins University Press, 1986). For Gilman's treatment of Heine's ambivalence toward his own Jewishness and that of his predecessor Ludwig Borne, see especially pp. 148–88.

14. For McGann's use of Heine to exemplify an approach to romanticism that is "analytic and critical," that assumes an "antithetical but non-Romantic point of view to its subject," see *The Romantic Ideology* (Chicago: University of Chicago Press, 1983), pp. 48–56.

15. References to "Jehuda ben Halevy" are to the translations of the poem by Margaret Armour in *Heine's Poetry and Prose* (London: Dent, 1966), pp. 139–56, and S. S. Prawer in his discussion of the poem in *Heine's Jewish Comedy* (Oxford: Clarendon Press, 1983), pp. 561–91. Prawer's study gives the most complete and detailed modern account in English of Heine's position toward Jewishness.

16. Jeffrey Sammons, *Heinrich Heine: The Elusive Poet* (New Haven: Yale University Press, 1969), p. 390.

3. Gilman

1. Mark Twain, *Concerning the Jews* (Philadelphia: Running Press, 1985). This edition has a good historical introduction. All quotations are to this edition. See also Carl Dolmetsch, "Mark Twain and the Viennese Anti-Semites: New Light on 'Concerning the Jews,'" *Mark Twain Journal* 23 (1985): 10–17; Guido Fink, "Al di qua della paroia: Gli ebrei di Henry James e di Mark Twain," in Guido Fink and Gabriella Morisco, eds., *Il recupero de testo: Aspetti della letteratura ebraico-americana* (Bologna: Cooperative Lib. Univ. ed. Bologna, 1988), pp. 29–50. The general background in Twain's work can be judged based on the extracts in Janet Smith, ed., *Mark Twain on the Damned Human Race* (New York: Hill & Wang, 1962), and Maxwell Geismar, ed., *Mark Twain and the Three R's: Race, Religion, Revolution* (Indianapolis: Bobbs-Merrill, 1973). The best overall discussion of Mark Twain's attitude toward the Jews is still to be found in Philip S. Foner, *Mark Twain, Social Critic* (New York: International Publishers, 1958), pp. 288–307, which documents in great detail the critical reception of this piece, including its use in the anti-semitic propaganda of the early twentieth century. On the overall question of the image of the Jew in nineteenth-century American culture see Louis Harap, *The Image of the Jew in American Literature from Early Republic to Mass Immigration* (Philadelphia: Jewish Publication Society, 1974).

2. Marion A. Richmond, "The Lost Source in Freud's 'Comment on Anti-Semitism': Mark Twain," *Journal of the American Psychoanalytic Association* 28 (1980): 563–74.

3. Cited by Foner, p. 300.

4. All references are to the edition: Mark Twain, *The Innocents Abroad/Roughing It* (New York: The Library of America, 1984). On the historical background for this volume see Dewey Ganzel, *Mark Twain Abroad: The Cruise of the "Quaker City"* (Chicago: University of Chicago Press, 1968), and Franklin Dickerson Walker, *Irreverent Pilgrims: Melville, Browne, and Mark Twain in the Holy Land* (Seattle: University of Washington Press, 1974).

5. See L. Belloni, "Anatomica plastica: The Bologna Wax Models," *CIBA Symposium* 8 (1960): 84–87; François Cagnetta, "La vie et l'oeuvre de Gaetano Giulio Zummo," *Cereoplastica nella scienza e nell'arte series: Atti del 1 congresso internazionale, Biblioteca della Revista di storia delle scienze mediche e naturali* 20 (1977): 489–501. On the religious background to this tradition see the following two catalogues and their general historical introductions: Benedetto Lanza et al., *La cere anatomiche della Specola* (Florence: Arnaud Editore, 1979), on the Florentine collection, and, on the Viennese collection, Konrad Allmer and Marlene Jantsch, eds., *Katalog der josephinischen Sammlung anatomischer und geburtshilflicher Wachspräparate im Institut für Geschichte der Medizin an der Universität Wien* (Graz-Cologne: Hermann Böhlaus Nachf., 1965).

6. Henry Wadsworth Longfellow, *Outre Mer: A Pilgrimage beyond the Sea* (London: C. Routledge, 1853), pp. 224–25.

7. Nathaniel Hawthorne, *Passages from the French and Italian Note-Books* (Boston: Houghton, Mifflin and Co., 1871), p. 380.

8. One must note that such a specific use of death and decay is quite different from Twain's metaphoric use of death. See Stephen Cooper, "'Good Rotten Material for a Burial': The Overdetermined Death of Romance in *Life on the Mississippi*," *Literature and Psychology* 36 (1990): 78–89.

9. Patrice Boudelais and Andre Dodin, *Visages du Cholera* (Paris: Belin, 1987).

10. *Mark Twain's Notebooks and Journals*, vol. 1 (1855–1873), ed. Frederick Anderson, Michael B. Frank, and Kenneth M. Sanderson (Berkeley: University of California Press, 1975), p. 438.

11. On Twain's theology, see Susan K. Harris, *Mark Twain's Escape from Time: A Study of Patterns and Images* (Columbia: University of Missouri Press, 1982).

12. Quoted by Ganzel, p. 222.

13. Quoted by Harap, p. 349.

14. *The Autobiography of Mark Twain*, ed. Charles Neider (New York: Harper and Row, 1975), p. 3.

15. See the discussion in Foner, pp. 288–89.

16. Friedrich Ratzel, *The History of Mankind*, trans. A. J. Butler, 3 vols. (London: Macmillan, 1896), 3:183. The German edition appeared between 1885 and 1888. For a more detailed discussion see my *Jewish Self-Hatred: Anti-Semitism and the Hidden Language of the Jews* (Baltimore: The Johns Hopkins University Press, 1986), pp. 216–17.

17. Richard Andree, *Zur Volkskunde der Juden* (Leipzig: Velhagen & Klasing, 1881), pp. 24–25; translation from Maurice Fishberg, "Materials for the Physical Anthropology of the Eastern European Jew," *Memoirs of the American Anthropological Association* 1 (1905–1907): 6–7.

18. Johannes Buxtorf, *Synagoga Judaica . . .* (Basel: Ludwig Königs selige Erben, 1643), pp. 620–22.

19. Johann Jakob Schudt, *Jüdische Merkwürdigkeiten* (Frankfurt am Main: S. T. Hocker, 1714–18) 2:369. On the later ideological life of this debate see Wolfgang Fritz Haug, *Die Faschisierung des bürgerlichen Subjekts: Die Ideologie der gesunden Normalität und die Ausrottungspolitiken im deutschen Faschismus* (Berlin: Argument Verlag, 1986).

20. Johann Pezzl, *Skizze von Wien: Ein Kultur- und Sittenbild as der josephinischen Zeit*, ed. Gustav Gugitz and Anton Schlossar (Graz: Leykam-Verlag, 1923), pp. 107–8.

21. On the meaning of this disease in the medical literature of the period see the following dissertations on the topic: Michael Scheiba, *Dissertatio inauguralis medica, sistens quaedam plicae pathologica: Germ. Juden-Zopff, Polon. Koltun : quam . . . in Academia Albertina pro gradu doctoris . . . subjiciet defensurus Michael Scheiba . . .* (Regiomonti: Litteris Reusnerianis, [1739]), and Hieronymus Ludolf, *Dissertatio inauguralis medica de plica, vom Juden-Zopff . . .* (Erfordiae: Typis Groschianis, [1724]).

22. Madison Marsh, "Jews and Christians," *The Medical and Surgical Reporter* (Philadelphia) 30 (1874): 343–44, here 343.

23. Marsh, p. 343.

24. See the debate following the presentation of Joseph Jacobs, "On the Racial Characteristics of Modern Jews," *The Journal of the Anthropological Institute* 16 (1886): 23–63, here 56, 61.

25. Marsh, p. 344.

26. Ibid.

27. Joseph Krauskopf, *Sanitary Science: A Sunday Lecture* (Philadelphia: S. W. Goodman, 1889), p. 7.

28. Ephraim M. Epstein, "Have the Jews Any Immunity from Certain Diseases?" *The Medical and Surgical Reporter* (Philadelphia) 30 (1874): 440–42, here 440.

29. Epstein, p. 441.

30. Ibid.

31. Carl Claus, *Grundzüge der Zoologie zum Gebrauche an Universitäten und höheren Lehranstalten sowie zum Selbststudium*, 2 vols. (Marburg: N. G. Elwerts Universitäts-Buchhandlung, 1872) 2:123.

32. Madison Marsh, "Have the Jews Any Immunity from Certain Diseases?" *The Medical and Surgical Reporter* (Philadelphia) 31 (1874): 132–34.

33. On the history of this concept see Sander L. Gilman and Steven T. Katz, eds., *Anti-Semitism in Times of Crisis* (New York: The New York University Press, 1991), p. 29.

34. Peter Charles Remondino, *History of Circumcision from the Earliest Times to the Present: Moral and Physical Reasons for its Performance, with a History of Eunuchism, Hermaphroditism, etc., and of the Different Operations Practiced upon the Prepuce* (Philadelphia: F. A. Davis, 1891), p. 186. Remondino notes in his introduction that the book was written decades before it was published.

35. Stuart Creighton Miller, *"Benevolent Assimilation": The American Conquest of the Philippines, 1899–1903* (New Haven: Yale University Press, 1982), p. 75.

36. Sander L. Gilman, "On the Nexus of Madness and Blackness," in my *Difference and Pathology: Stereotypes of Sexuality, Race, and Madness* (Ithaca, N.Y.: Cornell University Press, 1985), pp. 131–49.

37. See George Frederickson, *The Black Image in the White Mind: The Debate about Afro-American Character and Destiny, 1817–1914* (New York: Harper and Row, 1971).

38. Cited by Foner, p. 290.

39. See Eugene Levy, "'Is the Jew a White Man?' Press Reaction to the Leo Frank Case, 1913–1915," *Phylon* 35 (1974): 212–22.

40. Clara Clemens, *My Father, Mark Twain* (New York: Harper & Brothers, 1931), pp. 203–4.

41. Dolmetsch, p. 14.

42. Sander L. Gilman, "The Jewish Genius," in my *The Jew's Body* (New York: Routledge, 1991), pp. 128–49.

4. Baumgarten

1. Hannah Arendt, "Introduction," and "The Jew as Pariah," in *The Jew as Pariah: Jewish Identity and Politics in the Modern Age*, ed. Ron Feldman (New York: Grove Press, 1978).

2. J. Hillis Miller, "The Fiction of Realism: Sketches by Boz, Oliver Twist, and Cruikshank's Illustrations," *Victorian Subjects* (New York: Harvester Wheatsheaf,

1990), p. 153. Also see Robert Patten, *George Cruikshank's Life, Times, and Art* (New Brunswick, N.J.: Rutgers University Press, 1992).

3. Anthony Burton, "Cruikshank as an Illustrator of Fiction," in *George Cruikshank: A Reevaluation*, ed. Robert Patten (Princeton, N.J.: Princeton University Press, 1974), p. 127. See also Miller, p. 158: "Cruikshank's illustrations are based on complex conventions which include not only modes of graphic representation, but also the stereotyped poses of melodrama and pantomime."

4. Jonathan Grossman, personal communication. References to Dickens are to the Penguin edition; for textual issues concerning this and other editions of Dickens see Grossman.

5. Henry Mayhew, "Of the Street Jews," in *London Labour and the London Poor* (New York: Dover, 1968 [1861–62]), pp. 115–32.

6. *Typologies: 9 Contemporary Photographers*, exhibition organized by the Newport Harbor Art Museum, Newport Beach, Calif., shown at the San Francisco Museum of Modern Art, summer 1992.

7. Deborah Heller, "The Outcast as Villain and Victim: Jews in Dickens's *Oliver Twist* and *Our Mutual Friend*," in Derek Cohen and Deborah Heller, eds., *Jewish Presences in English Literature* (Montreal: McGill-Queen's University Press, 1990), pp. 40–42.

8. "An Address by Stanislaus de Clermont Tonnerre, December 23, 1789," in *Out of Our People's Past*, ed. Walter Ackerman (New York: United Synagogue of America, 1977), p. 240.

9. See Ed Eigner, *The Dickens Pantomime* (Berkeley: University of California Press, 1989).

10. John O. Jordan, "The Purloined Handkerchief," *Dickens Studies Annual* 18 (1989), p. 14.

11. Edward Alexander, "George Eliot's Rabbi," *Commentary* 92, no. 1 (July 1991), p. 29. Also see his *With Friends Like These. . .* (New Brunswick, N.J.: Transaction Press, 1992).

12. I use the Oxford World's Classics edition of Robert Tracy (Oxford: Oxford University Press, 1992).

13. Bryan Cheyette, *Constructions of "the Jew" in English Literature and Society: Racial Representations, 1875–1945* (Cambridge: Cambridge University Press, 1993), pp. 28–29.

14. Joan Mandel Cohen, *Form and Realism in Six Novels of Anthony Trollope* (The Hague, 1976), p. 84, quoted in Cheyette, *Constructions*, p. 29.

15. See John Bayley, "Things As They Really Are," in John Gross and Gabriel Pearson, eds., *Dickens and the Twentieth Century* (London: Routledge, 1962), p. 51.

16. Cheyette, pp. 22–32; also see Richard Mullen, *Anthony Trollope: A Victorian in His World* (London: Duckworth, 1990), p. 470.

17. Florian Krobb, "'*La Belle Juive*': 'Cunning in the Men and Beauty in the Women,'" *The Jewish Quarterly* 39, no. 3 (Fall 1992): 5–10. Also see Michael Galchinsky, "Romancing the Jewish Home," and Joseph Childers, "At Home in the Empire," in Murray Baumgarten and H. M. Daleski, eds., *Homes and Homelessness in the Victorian Imagination* (New York: AMS Press, in press).

18. See Livia Bitton-Jackson, *Madonna or Courtesan? The Jewish Woman in Christian Literature* (New York: Seabury, 1982). Also see Sander Gilman, "The Jewish Murderer: Jack the Ripper, Race, and Gender," in *The Jew's Body* (New York:

Routledge, 1991), pp. 104–27. Paul Goodman's story, "The Facts of Life," echoes these issues and is conveniently located in *Jewish-American Stories*, ed. Irving Howe (New York: New American Library–Mentor, 1977), pp. 222–35.

19. Robert Tracy, "'The Old Story' and Inside Stories: Modish Fiction and Fictional Modes in *Oliver Twist*," *Dickens Studies Annual* 17 (1988), pp. 4–5, 16.

20. Cynthia Chase, "The Decomposition of the Elephants: Double-Reading *Daniel Deronda*," *PMLA* 93 (1978), pp. 215–27.

5. Freedman

1. See, for example, Christopher Ricks's recent *T. S. Eliot and Prejudice* (London: Faber and Faber, 1988). I forbear even alluding to the spate of commentary from the 1940s to the present day on the antisemitism of Ezra Pound.

2. Maxwell Geismar, *Henry James and the Jacobites* (New York: Hill and Wang, 1962), pp. 349–50.

3. The best example of these is an essay by Leo Levy (author of a fine 1956 book on Jamesian melodrama) that was published, tellingly, in *Commentary* in 1958. But the very specialized audience of that journal, and the fact that Levy's work was not published in an academic venue that was, at that precise time, admitting Jews like Levy to its precincts, is telling of the social dynamics of academic Jamesianism. See Levy, "Henry James and the Jews," *Commentary* 26 (September 1958), pp. 243–49.

4. Posnock, *The Trial of Curiosity: Henry James, William James, and the Challenge of Modernity* (New York: Oxford University Press, 1991).

5. James, *The American Scene* (Bloomington: Indiana University Press, 1968), p. 131. Further citations in the text will refer to this edition.

6. The persistent and erroneous myth of the racial identity of the Jew is not only one of the most disturbing inheritances of post-Enlightenment race theory but a powerful reminder of the inadequacy of the very concept of race itself. On the former point, I hold with Ashley Montagu, who eloquently argues that

> the fact is that there is not now nor was there ever a Jewish race. . . . The Jewish religion is not a marker of any race whatsoever since any member of any race may belong to it. As for the people who are identified with "the" Jews, they are drawn from probably more heterogeneous sources than any other identifiable people in the world. The ethnic ingredients entering into the formation of the group called Jews have not undergone mixture in a common melting pot, but remain very various. Clearly, then, the Jews are not anything approaching a homogenous, biological entity, nor are they a race or an ethnic group.

To this vigorous argument, we can add Anthony Appiah's elegant marshaling of the relevant data on genetics — which reminds humanists of the fact that "racial characteristics" like skin color or nose shape are genetically insignificant markers of difference — to produce the formulation that the slippage between the signifier "Jew" as practitioner of religion and that of the signifier "Jew" as part of a "homogenous biological entity . . . race . . . or ethnic group" reproduces the slippage between culture and biology constitutive of the discourse on race itself.

For more on the genetic stew that constitutes Jewish identity, see Patai and Wing, *The Myth of the Jewish Race* (New York: Scribner's, 1975). For the genetic argument against theories of race, see Appiah, "The Uncompleted Argument: Du Bois and the Illusion of Race," in Henry Louis Gates, ed., *"Race," Writing, and Difference* (Chicago: University of Chicago Press, 1986).

7. Both this example and a larger treatment of the tendency of thought underlying it are provided by George Stocking, "Lamarckianism in American Social Science, 1890–1925," in *Race, Culture, and Evolution* (Chicago: University of Chicago Press, 1968, 1982), p. 244. And many other Jewish "racial" characteristics were often cited by American neo-Lamarckians as examples of acquired traits: "William Z. Ripley explained Jewish 'deficiency' in lung capacity as 'an acquired characteristic, the effect of long subjection to an unfavourable sanitary and social environment . . . [which] has nevertheless become a hereditary trait.'" (Stocking, p. 244). For more on the Enlightenment origins of the Jewish nose, see George Mosse, *Towards the Final Solution* (Madison: University of Wisconsin Press, 1978, 1985), p. 29.

8. Jean-Paul Sartre, *Anti-Semite and Jew*, trans. George Becker (New York: Schocken, 1948, 1965), pp. 38–39.

9. For these matters, the classic text remains John Higham, *Strangers in the Land: Patterns of American Nativism, 1860–1925* (New York: Atheneum, 1968), and Higham, "Social Discrimination Against Jews, 1830–1930," in Higham, ed., *Send These to Me: Jews and Other Immigrants in Urban America* (New York: Atheneum, 1975). But I also have reference below to a "revisionist" or non-mainstream body of historiography on this issue, including Walter Dombowski, *The Tarnished Dream* (Westport: Greenwood Press, 1968), and Robert Singerman's very useful essay, "The Jew as Racial Alien," in David Gerber, ed., *Anti-Semitism in American History* (Urbana: University of Illinois Press, 1986). This scholarship differs with Higham on a number of crucial specifics—his stressing of objective grounds for antisemitic prejudices (economic strains, *parvenu* behavior) and his understatement of the extensiveness of racial stereotyping in American popular culture and consciousness. But it differs more powerfully in its being explicitly informed by a sense of ethnic identity and political urgency lacking not only in Higham, but also in the "mainstream" history he represents. For a fine survey of the historiographical issues involved in this matter, see Gerber's introduction to his own volume, "Anti-Semitism and Jewish-Gentile Relations in American Historiography and the American Past," pp. 3–56 of *Anti-Semitism in American History*.

10. Paul Leland Haworth, *America in Ferment* (Indianapolis: Bobbs-Merrill, 1915), quoted by Singerman, pp. 108–9.

11. To give some sense of the similarity of James's language not just with the fantasies of the eugenicists, but with the commonly accepted representations of Jewish immigration, compare James's language here with that of *Frank Leslie's Weekly* from 1892:

> There exists on the east side of this town a great and coherent population of foreigners of a low order of intelligence, speaking their own languages, following their own customs, and absolutely blind or utterly indifferent to our ideals, moral, social and political. . . . Go and see them swarm in the streets

and the houses of the east side if you have any doubts on the subject, and form your own conclusions as to the availability of the material for manufacture into the sort of citizen which the founders and fathers of the republic had in mind. (*Leslie's Weekly*, Feb. 27, 1892, p. 57)

12. While James—properly—does not occupy a major place in the literature on fin-de-siècle antisemitism, he is routinely included in surveys of elite antisemitism of this era. In Higham's *Send These to Me*, for example, James's shadowy presence in the terrain of antisemitism is acknowledged by a footnote to the passage we have been discussing in *The American Scene*; and Walter Dombowski includes James on the roster of elite antisemites, though he spends the majority of his time discussing Edith Wharton, Vance Thompson, and the Adams family. See Dombowski, *The Tarnished Dream*.

13. Indeed, it of course can be argued that "western civilization" as a discursive category from Juvenal through Gibbon through Alan Bloom is composed largely of warnings about the decline and fall of that very civilization. See, inter alia, Patrick Brantlinger, *Bread and Circuses* (Ithaca: Cornell University Press, 1985), pp. 38–46.

14. Nietzsche continues: "The Jews are the counterparts of the *dècadents*: they have been compelled to *act* as *dècadents* to the point of illusion" (Nietzsche, *The Anti-Christ*); I encountered this question in Eve Sedgwick, *Epistemology of the Closet* (Berkeley: University of California Press, 1990), p. 177.

15. Sander Gilman, *Difference and Pathology: Stereotypes of Sexuality, Race, and Madness* (Ithaca: Cornell University Press, 1985), esp. pp. 150–63 and 191–217. Further citations in the text will refer to this edition.

16. On inbreeding, see Patai and Wing, pp. 99–118.

17. The notion of "mongrelization" and its implicit delineation of the lower classes or demonized races as less than human is built into racist discourse by Gobineau, and recurs throughout racist discourses of all varieties. Indeed, it is central to Lombroso's theory of degeneration, in which criminals and other deviants as well as "lesser" races are seen as literally members of another, less evolved species. To his credit, this is one of the aspects of Lombroso that Nordau does not echo in his own writings on degeneration.

18. Reprinted in Paul Popenoe and Roswell Johnson, *Applied Eugenics* (New York, 1918), p. 133, quoted in Singerman, p. 113.

19. For the currency of these sentiments, see, inter alia, Singerman, Solomon. The most fervent exponents of these ideas, it should be noted, were not only James's contemporaries Henry and Brooks Adams, but family friends and personal supporters like James Russell Lowell. Lowell's career as an antisemite provides a fascinating example of the ambivalence or lability that afflicts even the most egregiously antisemitic subject position. Early in his life, Lowell was an outspoken philosemite; later he shifted to a bitter and outraged antisemitism. But even at the apogee of his career as an antisemite, Lowell entertained the belief in the Jewish origins of all human races—a belief alluded to (if only to be disavowed) at a crucial moment in *The Tragic Muse*.

20. Henry Suskdorf, *Our Race Problems* (New York: The Shakespeare Press, 1911; rprnt. Miami: Mnemosyne Publishing Company, 1969), p. 8.

21. To quote again from the egregious Suskdorf: "There are only two solutions of the irritating problems [posed by the Jew]: either a complete fusion of the heterogeneous ethnic elements into heterogeneity, or extermination or expulsion of the weaker race by the stronger" (p. 8).

22. Daniel Pick, *Faces of Degeneration* (Cambridge: Cambridge University Press, 1989), p. 15. Significantly, most of the official biography of Nordau — written by his wife Anna and daughter, Maxa — is devoted not to his early anti-degeneration campaigns but to his later Zionist and internationalist political writing and activity. Lest my tone below betray a certain lack of respect, let me say here that Nordau was as thoroughly admirable, if frequently misguided, a figure as one could imagine; and that his Zionism was of a Utopian, humanist, flavor.

23. Nordau, *Degeneration* (New York: Appleton's, 1895), p. 19. Further citations in the text will refer to this edition.

24. The 1937 Munich exhibition of "degenerate art" (*Entartete Kunst*) organized at the behest of Goebbels himself, has been recently reassembled at the Los Angeles County Museum of Art; the catalogue cum commentary is entitled *Degenerate Art: The Fate of the Avant-Garde in Nazi Germany* (Los Angeles: Los Angeles County Museum of Art, 1991).

25. As quoted in Edwin Cady, ed., *W. D. Howells as Critic* (London: Routledge and Kegan Paul, 1973), p. 165.

26. See my *Professions of Taste* (Stanford: Stanford University Press, 1990) for a fuller version of this argument.

27. James, *The Tragic Muse* (Harmondsworth: Penguin, 1975), p. 590. Further citations in the text will refer to this edition.

28. James, *The Golden Bowl*, The New York Edition (New York: Scribner's, 1910), vol. 24, p. 196.

29. Julia Kristeva, *Powers of Horror: An Essay on Abjection*, trans. Leon Roudiez (New York: Columbia University Press, 1982), p. 1. Further citations in the text will refer to this edition.

30. Haviland, "James and DuBois Encounter the South," unpublished ms.

31. Kristeva, p. 191.

32. Consider the recrudescence of arguments about the genetic basis of I.Q. and the racial endowments thereof in Charles Murray and Richard Herrnstein's *The Bell Curve* (New York: Free Press, 1994). At first sight, these arguments would seem to be exempt from the charge of antisemitism (at least), since Herrnstein and Murray include "Ashkenazi Jews" in their lists of the genetically equipped elite. But to the contrary, they import into the construction of the Jew good old-fashioned nineteenth-century scientific racism through the modifier "Ashkenazi." And they inadvertently demonstrate the incoherence of their own theorizing at the very same time. For any sustained reflection on the categories of "Ashkenaz" would question Herrnstein and Murray's astonishingly naive sense of racial identity, since that very category is constructed by the interpenetration of genetic materials between people living in the same geographical terrain. If, to the contrary, the designation of "Ashkenaz" is to be seen (as I believe it should) as essentially a cultural one, a designation referring to the interpretation of western European Jews and their gentile compatriots, then the genetic determinism of Murray and Herrnstein's argument is

dealt a quite significant blow. In either case, one is called upon to wonder why Murray and Herrnstein are compelled to make the distinction in the first place; and the answers, while not attractive, are revealing: for Murray and Herrnstein, almost reflexively, skin color and proximity to Europe seem to be the chief determining factors of cognitive intelligence and hence of social success in a culture that rewards intellectual attainment.

6. Ellmann

1. Eliot reportedly denies the presence of antisemitism in any of his poetry in an unpublished letter to Edward Field, 17 March 1947, in the T. S. Eliot Collection of the University of Texas at Austin (G462). I have not seen this letter.

2. Michael Reck, "A Conversation between Ezra Pound and Allen Ginsberg," *Evergreen Review* 55 (June 1968), pp. 27ff.

3. Canto CXX, *The Cantos* (New York: New Directions, 1970), p. 803. Further references to *The Cantos* will be designated by the Canto number (in Roman numerals) and the page number (in Arabic numerals).

4. George Steiner, letter to *The Listener*, 29 April 1971; cited in Christoper Ricks, *T. S. Eliot and Prejudice* (London: Faber, 1988), p. 28.

5. Letter from Pound to Eliot [24 December 1921], in *The Letters of T. S. Eliot*, ed. Valerie Eliot (London: Faber, 1988), vol. 1, p. 498.

6. "Whatever you do . . . avoid piles," Eliot cautioned a friend after an operation to remove his own in 1951: see Peter Ackroyd, *T. S. Eliot* (Harmondsworth: Penguin, 1984), p. 303. See also T. S. Eliot, *Collected Poems and Plays* (London: Faber, 1969), pp. 37, 56, 41.

7. Ricks, p. 38.

8. I am grateful to John Simons for this suggestion. Another example of Jewish eye disease may be found in the abominable unpublished "Dirge" in T. S. Eliot, *The Waste Land: A Facsimile and Transcript*, ed. Valerie Eliot (London: Faber, 1971), p. [121]:

> Full fathom five your Bleistein lies
> Under the flatfish and the squids.
> Graves' Disease in a dead jew's eyes!
> When the crabs have eat the lids.

The whole passage in the manuscript was marked "?? doubtful" by Pound.

9. Cited in Colin Holmes, *Anti-Semitism in British Society, 1879–1939* (London: Edward Arnold, 1979), p. 37.

10. Sander Gilman, *The Jew's Body* (London: Routledge, 1991), ch. 2, esp. pp. 38–49.

11. For a powerful attack on this tradition, see Leo Bersani, *The Culture of Redemption* (Cambridge, Mass.: Harvard University Press, 1990).

12. Quoted by Ricks, p. 61.

13. T. S. Eliot, *Notes Towards the Definition of Culture* (London: Faber, 1948), p. 71.

14. I am grateful to Ronald Schuchard for drawing my attention to this alteration.

15. Letter from Eliot to Pound, 28 December 1959, in Pound Archive, Beinecke; quoted in Maud Ellmann, *The Poetics of Impersonality: T. S. Eliot and Ezra Pound* (Cambridge, Mass.: Harvard University Press, 1987), p. 35.

16. T. S. Eliot, *After Strange Gods* (London: Faber, 1934), p. 19.

17. Ibid., p. 18.

18. James Joyce, *Ulysses* (London: Bodley Head, 1986), pp. 271–72.

19. Hannah Arendt, *The Origins of Totalitarianism* (1951; rpt. New York: Harcourt Brace Jovanovich, 1973), Part I: "Antisemitism."

20. Letter to J. V. Healy, 19 June 1940, T. S. Eliot Collection, University of Texas at Austin (G334); discussed by Ricks, p. 54.

21. T. S. Eliot, Letter to J. V. Healy, 10 May 1940, in T. S. Eliot Collection (G333).

22. Ibid.; cited by Ricks, p. 44.

23. T. S. Eliot, *Selected Prose*, ed. John Hayward (Harmondsworth: Penguin, 1953), pp. 20–21; the four sentences that follow Hayward's excerpt are the most notorious. I am grateful to John Simons for drawing my attention to this ellipsis.

24. "Classical Inhumanism," rev. of Geoffrey Wagner, *Wyndham Lewis*, TLS, 2 August 1957, p. 466.

25. *TLS*, 6 September 1957, p. 533. The editorial cited by Logue is in *Criterion* 7 (1928?), p. 98: "The accusations made by *The British Lion* against British Communists may all be true, and *the aims set forth in the statement of policy are wholly admirable*. The *Lion* wishes to support 'His Majesty the King, his heirs and successors, the present Constitution, the British Empire and the Christian Religion'. These are cardinal points. We would only suggest that the British Lion might very well uphold these things without dressing itself up in an Italian collar." Christopher Logue quotes only the passage italicized above. Eliot's views are more clearly expressed in another editorial in *Criterion* 8 (1928), p. 288, where he declares his preference for Charles Maurras and *Action Française* over fascism: "I am all the more suspicious of fascism as a panacea because I fail so far to find in it any important element, beyond this comfortable feeling that we shall be benevolently ordered about, which was not already in existence. Most of the concepts which might have attracted me in fascism I seem already to have found, in a more digestible form, in the work of Charles Maurras. I say a more digestible form, because I think they have a closer applicability to England than those of fascism." He concludes with the statement: "Both Russian communism and Italian fascism seem to me to have died as political ideas, in becoming political facts" (p. 290). In general terms, Eliot seems to feel that fascism, whatever its success in Italy, cannot be imported into Britain because of its incompatibility with monarchism.

26. Eliot, "The Hollow Men," V (1925), *Collected Poems*, p. 85.

27. William Empson, *Using Biography* (1984); cited by Ricks, p. 47.

28. Letter to Healy, 10 May 1940, T. S. Eliot Collection, University of Texas at Austin; cited by Ricks, p. 44.

29. Extended versions of these arguments may be found in my book, *The Poetics of Impersonality*, pp. 23–61; 149–99; and in my essay "Ezra Pound: The Erasure of History," in Derek Attridge, Geoff Bennington, and Robert Young, eds., *Post-Structuralism and the Question of History* (Cambridge: Cambridge University Press, 1987), pp. 224–62.

30. T. S. Eliot, *On Poetry and Poets* (London: Faber, 1957), pp. 32–33.

31. T. S. Eliot, "The Varieties of Metaphysical Poetry," The Turnbull Lectures, ms., T. S. Eliot Collection, Houghton Library (bMS Am 1261), III; cited in Ellmann, *The Poetics of Impersonality*, p. 54.

32. Terry Eagleton, "Eliot and a Common Culture," in Graham Martin, ed., *Eliot in Perspective: A Symposium* (London: Macmillan, 1970), p. 281.

33. T. S. Eliot, "The Metaphysical Poets" (1921), in *Selected Essays* (London: Faber, 1951), p. 288; "Swinburne as Poet" (1920), *Selected Essays*, p. 327; "Milton I" (1936), in Frank Kermode, ed., *Selected Prose* (London: Faber, 1975), p. 262; "Swinburne as Poet," *Selected Essays*, p. 327.

34. "The Method of Mr Pound," *Athenaeum*, no. 4669 (1919), p. 1065.

35. J.-K. Huysmans, *Against Nature [A Rebours]*, trans. Robert Baldick (Harmondsworth: Penguin, 1959), p. 162.

36. T. S. Eliot, *The Use of Poetry and the Use of Criticism* (1933; rpt. London: Faber, 1971), p. 135.

37. T. S. Eliot, *Little Gidding* (1942), V, *Collected Poems*, p. 197.

38. Quoted by Peter Ackroyd, *T. S. Eliot* (Harmondsworth: Penguin, 1984), p. 304.

39. Henry James, *The American Scene* (Bloomington: Indiana University Press, 1968), p. 131.

40. Ezra Pound, "Hugh Selwyn Mauberley (Life and Contacts)," lines 37–38, in *Collected Shorter Poems* (London: Faber, 1968), p. 206. See, for instance, Tadeusz Zielinski, *Our Debt to Antiquity*, trans. Strong and Stewart (London: Routledge, 1909), p. 123.

41. See Robert Casillo, *The Genealogy of Demons: Anti-Semitism, Fascism, and the Myths of Ezra Pound* (Evanston, Ill.: Northwestern University Press, 1988), pp. 4–8.

42. Ezra Pound, *Antheil and the Treatise on Harmony* (1927; rpt. New York: Da Capo Press, 1968), p. 9.

43. Letter to Louis Zukofsky, TS (March? 1936), Pound Archive, Beinecke Library, Yale University.

44. Letter to Boris de Rachewiltz, TS (31 May? 1954), ibid.; cited in Ellmann, "Ezra Pound: The Erasure of History," p. 250.

45. Ezra Pound, *Selected Prose: 1909–1965*, ed. William Cookson (London: Faber, 1973), p. 21.

46. Ezra Pound, *Gold and Work*, Money Pamphlets by £, no. 2 (London: Peter Russell, 1951), p. 12; rpt. in *Selected Prose*, p. 346.

47. Ezra Pound, *Impact: Essays on Ignorance and the Decline of American Civilization*, ed. Noel Stock (Chicago: Henry Regnery, 1960), pp. 91–92. See also XCIX 706: "You forget the timing of budgets / That is to say you probably don't even know that / Officials exist in time."

48. Ezra Pound, Postscript to Rémy de Gourmont, *The Natural Philosophy of Love* (London: Casanova Society, 1926), pp. 179, 169, 174; rpt. in Pound, *Pavannes and Divagations* (Norfolk: New Directions, 1958), pp. 203–14.

49. XLV 233; LXXIV 468; see also *Selected Prose*, pp. 290, 308, 338; and Christopher Hollis, *The Two Nations* (London: Routledge, 1935), ch. 3.

50. Ezra Pound, *Guide to Kulchur* (1938; London: Peter Owen, 1952), p. 78.

51. *Impact*, p. 233; *Selected Prose*, p. 265.

52. XLV 230; Addendum for C 798.

53. *Ezra Pound Speaking: Radio Speeches of World War II*, ed. Leonard J. Doob (Westport, Conn.: Greenwood, 1978), pp. 176–77; see also *Selected Prose*, p. 318.

54. *Radio Speeches*, p. 176; cf. *Selected Prose*, p. 347.

55. Frederick Soddy, "The Role of Money" (1934), in Montgomery Butchart, ed., *Money* (London: Stanley Nott, 1945), p. 268.

56. Letter to Agresti, TS (5 July 1951), Pound Archive, Beinecke Library, Yale University.

57. Letter to Sister Bernetta Quinn, TS (1954), ibid.

58. Myron I. Scholnick, *The New Deal and Anti-Semitism in America* (New York: Garland, 1990), pp. 62–68.

59. Letter to Boris de Rachewiltz (1 August 1954), Berg Collection, New York Public Library; Pound, *Guide to Kulchur*, p. 185.

60. *Pound/Joyce: The Letters of Ezra Pound to James Joyce, with Pound's Essays on Joyce*, ed. Forrest Read (London: Faber, 1966), p. 157.

61. James Joyce, *Finnegans Wake* (1939; rpt. New York: Viking, 1967), p. 116.

62. *Guide to Kulchur*, p. 243; see also my "Floating the Pound: The Circulation of the Subject of *The Cantos*," *Oxford Literary Review* 3 (1979), p. 26; and Daniel Pearlman, "Ezra Pound: America's Wandering Jew," *Paideuma* 9 (1980), pp. 461–81.

63. John Berryman, "The Imaginary Jew," *The Freedom of the Poet* (New York: Farrar, Straus and Giroux, 1976), pp. 364–66.

64. "Group Psychology" (1921), in the Standard Edition of *The Complete Psychological Works of Sigmund Freud*, trans. James Strachey (London: Hogarth, 1953–74), vol. 18, p. 105; "Mourning and Melancholia" (1917), vol. 14, p. 253.

7. Reizbaum

1. All parenthetical citations for passages in *Ulysses* refer to the corrected text, ed. Hans Walter Gabler with Wolfhard Steppe and Claus Melchior (New York: Vintage Books, 1986).

2. Oliver St. John Gogarty, *Sinn Fein*, Dec. 1, 1906. Joyce read Gogarty's series "Ugly England" in *Sinn Fein* and thought his article on Jews was "drivel" (*Letters*, II, p. 200). Dominic Manganiello has cited this same conjunction of facts (*Joyce's Politics* [Boston: Routledge and Kegan Paul, 1980], pp. 131–32), as has Ira Nadel in his recent work, *Joyce and the Jews* (Iowa City: University of Iowa Press, 1989), p. 66, in which he documents my work on this general subject as a source for his own (see Reizbaum, Ph.D. diss., "James Joyce's Judaic 'Other': Text and Contexts," University of Wisconsin–Madison, 1985.

3. Leon Hühner, "The Jews of Ireland: A Historical Sketch," in *Transactions of the Jewish Historical Society of England*, vol. 5 (1902–5), p. 242. Louis Hyman (*The Jews of Ireland from Earliest Times to the Year 1910* [Shannon: Irish University Press, 1972], pp. 183–84) cites an item in *Notes and Queries*, May 11, 1867, as a possible source for Deasy's remark and, at any rate, as an indication of the relative absence of Jews from Ireland: "It is said that in Ireland the Jew was never persecuted! Was it from a more exalted view of civil and religious liberty, or because the Jew was an

absentee from that country? I am inclined to think that the Jew was a non-resident in Ireland until late years."

4. A more recent and provocative study of Irish nationalism in these terms, though not related to Jewish figuration within it, is David Lloyd's *Nationalism and Minor Literature: James Clarence Mangan and The Emergence of Irish Cultural Nationalism* (Berkeley: University of California Press, 1987).

5. The myth of blood libel—the superstition that Jews kill Christian children in order to use their blood to make "matzoth," the ritual unleavened bread used on Passover—is thought to have first emerged in Europe in the twelfth century. Over the centuries, and including the twentieth (in Kiev, 1911), thousands of Jews have been murdered in pogroms as a consequence of the blood libel accusation. Bloom thinks about blood libel in Hades, an issue that contributes more generally to the trope of false accusation in *Ulysses*. For a discussion of blood libel in *Ulysses*, see Reizbaum, ch. 1.

6. Many have documented Father Creagh's part in the Limerick boycotts, including Hyman and Manganiello, and Marvin Magalaner in "The Anti-Semitic Limerick Incidents and Joyce's Bloomsday," *PMLA* 68 (December 1953), pp. 1219–23. Accounts of the boycott and Creagh's comments appeared in all the major Irish newspapers.

7. Bonnie Kime Scott has pointed out that *Lyceum*, a University College publication, which was published monthly from 1887 to 1894 and which was possibly a source for Joyce, was decidedly antisemitic in its views on the developing Jewish community in Ireland. Hyman refers to a priest's letter that appeared in the *Irish Catholic* of July 1893, in which he "sought to lend currency to the heartless slander that the Jews had been driven out of Russia for impropriety of behaviour" (in Hyman, p. 162). And in Eumaeus, Bloom intimates the clergy's attitude: "That's the juggle on which the p.p.'s raise the wind on false pretences" (16.1130–31). ("Raise the wind" in Irish idiom means to incriminate publicly with the intention to harm.)

8. Parnell, the charismatic Irish leader for Home Rule (1846–49) was a product of the Protestant ascendancy in Ireland. His affair with and eventual marriage to the Catholic Kitty O'Shea gave his opponents the "moral" ammunition to bring him down and thereby defeat his political platform, proving once again the potency of the religious context in Ireland. In this instance, the parallel drawn throughout *Ulysses* between Parnell and Bloom suggests what would be the demise of the Jewish community in Limerick.

9. Gerald Goldberg, former mayor of Cork, has sent me recorded accounts of the attacks upon Jews in Limerick. His father was among the Jews attacked. One such account appeared in the *Limerick Leader*, July 22, 1904. The phrase "catechism of anti-Semitism" derives from Magalaner's article on the Limerick boycott.

10. For example, see *United Irishman*, July 15, 1899.

11. The Masonic Order and Judaism have been historically linked—as secret(ive) societies, for example, that promote anti-Christian feeling. In Irish letters see, for example, Rev. Denis Fahey, C.S.Sp., *The Rulers of Russia* (1938), which draws upon another work translated into English, Vicomte Leon De Poncins, *The*

Secret Powers Behind Revolution (Boswell Printing and Publishing Co. Ltd., 1929). The latter identifies the B'nai B'rith as a Masonic order and links the Masonic star with the star of David. Relevantly, the old Masonic temple of Dublin (now the School for Irish Studies) has a six-pointed star of David as its window emblem. To suspect Bloom of Freemasonry is to metonymically identify him as Jewish, despite the fact that others in the novel, such as Frederick Falkiner, are associated with the Masons (Bloom observes Falkiner entering Freemasons Hall, 8.1151).

12. As a historical people, Jews might be seen in symbolical, almost mythical terms, often analogized with other oppressed peoples (the Irish, the Hungarians) and thereby romanticized. Once the Jew steps out of this symbolic role and becomes the citizen of an actual place, he becomes at once detestable, no longer a symbol of the oppressed but the killer of Christ, usurper of Jerusalem, usurer, heathen. This condition created a documentable pathology for the Jewish self-concept (self-hatred). For a more extensive discussion of this topic, see Reizbaum, "James Joyce's Judaic 'Other,'" pp. 12–17. For a more general treatment, see Sander Gilman, *Difference and Pathology: Stereotypes of Sexuality, Race and Madness* (Ithaca, N.Y.: Cornell University Press, 1985) and *Jewish Self-Hatred* (Baltimore: Johns Hopkins University Press, 1986).

13. One such attacker, particularly relevant here, calling himself "A Black Northman," penned the following:

> Since Father Creagh, C.ss.R., delivered his anathema against the Parasites, there has been much talking, much writing, much holding up of hypocritical holy hands. We Irish find it hard enough work to maintain a merest living in a country that should be our own by every right of descent. . . . Yet, because one man in Ireland is of heart high enough to say a word in defence of his own—his beggarly own—he is condemned on all sides as a bigot and a fanatic. Ireland's body is a body diseased; there is a strange sickness upon her that saps herself while it feeds the Parasites. If she is to survive as a nation she must rouse herself and shake off the Parasites, who, if they could, would bleed her blue veins white. (*All-Ireland Review*, May 7, 1904)

It has already been well documented by Louis Hyman and Marvin Magalaner that when Bloom defends the Jews to Stephen in Eumaeus, he seems to echo a reply to "A Black Northman" that appeared in the *Review* in that same month. That reply, signed "A Jewess," rebuts the accusation that the Jews are parasites by pointing to the Spain of the day as being considerably impoverished in comparison to the Spain of the Golden Age, when Jewish intellectuals flourished. Bloom likewise uses this example:

> Jews, he softly imparted in an aside in Stephen's ear, are accused of ruining. Not a vestige of truth in it, I can safely say. History—would you be surprised to learn?—proves up to the hilt Spain decayed when the Inquisition hounded the jews out and England prospered when Cromwell, an uncommonly able ruffian, who, in other respects, has much to answer for, imported them. (16.1119–24)

14. Manganiello discusses and documents Joyce's attitudes toward Griffith and *Sinn Fein*, pp. 125–30.

15. Ellsworth Mason and Richard Ellman, eds., *Critical Writings* (New York: Viking Press, 1959), pp. 161–62. This passage is alluded to in *Ulysses* (16.1130–31).

16. Drumont was a spokesman for the ideals of the Royalist, anti-Republican Action Française, a group that specialized in assaults on liberals, Jews, and Protestants. In 1886, he wrote a best-selling book, *La France juive*, in which he identifies the Jews as the principal source of France's misfortunes. This, among other things, set the scene for the Dreyfus affair.

17. Augustin Daly's *Leah the Forsaken* (printed for the author, 1863) is an adaptation of Solomon Hermann von Mosenthal's *Deborah* (Leipzig: Philipp Reclaim, 1908). (Joseph Prescott discusses Joyce's use of Mosenthal's text in "Mosenthal's *Deborah* and Joyce's *Ulysses*.") *Leah* treats the love affair between a Jewish woman and a non-Jewish man that is thwarted by an apostate Jew who fears she will uncover his identity. By the end of the play he is exposed by her, and she dies a broken-hearted woman wrongly accused of opportunism in her desire to marry the gentile. Nathan, the Jewish apostate, can escape neither his identity nor his guilt for apostasy.

18. Griffith's *The Resurrection of Hungary* first appeared as a series of articles in the *United Irishman* (Jan. 30, 1904, p. 3; Feb. 6, 1904, p. 3; Feb. 13, 1904, p. 6; Feb. 20, 1904, p. 3) and then was published separately as a pamphlet in 1904.

19. Robert Tracy makes this claim and discusses generally the significance of Bloom's Hungarian background in "Leopold Bloom Fourfold: A Hungarian-Hebraic-Hellenic-Hibernian Hero," *Massachusetts Review* 6 (Spring–Summer 1965), pp. 523–38. Tracy also suggests, as I have, that the "over-patriotic" "are portrayed as paying lip service to liberty and democracy, and as having veneration for Jews and Hungarians as symbols but no tolerance for them as individuals" (p. 535).

20. Joyce followed trials in Dublin that involved Jews. In one particular case, *Wought v. Zeretsky*, a Jew is accused of masquerading as an emigration official and of obtaining money from another Jew for passage to Canada. It is less a matter of false accusation than a confirmation of the stereotype of the Jew as thief and swindler — the headline of the article in the *Evening Mail* (June 16, 1904) reads "ALLEGED IMMIGRATION SWINDLE — A JEW AND HIS FELLOWS." Joyce incorporates the case into the Cyclops chapter (12.1089–93) where Bloom is identified as a series of Jewish stereotypes, pilloried by prejudice, and, ironically, crucified for being a Jew (like Christ). Joyce replaces the judge of *Wought v. Zeretsky* (Swifte) with the Recorder Falkiner, who reappears in the trial scene in Circe.

21. I have copies of the letters, thanks to Gerald Goldberg, from Montefiore to Falkiner, dated Jan. 29, 1902, and from Falkiner to Montefiore, dated Jan. 30, 1902. Accounts of the exchange were reported in the press.

22. All parenthetical citations to page numbers in *Dubliners* refer to the Penguin edition (The Viking Critical Library, 1969).

23. In Circe especially, the text enacts the historical figuration of cultural inferiority in stereotypes of the feminine — the disempowerment of a culture is an emasculation. There is a litany of racist and sexist theories that use and reinforce such a

figuration. One such source for Joyce was Otto Weininger's *Sex and Character* (1903). These ideas are developed at some length in ch. 4 of "James Joyce's Judaic 'Other.'" For a more general discussion, see also Gilman, *Difference and Pathology* and *The Jew's Body* (New York: Routledge, 1991), as well as Andrew Parker, Mary Russo, Doris Sommer, and Patricia Yaeger, eds., *Nationalisms & Sexualities* (London: Routledge, 1992).

24. This observation has been made before by both Robert Boyle, S.J., "A Note on Reuben J. Dodd as a 'Dirty Jew,'" *James Joyce Quarterly* 3 (Fall 1965): 64–66; and Patrick A. McCarthy, "The Case of Reuben J. Dodd," *James Joyce Quarterly* 21, no. 2 (Winter 1984): 171.

25. Davitt, in two works—*The Boer Fight for Freedom* (New York: Funk and Wagnall, 1902) and *Within the Pale: The True Story of the Anti-Semitic Persecutions in Russia* (1903)—gave evidence of his own antisemitism. He could stand in opposition to the Jew where he might be a foe "to nationality, or against the engineers of a sordid war in South Africa, or as the assailant of the economic evils of unscrupulous capitalism everywhere."

26. Joyce has by now made famous John F. Taylor's speech of Oct. 24, 1901, in Dublin—"The Language of the Outlaw"—in which he analogizes the Irish plight with the Israelites' slavery under the Pharaoh. Part of that speech is reproduced in Aeolus (7.842–70).

27. Charles Vallancey was an eighteenth-century comparative mythologist who had a theory that the Irish were of Phoenician origin (*A Vindication of the Ancient History of Ireland* [1786]). Joyce mentions Vallancey's theories in "Ireland, Island of Saints and Sages," a lecture delivered in Trieste in 1907 (*Critical Writings*).

28. Edward Raphael Lipsett, a Dublin Jew, journalist, novelist, and playwright, recorded his impressions of the position of the Jew in Ireland, in the *Jewish Chronicle*, Dec. 21, 1906:

> There is an invisible but impassable barrier between Jew and Christian—a barrier which the one party will not, and the other cannot, break through. You cannot get one native to remember that a Jew may be an Irishman. The term "Irish Jew" seems to have a contradictory ring upon the native ear; the very idea is wholly inconceivable to the native mind. . . . Irish Jews feel that if they spoke of each other as Jewish Irishmen, it would meet with a cutting cynicism from the natives that the two elements can never merge into one, for any single purpose. . . . There is undoubtedly a mutual estrangement between the Jews and the Irish. The Jews understand the Irish little; the Irish understand the Jews less. Each seems a peculiar race in the eyes of the other; and, in a word, the position of Jews in Ireland is peculiarly peculiar.

Hyman cites this passage, p. 176.

8. Rose

1. Hannah Arendt, *The Origins of Totalitarianism* (1951; New York: Harcourt Brace Jovanovich, 1973), part 1, "Antisemitism."

2. Virginia Woolf, *Three Guineas* (1938; Oxford: Oxford University Press, World's Classics, ed. Morag Shiach, 1992), pp. 273, 313.

3. Henry James, *The Portrait of a Lady* (1881; Harmondsworth: Penguin, 1963), p. 196.

4. Dorothy Richardson, *Pilgrimage*, 13 vols. (J. M. Dent, 1915–67; rpt. London: Virago, 1979).

5. See, for example, Robert Casillo, *The Genealogy of Demons: Anti-Semitism, Fascism and the Myths of Ezra Pound* (Evanston: Northwestern University Press, 1988); Christopher Ricks, *T. S. Eliot and Prejudice* (London: Faber, 1988); Bryan Cheyette, *Constructions of "the Jew" in English Literature and Society: Racial Representations, 1875–1945* (Cambridge: Cambridge University Press, 1993).

6. May Sinclair, *Mary Olivier: A Life* (1919; London: Virago, 1980), *Life and Death of Harriet Frean* (1922; London: Virago, 1980).

7. Virginia Woolf, *The Years* (1937; Oxford: Oxford University Press, World's Classics, ed. Hermione Lee, 1992), p. 322; see essay here by Phyllis Lassner, "The Milk of Our Mother's Kindness"; Stevie Smith, *Novel on Yellow Paper* (1936; London: Virago, 1980), pp. 10–11, but see also p. 107; Djuna Barnes, *Ladies Almanack* (1928; Elmwood: Dalkey Archive Press, 1992), p. 15.

8. Cheyette, *Constructions of "the Jew"*; the discussion that follows is indebted to ch. 4, "The 'Socialism of Fools': George Bernard Shaw and H. G. Wells."

9. Cited in Cheyette, p. 144.

10. Ibid., pp. 144–48.

11. This is the title of one chapter of Colin Holmes's study of English anti-semitism, *Anti-Semitism in British Society, 1876–1939* (London: Arnold, 1979), "A Nation Within a Nation?"

12. Benjamin Kidd, "Individualism and After," Herbert Spencer Lecture (Oxford: Clarendon Press, 1908), p. 10; Arnold White, *The Modern Jew* (London: Heinemann, 1899), p. 199.

13. White, p. xvi.

14. James, *The Portrait of a Lady*, p. 196.

15. Kidd, "Individualism and After," p. 20.

16. See Geoffrey Alderman, *The Jewish Community in British Politics* (Oxford: Clarendon Press, 1983), ch. 4, "The Socialists Arrive," p. 53.

17. See Alderman, and Lloyd Gartner, *The Jewish Immigrant in England, 1870–1914* (London: Simon, 1960 [1973]).

18. Cited in Gartner, p. 134.

19. Jean Radford, *Dorothy Richardson* (Hemel Hempstead: Harvester, 1991), ch. 2, "A Form of Quest."

20. Richardson, *Clear Horizon* (1935; Virago), vol. 4.

21. Josef Kastein, *Jews in Germany*, trans. Dorothy Richardson, preface by James Stephens (London: Cresset, 1934); Robert Neumann, *Mammon (die Macht)*, trans. Dorothy Richardson (London: Peter Davies, 1933). This second translation appears to have the most bizarre publishing history: rejected first by the English publishers, then by the author, who objected to the pre-arranged cuts, described in Gloria Fromm's biography of Richardson as finally abandoned altogether, it is nonetheless

listed in Fromm's bibliography and was published by Peter Davies in 1933 (even more oddly, inside the cover of the translation it lists the original as first published in 1931, *Mammon*, i.e., the translation as published in 1926, which would make this a novel, not impossibly, whose English translation preceded its German publication); see Gloria Fromm, *Dorothy Richardson: A Biography* (Urbana: University of Illinois Press, 1977), pp. 266–68.

22. Richardson, *Deadlock* (1921; Virago), vol. 3.

23. Kastein, p. 61, pp. 54–55.

24. Cited in Fromm, p. 222. Oscar Wilde gives these terms his own pro-decadent turn in *The Picture of Dorian Gray* (1891), in a conversation between Lord Henry Wotton and a duchess: "'I believe in the race,' she cried. 'It represents the survival of the pushing.' 'It has development.' 'Decay fascinates me more'" (Oxford, World's Classics, ed. Isobel Murray), p. 195.

25. Sigmund Freud, "Some Psychical Consequences of the Anatomical Distinction Between the Sexes," 1925 (Standard Edition of the Complete Psychological Works, vol. 19, p. 257; Penguin Freud, vol. 7, p. 341); *Three Essays on the Theory of Sexuality*, 1905 (Standard Edition, vol. 7, p. 207; Penguin Freud, vol. 7, p. 128).

26. Freud, *Beyond the Pleasure Principle*, 1921 (Standard Edition, vol. 19, Penguin Freud, vol. 11).

27. Richardson, *Dawn's Left Hand* (1931; Virago), vol. 4, p. 155.

28. Ibid., p. 288.

29. Beatrice Potter, "The Jewish Community," in Charles Booth, ed., *Life and Labour of the People in London*, 1st ser. (London, 1902), vol. 3, "Poverty," p. 192.

30. Cited by Bryan Cheyette, "Anglo-Jewish Fiction," in David Cesarani, ed., *The Making of Modern Anglo-Jewry* (Oxford: Blackwell, 1990), p. 110.

31. White, p. 209.

32. Claire Buck, paper presented at Cambridge "Modernism" conference, July 1993.

33. Kastein, p. 78.

34. Otto Weininger, Viennese turn-of-the-century author of *Sex and Character* (1903) who killed himself shortly after completing this "Jewish self-hating" and misogynistic text; see Sander Gilman, *The Jew's Body* (London: Routledge, 1991), pp. 131–37; and Jean Radford, paper presented at Cambridge "Modernism" conference, July 1993.

35. Potter, pp. 190, 168.

36. Kastein, p. 61.

37. Fromm, p. 153.

38. Kidd, p. 25.

39. Richardson, *Deadlock*, p. 150.

40. Gayatri Spivak, "Three Women's Texts and a Critique of Imperialism," in Catherine Belsey and Jane Moore, eds., *The Feminist Reader* (London: Macmillan, 1989).

41. White, p. 193.

42. Potter, p. 182.

43. Gartner, pp. 264–65.

44. Alderman, p. 65.

45. Cited by John Rosenberg, *Dorothy Richardson, The Genius They Forgot: A Critical Biography* (London: Duckworth, 1973), p. 64.

46. Cited in Cheyette, *Constructions of "the Jew,"* p. 144.

47. This analogy between woman and Jew, between racial and sexual oppression, has also taken the most concrete of forms; in June 1914, a demonstration at the Brighton synagogue on the part of Jewish suffragettes—who were particularly incensed at the role of established Jewish MPs such as Herbert Samuel and Rufus Isaacs in incarcerations and force-feedings—compared British treatment of suffragettes to the Russian treatment of Jews (Alderman, p. 87).

48. Richardson, *The Quakers Past and Present* (London: Constable, 1914), p. 5.

49. Richardson, *Deadlock*, p. 218.

50. Richardson, *Dimple Hill* (1938; Virago), vol. 4, p. 427.

51. Compare, too: "We all live under a Metaphocrasy. Tell her I'm giving up thinking in words. She will understand. Will agree that thought is cessation, cutting one off from the central essence, bearing an element of calculation." Richardson, *March Moonlight* (1967; Virago), vol. 4, p. 607.

52. Richardson, *Clear Horizon*, p. 292.

53. Arendt, *The Origins of Totalitarianism*, part 3, "Totalitarianism," p. 438. Compare, however, Marx in "Estranged Labour": "Man is a species being, not only because in practice and in theory he adopts the species as his object, but also because he treats himself as the actual, living species: because he treats himself as a *universal* and therefore a free being. *Economic and Philosophical Manuscripts of 1844* (London: Lawrence and Wishart, 1973), p. 112.

54. Arendt, *The Human Condition* (Chicago: University of Chicago Press, 1958), p. 312, cited Mary G. Dietz, "Hannah Arendt and Feminist Politics," in Mary Lyndon Shanley and Carole Pateman, eds., *Feminist Interpretations and Political Theory* (Cambridge: Polity, 1991), p. 244.

55. Elizabeth Young-Bruehl, *Hannah Arendt: For Love of the World* (New Haven: Yale University Press, 1982). For a discussion of the way this difficulty traces itself out in Arendt's own writing, see Gillian Rose, *The Broken Middle: Out of Our Ancient Society* (Oxford: Blackwell, 1992), ch. 5, "Love and the State—Varnhagen, Luxemburg and Arendt."

56. For discussion of these criticisms, see Dietz.

9. Lassner

1. Jane Marcus, *Virginia Woolf and the Languages of Patriarchy* (Bloomington: Indiana University Press, 1987), pp. 55, 78.

2. For an account of the debate about *Three Guineas* that originally appeared in *Time and Tide* (25 June 1938), pp. 887–88, see Jane Marcus, "'No More Horses': Virginia Woolf on Art and Propaganda," *Women's Studies* 4 (1977): 203–14.

3. Brenda R. Silver, "*Three Guineas* Before and After: Further Answers to Correspondents," in Jane Marcus, ed., *Virginia Woolf: A Feminist Slant* (Lincoln: University of Nebraska Press, 1983), p. 269.

4. *The Diary of Virginia Woolf*, ed. Anne Olivier Bell (New York: Harcourt Brace, 1984), vol. 5 (1936–1941), pp. 142, 169; *The Letters of Virginia Woolf*, ed. Nigel Nicolson and Joanne Trautmann (New York: Harcourt Brace, 1975), vol. 6, p. 379.

5. "Thoughts on Peace in an Air Raid," in *Collected Essays* (New York: Harcourt Brace, 1967), p. 174; *Letters*, vol. 6, p. 379.

6. *Three Guineas*, p. 103. Catherine F. Smith observes that in *Three Guineas* "ideas are imaged and dramatised" as a "visionary method" of "making society equitable and just" through the mind and writing of the woman narrator (*"Three Guineas*: Virginia Woolf's Prophecy," in Jane Marcus, ed., *Virginia Woolf and Bloomsbury* [Houndmills: Macmillan, 1987], p. 226). Beverly Ann Schlack sees precursors of Woolf's "explicitly bitter anger of *Three Guineas* towards 'manhood and patriotism, politics, and war' throughout her career" ("Fathers in General," in Jane Marcus, ed., *Virginia Woolf: A Feminist Slant*, p. 70.

7. *Virginia Woolf and the Languages of Patriarchy*, p. 120. For an analysis of the Woolfs' political disagreements, see Laura M. Gottleib, "The War Between the Woolfs," in Marcus, *Virginia Woolf and Bloomsbury*, who opts for Virginia's approach.

8. See "The Duchess and the Jeweller," unsigned and undated typescripts, at the Berg Collection of the New York Public Library, quoted with their permission and that of Quentin Bell.

9. Editorial note, *The Complete Shorter Fiction of Virginia Woolf*, 2nd. ed., ed. Susan Dick (New York: Harcourt Brace, 1989), p. 309; my emphasis.

10. For analyses of these literary stereotypes, see Harold Fisch, *The Dual Image: A Study of the Jew in English and American Literature* (London: World Jewish Library, 1971); Esther Panitz, *The Alien in Their Midst: Images of Jews in English Literature* (East Brunswick, N.J.: Assoc. University Press, 1981); Anne A. Naman, *The Jew in the Victorian Novel* (New York: AMS Press, 1980); Bryan Cheyette, "Jewish Stereotyping and English Literature," in Tony Kushner and Ken Lunn, eds., *Traditions of Intolerance* (Manchester: Manchester University Press, 1989).

11. Quoted by Sander Gilman in his discussion of the Jew's nose as "the iconic representation of the Jew's phallus" as a carrier of disease, *The Jew's Body* (New York: Routledge, 1991), p. 126.

12. Margery Allingham, "The Hat Trick," in *Mr. Campion and Others* (1939; Harmondsworth: Penguin, 1959), pp. 52–53.

13. I am grateful to Karen Alkalay-Gut for this insight. Naman argues that using Jewish or other typed traits to define Jewish character and focusing on the Jew's "moral traits and social roles rather than psychological complexities and environmental circumstances" suffuses his character with prejudice (p. 10).

14. *Three Guineas*, p. 103; "Thoughts on Peace," p. 174.

15. Phyllis Grosskurth, "Between Eros and Thanatos," review of vol. 6 of *Letters of Virginia Woolf, Times Literary Supplement*, Oct. 31, 1980, p. 1225; *The Journey Not the Arrival Matters* (London: Hogarth, 1970), p. 12. Leonard Woolf's youthful "bitterness and ambivalence" toward his Jewish identity developed into pride as he became concerned with antisemitism, beginning with his novel *The Wise Virgins* and story "Three Jews" and concluding with his account of his visit to Israel in 1957 (*Sowing: An Autobiography of the Years 1880–1904* [New York: Harcourt Brace, 1969],

p. 196). See Freema Gottlieb, "Leonard Woolf's Attitude to his Jewish Background and to Judaism," *Transactions of the Jewish Historical Society of England, 1973–75,* pp. 25–38, for an analysis of Leonard Woolf's ambivalence.

16. Critics have used the Woolfs' complex marriage to explain their intellectual and political differences. Both Grosskurth and Cynthia Ozick ("Mrs. Virginia Woolf," *Commentary* [August 1973]: 33–44) link their marital tensions both to Leonard's attitude toward Virginia's illness and to Virginia's ambivalence about Jews. Louise de Salvo notes Virginia's "repulsion" toward Leonard's family, but then, stringing together bits and pieces from Leonard's letters and from various intensely invested and therefore biased sources, states, as definitive and incontrovertible truth, that Leonard's "cruelty" and "betrayal" were to blame for the Woolfs' tensions. Virginia, by contrast, is beatified as his forgiving victim (*Conceived with Malice* [New York: Dutton, 1994], pp. 69, 59, 87). Though de Salvo allows for the marriage to develop productively, nowhere does she consider the historic and political implications of Virginia's "rabid anti-Semitism," p. 69.

17. Leonard felt that Germany's harsh punishment at the end of World War I led to an inevitable rise of militarism, but also felt that the Labour Party should "commit itself to a policy of resisting any further acts of aggression by Hitler" by ensuring Britain's military strength; see *Downhill All the Way* (London: Hogarth Press, 1970), p. 243.

18. Laura Gottlieb purports to compare the political writing of both Woolfs, but she analyzes only *The Intelligent Man's Way to Prevent War,* whose approach to ending war she finds "narrow" but to which she admits Leonard had only "limited involvement" (p. 247), and ignores his *Barbarians at the Gates.* Her argument that Leonard was jealous of Virginia's "intrusion into the field he had designated as his own" dismisses the validity of their different approaches as well as the possibility of taking his response to *Three Guineas* seriously (p. 242). Alex Zwerdling offers a careful analysis of the intellectual, political, and emotional bases of the Woolfs' different views about the coming war in *Virginia Woolf and the Real World* (Berkeley: University of California Press, 1986).

19. Wayne K. Chapman and Janet M. Manson show how the Woolfs collaborated and influenced each other's thinking about war and peace throughout the period of World War I and afterwards in their hopes for the League of Nations; see "Carte and Tierce: Leonard, Virginia Woolf, and War for Peace," in Mark Hussey, ed., *Virginia Woolf and War* (Syracuse: Syracuse University Press, 1991).

20. *The Years* (London: Hogarth Press, 1937), p. 366. Freema Gottlieb also shows that this representation coincides with a "Nazi typology," which justified closing swimming baths to Jews in 1933 because, as Sartre showed in his study of antisemitism, "the body of the Jew would render the bath wholly unclean" (p. 29).

21. In *The Elephant and My Jewish Problem* (New York: Harper & Row, 1988), Hugh Nissenson reports a conversation with Quentin Bell, who said that "when she was young, Virginia had a Jewish problem. Leonard, too, if the truth be told. It's a common English ailment. It doesn't mean much" (p. 156).

22. Preparing for *Three Guineas,* Woolf carefully searched the daily newspapers for evidence of masculinity and militarism. See Zwerdling, p. 299, and Brenda Silver, *Virginia Woolf's Reading Notebooks* (Princeton: Princeton University Press,

1983). The hostility and aggression that Sara shares with North challenge Patricia Cramer's thesis that the novel expresses "feelings of peace and love that Woolf associated with maternal and woman-to-woman love" ("Loving in the War Years," *Virginia Woolf and War*, p. 206).

23. Leonard Woolf felt that though "the hero of this novel — is England and the pageant of English history . . . the war itself is not referred to except once obliquely"; quoted in Zwerdling, p. 353, from the Leonard Woolf Papers, I R, University of Sussex Library.

24. *Virginia Woolf: Feminist Destinations* (Oxford: Blackwell, 1988), pp. 149–50. Elizabeth Abel compares the novel to Freud's conception of a progressive patriarchal order that ignores the relationship between Hitler, antisemitism, and the powerful authority Freud himself invokes. Although she sees the novel's "present-time reality" recreating an oppressive patriarchal past, she never mentions the presence and absence of Jews, *Virginia Woolf and the Fictions of Psychoanalysis* (Chicago: University of Chicago Press, 1989), p. 116. Judith Johnston sees the novel challenging "the humanist myth of a continuous cultural lineage from Greek to . . . British empires" ("The Remediable Flaw," in *Virginia Woolf and Bloomsbury*, p. 260).

25. *Letters of Vita Sackville-West to Virginia Woolf* (New York: William Morrow, 1985), p. 415. Sackville-West offers a different view of responsibility for World War II in her dystopic novel, *Grand Canyon* (London: Michael Joseph, 1942), which was a plea for the United States to enter the war and save itself and the world from repeating a politics of appeasement. Woolf's use of combative language has been noted by Zwerdling, among others.

26. Pamela Caughie argues in *Virginia Woolf and Postmodernism* (Bloomington: Indiana University Press, 1991) that more important than resolving conflict is to recognize "how our descriptions create them" (p. 207), but Deborah Guth, "Fiction as Self-Evasion in *Mrs. Dalloway*," *Modern Language Review* 84 (Jan. 1989), shows how Woolf's evasiveness prevents this. Brenda R. Silver shows how "the authority of anger" in *Three Guineas* is emotionally and ideologically directed (*"Three Guineas* Before and After"). I would insist that Woolf's representation of Jews is both evasive and directed; while her anger at patriarchal oppression is justified, the vituperative tone embedded in her portraits of Jews is dangerous and questions her authority.

27. Louise de Salvo asserts that Woolf's final depression results from being unable to reconcile Freud's insistence on unconscious fantasy with her experiences and memory of childhood sexual abuse, *Virginia Woolf: The Impact of Childhood Sexual Abuse on Her Life and Work* (New York: Ballantyne, 1989). I maintain that her despair is overdetermined, that the war meshes with memories of abuse and loss, and that reading Freud was disturbing because it also made her recognize so much of her unresolved ambivalence. Andrea Freud Loewenstein's psychological model of ambivalence toward the Jew in modern British writers such as Graham Greene and Wyndham Lewis, *Loathsome Jews and Engulfing Women* (New York: New York University Press, 1993), is very useful in pointing to the convergence of political attitudes and rhetorical strategy.

28. Nora Eisenberg, "Virginia Woolf's Last Words on Words: *Between the Acts* and 'Anon,'" in Jane Marcus, ed., *New Feminist Essays on Virginia Woolf* (Lincoln: University of Nebraska Press, 1981), p. 257.

29. Joyce Carol Oates sees Pompey's voice as "quirky, rambling, ingenuous, stubborn, funny-peculiar." See "A Child with a Cold, Cold Eye," *New York Times Book Review*, Oct. 3, 1982, p. 11. David Garnett discusses her candor in *The New Statesman and Nation*, Sept. 5, 1936, p. 321.

30. Frances Spalding notes Smith's criticism of George Orwell, who, as Loewenstein shows in this volume, expressed ambivalence toward the Jews despite his avowed sympathy for them and his analysis of British antisemitism. See *Stevie Smith: A Biography* (New York: Norton, 1988). Sanford Sternlicht maintains that Smith is not interested in politics, but despite her own disclaimer, the discourse on antisemitism in *Over the Frontier* is thoroughly politicized. For Smith's political values in relation to Storm Jameson, see my essay, "A Cry for Life," in M. Paul Holsinger and Mary Anne Schofield, eds., *Visions of War* (Bowling Green: Popular Press, 1992).

31. Paul Rich sees "the British right in the inter-war years as dominated by a more traditional Victorian idea of status and gentility" ("Imperial Decline," in *Traditions of Intolerance*, p. 37).

32. Tony Kushner discusses the survival of British antisemitism during the war, despite the decline of Oswald Moseley's British Union of Fascists ("The Paradox of Prejudice," in *Traditions of Intolerance*). Hermione Lee notes Pompey's lack of "patience with pacifism in the face of the Nazis" in relation to her concern with the aggression of men and women; see "Stevie Smith," in Harold Bloom, ed., *British Modernist Fiction, 1920–1945* (New York: Chelsea House, 1986), p. 320.

10. Loewenstein

1. Sander Gilman, *Difference and Pathology: Stereotypes of Sexuality, Race, and Madness* (Ithaca: Cornell University Press, 1985) pp. 20–22.

2. For a good short summary of the muscular Christianity code, see Daphne Patai, *The Orwell Mystique: A Study in Male Ideology* (Amherst, Mass.: University of Massachusetts Press, 1984), p. 273, n. 2. More detailed histories and descriptions of this idea can be found in John Reed's *Old School Ties: The Public Schools in British Literature* (Syracuse, N.Y.: Syracuse University Press, 1964). Also see J. A. Magnan and James Walvin, eds., *Manliness and Morality: Middle-Class Masculinity in Britain and America, 1800–1940* (Manchester, Eng.: Manchester University Press, 1987).

3. George Orwell, "Such, Such Were the Joys," in Sonia Orwell and Ian Angus, eds., *The Collected Essays, Journalism, and Letters of George Orwell* (New York: Harcourt, Brace and World, 1986), vol. 4, p. 359.

4. Karen Horney, "The Dread of Women," *International Journal of Psychoanalysis* (1932), p. 357. For other gynocentric theorists, see Melanie Kline, "Notes on Some Schizoid Mechanisms," in *Envy and Gratitude and Other Works, 1946–1963* (1975; New York: The Free Press, 1984); Margaret Mead, *Male and Female* (New York: William Morrow, 1949); Dorothy Dinnerstein, *The Mermaid and the Minotaur: Sexual Arrangements and Human Malaise* (New York: Harper and Row, 1976); Jessica Benjamin, *The Bonds of Love: Psychoanalysis, Feminism, and the Problem of Domination* (New Haven: Yale University Press, 1989); Nancy Chodorow, *Feminism and Psychoanalytic Theory* (New York: Princeton University Press, 1989).

5. Mead, *Male and Female*, p. 303, quoted by Chodorow, *Feminism and Psychoanalytic Theory*, p. 40.

6. For men such as Charles Williams and William Gerhardi who longed to attend a public school but were never able to, the ideals of muscular Christianity were sometimes even more pervasive than for those who actually lived the ideal.

7. For a summary of this literary history see Edgar Rosenberg, *From Shylock to Svengali: Jewish Stereotypes in English Fiction* (Stanford, Calif.: Stanford University Press, 1960), and Leslie Fiedler, "'What Can We Do About Fagin?' The Jew-Villain in Western Tradition," *Commentary* 7 (May 1949). See also chap. 3 of my book, *Loathsome Jews and Engulfing Women: Metaphors of Projection in the Works of Wyndham Lewis, Charles Williams and Graham Greene* (New York: New York University Press, 1993).

8. For a quick historical summary of this history of Anglo Jewry, see ch. 3 of Loewenstein, *Loathsome Jews*, or Solomon Grayzell, *A History of the Jews: From the Babylonian Exile to the Present* (New York: New American Library, Mentor, 1947, 1968).

9. For an excellent summary of these characteristics, see Rosenberg, pp. 35–36.

10. David Shapiro, *Autonomy and Rigid Character* (New York: Basic Books, 1981), pp. 101–2.

11. Ibid., p. 107. This pervasive relational sadism should be distinguished from consensual sexual sado-masochism, which is often confined to sexual behavior only.

12. Robert Stoller, *Perversions: The Erotic Form of Hatred* (Washington, D.C.: American Psychiatric Press, 1975), p. 27.

This symbolic strategy has historically been used against Jews. In *The Dual Image* (London: World Jewish Library, 1971), Harold Fisch attempted to explain the "blood libel" myth that appears over and over in oral and written literature and that was used, as late as the Second World War, for the justification for countless pogroms and expulsions. Fisch calls it "a simple example of guilt transference or substitution" in which

> the guilt one feels in one's own conscience . . . is transferred imaginatively to the victim who is made guilty of precisely the same crime. It is no accident that the revival of the blood libel charge has always been associated with actual outbreaks of violence against Jews: the myth is clearly produced to justify by anticipation the crime already mediated by the unconscious. (p. 22)

A more modern instance of such a substitution can be found in the minutes of the British Foreign Office, Colonial Office, and Ministry of Information during World War II. The officials in these offices took passive but lethal action congruent with their perceived role of oppressed victims of the Jews. J. S. Bennett, one of the Colonial Office's Middle East experts, complained in the Minutes for April 18, 1941: "The Jews have done nothing but add to our difficulties by propaganda and deeds since the war began . . . when coupled with unscrupulous Zionist 'sob stuff' and misrepresentations, it is very hard to bear" (Public Record Office, Colonial Office. 733/445/ Part II 76021/308; in Bernard Wasserstein, *Britain and the Jews of Europe, 1939–1945* [Oxford: Oxford University Press, 1988], p. 50).

Officials like Bennett, even in the face of the most overwhelming evidence of victimization, continued to perceive themselves and the country they identified with as the real victims and the Jews as oppressors. Their "defensive" reactions included delays, lies, and inaction used to counter schemes to provide aid to the Jews of Europe and to countermand instructions from the Prime Minister and Foreign Secretary to bomb Auschwitz.

13. William Gerhardi, in a letter to Oliver Stonor of May 31, 1941. Quoted in Dido Davies, *William Gerhardi* (Oxford: Oxford University Press, 1990), p. 313.

14. William Gerhardi, *Memoirs of a Polyglot* (London: Macdonald, 1931).

15. For Wyndham Lewis, see Loewenstein, *Loathsome Jews*.

16. From an undated letter to Prince Leopold Loewenstein, in Davies, p. 365.

17. In contrast, George Orwell and Graham Greene, who did have the capacity to envision other people as human, were able to create some convincing (male) characters.

18. William Gerhardi, "In the Wood," in *Pretty Creatures* (New York: Duffield, 1927), p. 139.

19. William Gerhardi, "Tristan and Isolde," in *Pretty Creatures*, p. 189.

20. William Gerhardi, *My Wife's the Least of It* (London: Faber and Faber, 1938), p. 289.

21. See Wyndham Lewis, *The Apes of God* (1930; Santa Barbara: Black Sparrow, 1981), pp. 425–473. See also Loewenstein, *Loathsome Jews*, pp. 183–87.

22. Both Gerhardi and Lewis, of course, saw themselves as the only true example of such a category.

23. V. S. Pritchett, "George Orwell," *New Statesman and Nation*, Jan. 28, 1950, p. 96. Quoted by Patai, p. 13. I am heavily indebted to Daphne Patai's ideas for my thinking on George Orwell in this paper.

24. Humphrey Dakin to Ian Angus, interview, April 1965, in Michael Sheldon, *Orwell: The Authorized Biography* (New York: Harper Collins, 1991), p. 19.

25. George Orwell, unpublished notebooks, quoted in Sheldon, p. 22.

26. George Orwell, *Coming Up for Air* (New York: Harcourt Brace, 1939; 1950), p. 54.

27. Homosexuals, Indians, nudists, Quakers, vegetarians, divorce reformers, pacifists, birth control "fanatics," feminists, and Jews, to name only a few of his common targets.

28. For this attraction, see Daphne Patai on *The Road to Wigan Pier* and *Down and Out in Paris and London*.

29. The text of the letter Eileen wrote to him before entering the hospital, where she died under anesthetic, is a frightening document, part of whose text follows:

> One very good thing is that by the time you get home I'll be convalescent . . . and you won't have the hospital nightmare you so much dislike. You'd more or less have to visit me, and visiting someone in a ward really is a nightmare . . . particularly if they're badly ill as I shall be at first of course. I only wish I could have had your approval as it were. . . . The surgeon will finish me off as quickly as anyone in England, as well as doing the job properly—so

he may well come cheaper in the end. I rather wish I'd talked it over with you before you went away. I knew I had a "Growth." But I wanted you to go away peacefully. (Crick, p. 330)

30. For the texts of letters sent to both wives and letters proposing marriage to several women, see Crick.

31. In this chapter I owe an enormous debt to Patai and to David Walton, "George Orwell and Antisemitism," "*Patterns of Prejudice*," vol. 16, no. 1 (1982), pp. 19–34. Walton pointed me directly to almost all of Orwell's references to Jews to which I refer in this paper.

32. George Orwell, "Hop Picking," in *Collected Essays* 1:55.

33. George Orwell, *A Clergyman's Daughter* (London: Gollancz, 1935), p. 161.

34. George Orwell, *Down and Out in Paris and London* (London: Penguin; 1933), p. 118.

35. Jewish and gentile homosexuals, were, of course, also murdered by Hitler, but either the facts were insufficiently publicized or Orwell's own fears were too strong for him to act upon his knowledge in this case.

36. George Orwell, *Tribune*, Aug. 23, 1940, in Walton, p. 24.

37. George Orwell, "Marrakech," in *Collected Essays* 1:390.

38. George Orwell, review of *Mein Kampf*, *New English Weekly*, March 21, 1940, in *Collected Essays* 2:12–13.

39. See George Orwell, "Notes on Nationalism," ibid. 3.

40. In this identification and projection, Orwell exactly resembles his arch-enemy, Wyndham Lewis, deeply critical of Britain, though in different ways.

41. George Orwell, "Wartime Diary," Oct. 25, 1940, in *Collected Essays* 3:340–41. For the same sentiments, see letter to *Partisan Review*, August 1943, ibid. 2:290–291. Here, Orwell refers to "the incredible tactlessness of some refugees," citing as "objective truth" that "Jewish refugees use this country as a temporary asylum but show no loyalty to it."

42. See, for example, his defensive response to T. R. Fyvel's statement about T. S. Eliot's antisemitism: he calls the statement nonsense, and complains "some people go round smelling after antisemitism all the time. I have no doubt Fyvel thinks I am antisemitic. More rubbish is written about this subject than any other I can think of." Letter to Julian Symons, Oct. 29, 1948, in *Collected Essays* 4:450.

43. George Orwell, "Antisemitism in Britain," ibid. 3:340–41.

44. Orwell's friend, T. R. Fyvel, felt that his friend was remarkable in his lack of "Jew consciousness in his personal relationships," but commented in 1978: "Concerning the Holocaust, Auschwitz, the desire of the survivors of the death camps to get to Israel—on all this he had something of a blind spot." Walton, p. 30.

45. Orwell does mention Asian and Eurasian faces shown as enemies in the Three Minute Hate newsreel.

46. Letters and journal entries in which Orwell brainstormed about his new book make this connection clear. See "Letter to J. J. Wilmett, May 18, 1944," in *Collected Essays* 3:149–50, and "The Last Man in Europe," which contains notations such as "Antisemitism & terrible cruelty of war etc." and "extracts of anti-Jew propaganda."

47. George Orwell, *Nineteen Eighty-Four* (New York: Signet, 1949), pp. 13, 15.

48. For instance, Goldstein is reminiscent of Sir Marcus in Graham Greene's *A Gun for Sale* (1936) and of Simon the Clerk in Charles Williams's *All Hallows Eve* — evil and dangerous Jewish characters designed to be accepted at face value by the reader.

11. Homberger

1. Jonathan Kellerman, *The Butcher's Theatre* (London: Macdonald, 1988), pp. 249, 251.

2. Sander L. Gilman, *Jewish Self-Hatred: Anti-Semitism and the Hidden Language of the Jews* (Baltimore: The Johns Hopkins University Press, 1988).

3. Lionel Trilling, "Under Forty: A Symposium on American Literature and the Younger Generation of American Jews," *Contemporary Jewish Record* 7 (February 1944), p. 17; and the discussion of this in Mark Krupnick, *Lionel Trilling and the Fate of Cultural Criticism* (Evanston, Ill.: Northwestern University Press, 1986), pp. 29–32.

4. *The Ritual Bath* (1986), *Sacred and Profane* (1987), etc. There have been occasional Jewish policemen and detectives in Jewish American writing (such as Bruce Jay Friedman, *The Dick*, and Irvin Faust, *The File on Stanley Patton Buchta*, both published 1970), but Faye Kellerman is the first to spin a commercially successful series of novels out of this theme. The amateur detective work of Harry Kemelman's *Rabbi* novels prepared the way.

5. As an attentive reading of Norman Podhoretz's "My Negro Problem—And Ours," *Doings and Undoings: The Fifties and After in American Writing* (London: Rupert Hart-Davis, 1965), and of the magazine he edits, *Commentary*, makes abundantly clear.

6. The first volume of Ludwig Lewisohn's autobiography, *Up Stream* (1922), is a rich source of what the author later regarded as a false consciousness about his religion and people. Emma Goldman's *Living My Life* (1933) is also relevant to this question, as is shown by David Waldstreicher, "Radicalism, Religion, Jewishness: The Case of Emma Goldman," *American Jewish History* 80 (Autumn 1990), pp. 74–92.

7. Roth in conversation, 1973, quoted in Henry Roth, *Shifting Landscapes*, ed. Mario Matcrassi (Philadelphia: Jewish Publication Society of America, 1982), p. 170.

8. *The Education of Abraham Cahan*, trans. Leon Stein, Abraham P. Conan, and Lynn Davidson (Philadelphia: Jewish Publication Society of America, 1969), p. 225.

9. Abraham Cahan, "The Russian Jew in America," *Atlantic Monthly,* July 1898, pp. 128–39.

10. This struggle was largely rewritten by Anzia Yezierska in the 1920s, in *Hungry Hearts* (1920) and *Children of Loneliness* (1923), with a similar sense of the entrapment of tradition and the impossibility of self-liberation.

11. Michael Gold, *Jews Without Money* (New York: Horace Liveright, 1930; rpt. New York: Carroll & Graf, 1984). Further references in the text.

12. Cahan, *Yekl: A Tale of the New York Ghetto* (New York: Appleton, 1896).

13. Irwin Granich, "Surveys of the Promised Land," *The Liberator* 1 (July 1918): 5.

14. Barbara Kirshenblatt-Gimblett, "Imagining the *Shtetl*: Jews as an Anthropological Subject During the Cold War," lecture delivered at the University of New Hampshire, April 8, 1992, suggests that the celebrated study of the *shtetl* by Mark Zborowsky and Elizabeth Herzog, *Life Is with People: The Jewish Little Town in Eastern Europe* (1952), reflects a politically guided process of establishing an acceptable image of the Jewish national character. Her analysis corresponds closely to the sentimental re-creations of the shtetl in post-Holocaust writing like *Fiddler on the Roof*. The most significant difference between imaginative literature and social anthropology lies in the ironic counterpointing of shtetl piety and American assimilation and materialism in Cahan, a note lacking in Zborowsky and Herzog.

15. Kenneth William Payne, "Michael Gold to *Jews Without Money*," Ph.D. thesis, University of Sussex, 1975, ch. 1.

16. Irwin Granich, "Towards Proletarian Art," *Liberator*, February 1921, pp. 20–24; reprinted in Michael Folsom, ed., *Mike Gold: A Literary Anthology* (New York: International Publishers, 1972).

17. Cahan, *Education*, p. 221.

18. Morris Raphael Cohen, *A Dreamer's Journey* (Boston: Beacon Press, 1949), p. 79; Samuel Chotzinoff, *A Lost Paradise: Early Reminiscences* (London: Hamish Hamilton, 1956), 64–65; Joseph Freeman, *An American Testament: A Narrative of Rebels and Romantics* (New York: Farrar & Rinehart, 1936), p. 15; Alfred Kazin, *A Walker in the City* (London: Victor Gollancz, 1952), p. 61.

19. Riis, who had a crash course in the city slums after his emigration from Denmark in the early 1870s, tried with at best limited success in *How the Other Half Lives* (1880) and other books to sustain a balanced view of the slums and those who lived in them. Hutchins Hapgood, author of *The Spirit of the Ghetto* (1902), one of Cahan's colleagues on the *New York Commercial Advertiser*, had the advantage of coming to the ghetto with little or none of Riis's anger or bigotry.

20. Herbert Asbury, *The Gangs of New York: An Informal History of the Underworld* (New York: Knopf, 1927), pp. 252–53; Eric Homberger, *The Historical Atlas of New York City* (New York: Henry Holt, 1994), pp. 130–31.

21. Published with the Lusk Committee report, Legislature of the State of New York, *Revolutionary Radicalism: Its History Purpose and Tactics . . . Report of the Joint Legislative Committee Investigating Seditious Activities . . .* , 4 vols. (Albany, 1920); Homberger, *The Historical Atlas of New York City*, pp. 136–37.

22. Such as the milieu so richly portrayed in Theresa Serber Malkiel, *The Diary of a Shirtwaist Striker*, with an introductory essay by Françoise Basch (Ithaca, N.Y.: ILR Press, School of Industrial and Labor Relations, Cornell University, 1990); and Leon Stein, ed., *Out of the Sweatshop: The Struggle for Industrial Democracy* (New York: Quadrangle/The New York Times Book Co., 1977).

23. In addition to Cahan's memoirs, see Jules Chametzky, *From the Ghetto: The Fiction of Abraham Cahan* (Amherst: University of Massachusetts Press, 1977), ch. 1.

24. On Gold see Daniel Aaron, *Writers on the Left* (New York: Harcourt Brace, 1961); Michael Brewster Folsom, "The Education of Michael Gold," in David Madden, ed., *Proletarian Writers of the Thirties* (Carbondale: Southern Illinois Univer-

sity Press, 1967), pp. 227–51; James Burkhardt Gilbert, *Writers and Partisans: A History of Literary Radicalism in America* (New York: Wiley, 1968); John M. Reilly, "Two Novels of Working Class Consciousness," *Midwest Quarterly* 14 (January 1973), pp. 183–93; Alan Wald, "Mike Gold and the Radical Literary Movement of the 1930s," *International Socialist Review* 34 (March 1973), pp. 34–37; Marcus Klein, *Foreigners: The Making of American Literature, 1900–1940* (Chicago: University of Chicago Press, 1981); Leslie Fishbein, *Rebels in Bohemia: The Radicals of "The Masses," 1911–1917* (Chapel Hill: University of North Carolina Press, 1982); Eric Homberger, *American Writers and Radical Politics, 1900–1939* (London: Macmillan, 1986); Cary Nelson, *Repression and Recovery: Modern American Poetry and the Politics of Cultural Memory, 1910–1945* (Madison: University of Wisconsin Press, 1989); James F. Murphy, *The Proletarian Moment: The Controversy Over Leftism in Literature* (Urbana: University of Illinois Press, 1991); Barbara Foley, *Radical Representations: Politics and Form in U.S. Proletarian Fiction, 1929–1941* (Durham: Duke University Press, 1993).

25. Introduction by Gold to a 1935 reissue of *Jews Without Money*, reprinted in Sun Dial Press edition, 1946. Katie Gold died in 1935.

26. Ibid., 12.

27. See the review by Melvin P. Levy in *The New Republic*, March 26, 1930, and the discussion of this issue in Edmund Wilson, "The Literary Class War," *The New Republic*, May 4, 1932. The same complaints, though by no means universally expressed on the left, were made about Henry Roth's *Call It Sleep* in 1934–35.

28. Murphy, *The Proletarian Moment*, p. 65.

29. This was virtually a commonplace among all immigrant groups, with Jews and Catholics among the most suspicious of the proselytizing intent of Protestant charities. See Konrad Bercovici, *Crimes of Charity* (New York: Knopf, 1917).

30. John Higham, *Send These to Me: Immigrants in Urban America*, rev. ed. (Baltimore: The Johns Hopkins University Press, 1984), chs. 5–7, esp. pp. 112–15.

31. Irving Howe, with the assistance of Kenneth Libo, *World of Our Fathers* (New York: Simon & Schuster, 1976), p. 343.

Index

Index

In this index an "f" after a number indicates a separate reference on the next page, and an "ff" indicates separate references on the next two pages. A continuous discussion over two or more pages is indicated by a span of page numbers, e.g., "57—59." *Passim* is used for a cluster of references in close but not consecutive sequence.

Abrams, M. H., 17
Adams, Brooks, 193n19
Adams, Henry, 193n19
African-Americans, 40ff, 168
Allingham, Margery, 4
allo-semitism, 14—15, 185n19
ambivalence, 4—5, 11f, 165, 175
Andree, Richard, 36
Anti-Alien Bill (1905), 118, 123
antisemitism: and feminism, 115, 122, 128;
   Irish, 103—13, 198n3, 199n7, 200n13,
   201n20, 202n25; and modernism, 115; rela-
   tion to philosemitism, 12—14, 18ff, 193n19;
   and romanticism, 16—26. *See also* Eliot,
   T. S.; James, Henry; Orwell, George;
   Pound, Ezra; self-hatred, Jewish; Twain,
   Mark; Woolf, Virginia
Appiah, Anthony, 191n6
Arabs, 33—36 *passim*
Arendt, Hannah, 17, 88, 114, 127f

Arnold, Matthew, 6, 92
art: anatomical, 29—31; avant-garde, as degenerate, 72—75, 83
Asher, Dr., 38
assimilation, 4, 13, 70, 114, 118f, 123ff

Balzac, Honoré de, 59
Bannister, Joseph, 133
Barnes, Djuna, 4, 115—16
Bauman, Zygmunt, 14
Baumgarten, Murray, 5, 7f, 11
Benjamin, Walter, 49
Bergson, Henri, 95
Berryman, John, 100
Black, as Other, 9—12 *passim*
blood libel, 199n5, 210n12
Bloom, Alan, 73, 193n13
Bloom, Harold, 17—18
Boehmer, Elleke, 4—5
Booth, Charles, 121

Library of Congress Cataloging-in-Publication Data

Between "race" and culture : representations of "the Jew" in English
    and American literature / edited by Bryan Cheyette.
        p.   cm. — (Stanford studies in Jewish history and culture)
    Includes bibliographical references and index.
    ISBN 0-8047-2635-3 (cloth : alk. paper). — ISBN 0-8047-2853-4 (pbk: alk. paper)
    1. Jews in literature.   2. Antisemitism in literature.   3. English
literature — History and criticism.   4. American literature — History
and criticism.   I. Cheyette, Bryan.   II. Series.
PR151.J5B48   1996
820.9'35203924 — dc20   96-12895   CIP

Original printing 1996

Last figure below indicates year of this printing:

05   04   03   02   01   00   99   98   97   96